# EPICUREAN ETHICS

## *Katastematic Hedonism*

Peter Preuss

Studies in the History of Philosophy
Volume 35

The Edwin Mellen Press
Lewiston/Queenston/Lampeter

**Library of Congress Cataloging-in-Publication Data**

Preuss, Peter, 1939-
    Epicurean ethics : katastematic hedonism / by Peter Preuss.
       p.    cm. -- (Studies in the history of philosophy ; v. 35)
    Includes bibliographical references (p. xxx-xxx) and indexes.
    ISBN 0-7734-9124-4
    1. Epicures. 2. Ethics, Ancient. 3. Pleasure. I. Title.
 II. Series: Studies in the history of philosophy (Lewiston, N. Y.) :
 v. 35.
 B573.P74  1994
 171'.4--dc20                                93-48974
                                          CIP

| This is volume 35 in the continuing series |
| Studies in the History of Philosophy |
| Volume 35 ISBN 0-7734-9124-4 |
| SHP Series ISBN 0-88946-300-X |

A CIP catalog record for this book is available from the British Library.

The Edwin Mellen Press
Box 450
Lewiston, New York
USA 14092-0450

The Edwin Mellen Press
Box 67
Queenston, Ontario
CANADA L0S 1L0

The Edwin Mellen Press, Ltd.
Lampeter, Dyfed, Wales
UNITED KINGDOM SA48 7DY

Printed in the United States of America

# Table of Contents

# Chapter One

# Introduction

Greek philosophy began in what Plato and Aristotle called "wonder"[1], an intellectual curiosity and a sense of ignorance about how things are and what causes them to be as they are. The examples given by Aristotle of the kind of thing that may bring on this sense of wonder are marionettes, the familiar return of the solstices, and the more technical matter of the incommensurability of the diagonal of the square. Such initial perplexities led the way to philosophy when they generated inquiry into greater issues such as the changes of the moon and the sun, and even the origin of the universe.

Aristotle thought that human beings had a natural desire to know[2] and to escape ignorance, a desire they could afford to indulge as a "recreation and a pastime" when all the needs of life had been provided for. Philosophy, as a response to perplexity and the natural need to know, was therefore carried on simply for the sake of knowledge and not for any practical utility. The physical speculations of the ancient Ionians, however, had far-reaching consequences, for they produced a new understanding of reality, a gradual replacement of a religious by a scientific world view. The basic difference between these two world views is that in the religious view natural events are understood as in some way expressive of the will of the gods and so as a drama of divine agency, while in the scientific view those

---

[1]For Plato see Theaetetus 155d; for this and the following related references to Aristotle see Metaphysics 982b to 983a.

[2]Met. 980a.

2

events are understood as the operation of causal laws devoid of divine intention. The transition[3] was not abrupt, and a moral or religious tinge continued to cling to natural philosophy for a long time. Greek atomism, however, was entirely free from it. Atomism was a radical system of natural physics which produced a strictly scientific conception of the world.

This new conception was of a world of tiny indestructible bits of matter called atoms constantly moving in space. These atoms come together to form compounds and separate again, whereupon the compounds, though not the atoms, simply cease to exist. All things in the universe, with the sole exception of atoms and the space in which they move, are compounds of atoms. This is true of grains of sand as much as of the bodies and souls of human beings and of the gods themselves. All things come to be as structured atomic aggregates, and cease to be again when the atoms disperse. The atoms are constant, like cards in a deck, but compounds come and go, like houses of cards being assembled and disassembled. The objects in the familiar world are brought into being and destroyed again, not by divine design, but as a result of blind causality. Things come to be and cease to be through causal processes, that is all: the world, and everything in it, is a fact without meaning.

Such a world is scientifically intelligible, it answers to and satisfies our natural desire for knowledge. But we not only have a natural desire to know, we also have a natural desire to evaluate. The need to distinguish between good and bad

---

[3]For studies of this transition see for example: F.M. Cornford, From Religion to Philosophy, New York: Harper and Row 1957 (first published in 1912); Wilhelm Nestle, Vom Mythos zum Logos, Stuttgart: Alfred Kröner Verlag, 1942; Giorgio de Santillana, The Origins of Scientific Thought: from Anaximander to Proclus, 600 B.C. to 300 A.D., The University of Chicago Press, 1961; E.J. Dijksterhuis, The Mechanization of the World Picture, Oxford: The Clarendon Press, 1961.

is no less natural than the need to distinguish between true and false. We not only seek to know reality, we also seek to make sense of life, to distinguish between a good life and a life not worth living.

The new philosophical conception of the world gave a new context within which to address the problem of the sense of life. The results of physics or natural philosophy are not irrelevant to ethics, the branch of philosophy that inquires into the good life. The dominant concern of early Ionian speculation had been the nature of reality, but by the time we get to Epicurus and the Hellenistic period the dominant concern has become ethical. The most important question has become: if the world is as our best natural philosophy says it is, how is it possible to live well and be human in such a world?

The scientific conception of the world never replaced the moral-religious conception as the sole world view of everyone, either in ancient Greece or at any time between then and our own day. In fact, during the long Christian middle ages the scientific conception suffered a near total eclipse for many centuries and was only revived by the rise of modern science in the fifteenth and sixteenth centuries. Even though today it is the more or less official conception, the religious conception is surely as widespread now as it was in the third century B.C.

There are, of course, many differences of detail between that ancient Greek religious conception of the world and the current version or versions, differences having to do with the nature and the number of the gods, for example, or the relation between god and nature. But they are the same in principle in that both conceive of a providential presence of the divine in the world, of human life as having a purpose related to god, and of human beings as having a post-mortem destiny related to the quality of life in relation to that purpose. And similarly there are, of course, also many differences of detail and a great difference in sophistication between ancient Greek atomism and twentieth century physical science, but they are the same in principle and in their relevance to ethics. If, therefore, Epicurus had something true and important to say about the sense of human life in the context of the scientific world view twenty-three hundred years ago, it is still of philosophical interest today.

I say "of philosophical interest" because I mean to distinguish it from the philological interest of the pure scholar.[4] The scholar is in the first place interested in the text and in whether or not a certain interpretation is an accurate reading of the text. The philosopher is in the first place interested in the doctrine and in whether or not the doctrine is important and true. It should be clear that the philosophical concern with an ancient author is in some respects parasitic upon the scholar's work, especially if, as in the case of Epicurus, the remains are fragmentary, because the doctrine in which the philosopher is interested is precisely that accurate interpretation of the text. The philosopher interested in Epicurean philosophy must, therefore, use the work of the scholar to find the doctrine he wishes to consider. But this may well be selective because the philosopher is not interested in everything equally. Some parts of an ancient philosopher's work are bound to be museum pieces, of justifiable interest to the scholar but of no, or only marginal, interest to the philosopher. A difficulty may, however, occur for the philosopher when there is disagreement among scholars on

---

[4]The distinction between philosophers and philologists is not a recent one but can already be found in antiquity. See, for example, Porphyry, The Life of Plotinus 14. 19-20 where Plotinus, upon having had some works of Longinus read to him, remarks: "Longinus is a scholar (philologos), but certainly not a philosopher."

points central to the doctrine, disagreement which perhaps cannot be settled by reference to the text alone. At such times, if it is important, the philosopher may try to understand the doctrine with an effort of philosophical thinking compatible with the extant text but not fully attestable. It is important, of course, that this be done insightfully and responsibly. It is a good working rule at such times to grant that the ancient author is a good philosopher, so that when a text is unclear enough to allow several interpretations of different philosophical quality we can choose the best, all things considered.

Let me give some examples here without going into detail at this point. In the case of Epicurus it is important to bear in mind not only that he is writing within the context of a world view much like our own, but also that the core of his philosophy is about pleasure and pain, something very familiar. He may or may not have had strange views about the place and value of pleasure and pain in the moral life. But when he is discussing the nature of pleasure and pain, then what he says can be checked against a familiar part of our experience. We must guard against interpreting him as saying something that is importantly inconsistent with our own experience, unless it can be clearly and explicitly attested in the text, otherwise we should try to make his views consistent with experience. For example, the view that every pleasure comes to be in the satisfaction of some desire is just too obviously false for us to ascribe it to Epicurus without being forced by a clear text. Similarly with the view that while pain has degrees of intensity, pleasure does not; or the view that pleasure is in its nature negative, being the absence of pain; or the view that while Epicurus thinks it appropriate to distinguish pleasure into kinetic and katastematic, he recognizes no such distinction in pain.

6

Epicurus did not invent atomism but found the doctrine in the work of Democritus. But Epicurus worked it out at length and in great detail, asked most of the right questions, and made some important changes.[5] The large questions that preoccupied Epicurus include whether or not there are gods in a mechanistic universe and, if so, what is their relation to nature and human life? Do human beings cease to exist at death as thoroughly as a house of cards after the cards are put back into the deck and, if so, what difference does that make to the value of human life? Is human action free and responsible, or is it causally as determined as any natural event? Given that we are natural beings who live and die in an indifferent world, can we live deliberately and well, and what shall we do with our humanity if that is our condition? These questions will also concern us in the following chapters.

Even though Epicurus spent most of his time and effort on natural philosophy[6], his last purpose was ethical. Indeed, he thought that the purpose of philosophy was above all to be a guide to life.[7] The key, however, to Epicurean ethics, to the good life of a mortal being, is pleasure. Many people, when they first hear that a philosophy makes pleasure the basis of the good life, feel a certain disappointment. Chances are that a life spent pursuing pleasure will in the long run fail even to be fun, but bring instead dissipation and ruin. And even if we could succeed in finding pleasure and having fun most of the time there would, in the minds of many people, still be something wrong. Somehow life is thought to

---

[5]For a thorough study of these issues see Cyril Bailey, The Greek Atomists and Epicurus, New York: Russell and Russell, 1964 (first published in 1928).

[6]Ep. Hdt. 37.

[7]Epicurus declared that 'philosophy is an activity which secures the happy life by arguments and discussions'. M 9.169; cf. Ep. Men 122.

be more serious than that. Pleasure is for holidays and relaxation, but when we return to the real business of life, pleasure and fun are set aside. We may look back on a day or a week of serious work and achievement and find that it was a pleasure, but pleasure was the furthest thing from our minds at the time. If it hadn't been, it surely would have interfered. When we're out for pleasure we tend to be less concerned about doing a good job, our standards of quality slip, we are less attentive, less ambitious, less concerned with success. Would you hire a foreman in your firm who admitted that his chief concern is that those under his supervision be having fun? This kind of reservation does not apply only to the job site, but to the whole of life. We are all the descendants of people who for generations and centuries have worked for other people, who have led and been bred and educated to lead useful lives of service. And the life of service, whether to the boss or the board or governments or kings or God himself, has become the paradigm of real life. In ancient Greece the story of the life of Hercules epitomized this view, and·he became the hero and model of philosophers for whom the steadfast life of service and its virtues, even if the service is given to no human master, became the foundation of ethics. I mean the Cynics, the first of whom were contemporaries of Plato, and the Stoics, who built on the Cynic ethical stance. Well yes, to the extent that Epicurus sets aside our inbred admiration for the unselfish heroism of service, he must expect some reservations and reluctance, indeed opposition. But this opposition becomes properly interesting to us only so far as it is philosophical, that is, considered and fundamental rather than just a matter of taste and style. It is indeed difficult to maintain serious and considered opposition to the Epicurean ethical stance, which is both simple and persuasive, perhaps even self-evident, once it is understood. The basic Epicurean view is that the good life is a happy, fulfilled, good-to-be-alive affair, rather than a miserable, anxious, painful burden to carry from birth to death, even if as though on a mission from higher powers. Whatever else we do, the life of service and its virtues included, has no intrinsic value, but finds its justification, when it does, only as a means to the Epicurean ideal. The question is one of the nature of the good, which we shall have to discuss at some length in due course.

The role of pleasure and pain in the philosophy of Epicurus is of the first importance and absolutely fundamental. They are the criteria of right and wrong, good and bad, and thus the foundation of all value. We shall have to discuss their status and function as criteria in due course, but for the present we can notice that as the foundation of all value they become the basis not only of the practical life but of the theoretical life as well. Even though they don't function as epistemological criteria they are still more basic in theory than truth itself, since the truth of a proposition is not what makes it worth knowing. We must value theoretical inquiry in the first place in order to engage in it, and not all objects of theoretical inquiry are equally worth being informed about. There are trivial truths as well as important truths, and not all important truths are equally important to everyone, though the propositions that express them are all equally true. There are indefinitely many true propositions not worth knowing, propositions which are part of no theory and devoid of interest. Something other than truth must supplement the truth of propositions to assemble them into a theory and make them the object of theoretical pursuit. Epicurus believed the justification for engaging in theoretical inquiry to be ethical and thus sees pleasure and pain, as the foundation of ethics, to be decisive even here.

We can begin to appreciate how pleasure and pain function as a last foundation in the philosophy of Epicurus when we consider that he was very much aware of philosophical skepticism. When he was a pupil of Nausiphanes in Teos he showed constant interest in Pyrrho, the most thorough practical skeptic of ancient Greece, whose pupil Nausiphanes had been.[8] And Nausiphanes had also been a pupil of Democritus to whose work he introduced the young Epicurus who found there not only the atomic theory, but also a powerful skeptical strain.[9] The skepticism of Pyrrho and Democritus, and Greek skepticism in general during the Hellenistic period, developed around the problem of appearance and reality. We may assume[10] that Epicurus was fully aware of this and of the seriousness of the skeptical challenge to any dogmatic philosophy. He realized that if his philosophy was to have a secure foundation it had to be skeptic-proof. He saw such a foundation in pleasure and pain. They were immune to the skeptical challenge, for their reality is their appearance, and their appearance is their reality. Whatever a closer philosophical consideration may show pleasure and pain to be, they cannot be unreal illusions. Platonic forms and Aristotelian substances are

---

[8]D.L. 9.64.

[9]On Epicurus' debt to Pyrrho see D. Sedley, *"Epicurus and his Professional Rivals"*, in Etudes sur l'epicurisme antique, ed., Jean Bollack and André Laks (Lille 1976) 121-159; for his attitude to Democritus, see P.M. Huby, *"Epicurus' Attitude to Democritus"*, Phronesis 23 (1978) 80-86. For a recent and insightful discussion of the development of Greek skepticism see Leo Groarke, Greek Scepticism, McGill-Queen's University Press, 1990.

[10]M.F. Burnyeat writes that "It is a fact of central importance that truth, in the skeptics' vocabulary, is closely tied to real existence as contrasted with appearance", ("Can the Skeptic Live His Skepticism?", in M.F. Burnyeat ed., The Skeptical Tradition, University of California Press 1983, p. 121.) Even if the skepticism of Pyrrho presented to Epicurus by Nausiphanes was basically practical, the skeptical strain found in Democritus is plainly theoretical. And we have no reason to think that Epicurus was unaware of the cosmological work On Nature by Democritus' pupil Metrodorus of Chios, the opening sentence of which was "None of us knows anything, not even whether we know anything or not". (Diels-Kranz 70 B1). In this connection Long and Sedley (The Hellenistic Philosophers. Cambridge University Press 1987, Vol. I, p. 83) write: "Democritus' doubts about the validity of sense perception had been developed into a full-scale skepticism by his fourth-century followers, such as Metrodorus of Chios and Anaxarchus, and the reversal of this trend in atomist philosophy is one of Epicurus' principal goals". Also Epicurus would surely have been aware of the subjective skepticism of the Cyrenaics (D.L. 2.92).

shadows by comparison.

Epicurean ethics is, of course, not the simple rule to pursue pleasure and shun pain. Just because something is a pleasure is not sufficient reason for pursuing it, nor is something's being a pain sufficient reason for avoiding it. It doesn't take deep philosophical insight to realize that our acts have consequences and that the act of pursuing and enjoying some pleasure may bring painful consequences in its train. And similarly with pains. Some pains may bring about later pleasures for the sake of which they are worth enduring. At the very least a hedonistic ethics will involve the prudent life management of maximizing pleasure and minimizing pain, and of calculating when a pain is worth enduring for the greater pleasure it will bring and when a pleasure holds the threat of painful consequences which will make it prudent to forego it. This much is pretty elementary and already known to and practiced by the Cyrenaics, a group of hedonists from whom Epicurus insists that he be distinguished, for the differences are important. Not only is the style of an Epicurean life quite different from the style of a Cyrenaic life, though both are hedonistic, there is also a fundamental difference in the theory of pleasure which it is important to understand correctly. The key to this theoretical difference is the Epicurean distinction between kinetic and katastematic pleasure, which the Cyrenaics did not recognize. We shall have to be all the more careful in making that distinction since, despite its importance to a proper understanding of Epicurus, it has been found to be problematical by commentators from the time of Cicero on. It is no exaggeration to say that only if we understand what Epicurus meant by katastematic pleasure will it be possible for us to do justice to his bread and water hedonism which, without such understanding, must strike us as the eccentric extravagance of an ailing recluse.

Epicureanism is sometimes labelled "egotistic hedonism" in textbooks. I suppose that the writers of such textbooks need a foil to utilitarianism, and Epicurus seems to them to be the only philosopher of some historical stature to fit the bill. But the label really is unfortunate, if only because it quite fails to take into account the Epicurean theory of the social life. True, the Epicurean individual is not an instrument but an end in himself, and must appear in ethics, and in particular in his own ethical life, as an end. But to treat myself as the ultimate end of my ethical life does not somehow imply or require me to treat others as instruments or means to my individual ends. Whether I do so or not is a separate matter and, initially at least, a matter of prudence. The basis of citizenship in a political organization is nothing more nor less than the prudential agreement not to harm other members of this organization, and the agreement is reciprocated so that it holds between all members of the group as a social contract. This much holds between people who may be utter strangers. But we find that there are other people who are more than strangers, who are acquaintances, family, friends. The relation of friendship is a natural bond which may grow between people beyond any agreement or contract. It may begin in relations of prudence, but develops into a good thing worth cultivating for its own sake and, at its best, the love between friends may grow so strong as not to make it unthinkable for an Epicurean to give his life for a friend.

The basic themes of Epicurus' philosophy speak to us today as much as they did to his contemporaries over two millennia ago because they address themselves to timeless human issues which retain their identity and their urgency within the flow of historical change. They speak of human beings engaged in living lives filled with misery or joy, success or failure, meaning or bleak pointlessness; of human beings at a loss about what really matters in life, or declaiming about it with a confidence got from finding their wisdom in fashionable platitudes. They speak of human beings driven by ambition, chasing reputation, luxury, and the goods dictated by convention, all those things which are indispensible if you're going to amount to anything in this world. They speak of people trained to wear our their lives in service, whether of worldly or otherworldly expectation. And they speak with a philosophical simplicity which rejects mere complexity and subtlety in favour of a kind of candid directness with which one feels that what is true and important can be stated.

Epicureanism presents a reasoned portrait of a human possibility. Whether this possibility can be finally enough, or whether we have perhaps really outgrown it in the intervening centuries, is something we shall have to consider after we have come to grips with this philosophy and done our best to understand it. The structure of this book is based on the Epicurean tetrapharmakos. Thus, one chapter is devoted to the gods and one chapter to death. Pleasure and pain, since they are the heart of the matter in any account of Epicurean ethics, are given more extended treatment in three chapters. Then a chapter is devoted to Epicurean social philosophy and its two central concepts, justice and freedom, and we end with a concluding chapter on the present day viability of Epicureanism.

# Chapter Two

# The Gods

The central place in Epicurean ethics is occupied by the four most important topics, the so-called tetrapharmakos: the gods, death, pleasure, and pain. Whenever Epicurus deals with them,[11] the gods come first, indicating that this topic either is the most important or, at least, the one that must be dealt with before the others. A right understanding of the gods and a proper attitude to them seem to be preconditions for a successful Epicurean life and, in that sense at least, are of the first importance.

But Epicurus is writing in the context of ancient Greek religion and its gods, which, for better or for worse, are today genuine museum pieces of no more than historical and aesthetic interest. His concern, therefore, that we have an accurate idea of the gods seems to be the most dated of his concerns, one that separates him from us by an important stretch of history dominated by a different God, one whose existence seems not in the least to be marked by blessedness and tranquility, but rather by a tempestuous history of wrath and revolt, love and atonement, culminating in the agony of the crucifixion and the triumph of resurrection.

Epicurus was aware, of course, that the religion of his day and locale was one among others. He was aware that others have different beliefs, but also that human beings always and everywhere have had a belief in gods. There does,

---

[11]eg. K.D. 1-4; Ep. Men.

therefore, seem to be something natural and not merely conventional about human belief in gods. In fact Epicurus tries to understand the divine nature beneath the mythological garb in which popular culture dresses it and say something of timeless philosophical interest about god. To the extent that he succeeds in this, what he has to say will not be outdated but remains of perennial interest.

What remains of interest in Epicurus' theology, I think, are his arguments that, first, the gods exist, second, they are quite unconcerned about the course of nature and human affairs, and third, we are quite safe from them, may contemplate them with pleasure, and make them our ethical models. What is no longer of genuine philosophical interest, on the other hand, is, for example, that Epicurus seems to have recognized two classes of gods; or that he had a principle of isonomy which implied that in an infinite universe the best, i.e. god, was bound to occur, or even that there were as many gods as there were people, or some such thing. Matters such as these can occupy us, if at all, only in passing.

Epicurus' arguments for divine indifference are so strong that one wonders why he didn't simply develop them into arguments for the non-existence of gods. Epicurus was aware, for example, of the argument from evil, one of the most powerful arguments for the non-existence of god, but apparently used it to prove that the gods do not care rather than that they don't exist. He must have thought that his reasons for affirming the gods' existence were very good, unless the affirmation had more to do with the prudence of not proclaiming atheism in a society which took its gods very seriously. However that may be, his reasons are worth looking at.

## The Universality of Belief in Gods

If Cicero reports him correctly, Epicurus saw in the universal belief in gods sufficient reason for the critical philosopher to accept the existence of gods. At first glance this seems naive. It is clear that there may well be universal agreement about a falsehood such as, for example, that the earth is flat. The simple circumstances that all men once believed, if they did, that the earth was flat would not constitute sufficient reason for the critical philosopher to accept that view. But if it is not sufficient reason in the case of the shape of the earth, why should it be in the case of the gods? The Epicurean argument is that there is an important difference. It is possible for a particular belief to be arrived at originally by faulty inference from sensory data and then spread by education until all, or nearly all, shared this belief. But suppose for a moment that we find a great many different beliefs about the shape of the earth in various cultures. We find, let's suppose, that some believe it to be a disc, others a cube, yet others a sphere, and so forth. They can't all be right, but it would surely be hasty for the critical philosopher simply to dismiss all these beliefs as false. For surely they are not completely false. These beliefs share the true common element that there is an earth and that this earth has a shape, and falsehood only enters, when it does, in the development of further details through inference and education. Epicurus saw the case of the gods to be similar to the example just given in that the great variety of beliefs in gods have a true common element which is natural and prior to all inference and education.

> For he alone perceived, first, that the gods exist, because nature herself has imprinted a conception of them on the minds of all mankind. For what nation or what tribe of men is there but possesses untaught [sine doctrina] some preconception of the gods? Such notions Epicurus designated by the word prolēpsis.[12]

---

[12]N.D. 1.43.

In every tribe or culture we find a developed common conception of the gods. These conceptions vary greatly from culture to culture, but, thought Epicurus, all of these different religious conceptions have their origin in a prolēpsis, a preconception, a fundamental concept or basic grasp of the nature of divinity that all human beings have, that is the same for all, and that we did not get by education but by the natural cognitive process with which we are all endowed by nature. Human beings are cognitive by nature. We not only see (etc.), but retain a memory of seeing and, so, come to see something we have seen before as something familiar, something we recognize and understand as a certain kind of thing. All this happens naturally, and basic concepts are a pre-deliberative, non-volitional, natural product of the human mind from original sensory experience. This fundamental concept, which is the first and most basic understanding we have of anything and without which no further inquiry would be possible, Epicurus calls a prolēpsis. A prolēpsis is produced as naturally by a healthy human mind that is given sensory experience as body tissue is produced by a healthy human stomach (etc.) that is given food. Because of this fundamental position in the natural process of human cognition, a prolēpsis is an epistemologically privileged concept. What this privilege amounts to we can best appreciate after a brief look at Epicurean epistemology. We need to look at this epistemology in any case, for Epicurus' claim that the gods exist is just a special case of the general claim that something exists, and we need to understand the status of Epicurean existence claims in general before we can understand the special claim about the gods.

## Epistemology: The Skeptical Background

Epicurus was aware of the developing skeptical strain in Greek philosophy and rejects it because, as human beings trying to live in a natural environment, we need cognition as much as we need digestion. The skeptics of the time when skepticism had reached its maturity[13] in the ancient world understood this need as well, of course. But they thought that this need could be met by living by appearances and sense impressions alone without any further inferences about the nature of the underlying reality that appears to us in sensation. This life by appearances was not restricted to the instantaneous subjective impression of the moment but, since skeptics are human beings with the same natural cognitive apparatus as Epicureans, it included concepts as well, that is, classes or kinds of appearances. Thus a skeptic will admit with a clear epistemological conscience that honey appears sweet,[14] and will buy honey from his grocer or collect it from his beehive if he wants a sweet spread on his bread. What they refused to affirm was that the appearance of sweetness in honey corresponded to a real sweetness in honey. They worked within a philosophical model in which there was a world of reality that exists independent of our knowledge of it, but that appears to us in our experience of it. Whether the world really is as it appears to us, is something they claimed not to know, nor could they see how it could be known. There was, therefore, no justification for treating appearances as accurate revelations of the nature of things. This skeptical withholding of assent they extended to all other proposed means of access to the real nature of things. They worked, it should be

---

[13]This may well already be true of the Academics Arcesilaus and Carneades (cf M. 7.150-190), but is clearly true of the Pyrrhonic skeptics from Aenesidemus on as represented principally by Sextus Empiricus.

[14]P.H. 1.19-20.

clear, within a correspondence theory of truth, even if only tacitly. Because by the time Sextus Empiricus was writing skeptics were perfectly aware that a skepticism which denied that we could know anything was self-refuting, they rather struck the pose of inquirers who suspend judgement until convinced of one among several contending claims. To choose to accept as true one among several contending claims requires that we have a standard of choice, a criterion of truth. And to adopt a criterion of truth from among several contending ones put forth by rival schools requires that we have a criterion for choosing among criteria and so on in an infinite regress.[15] It seems, then, that we have nothing that has shown itself to be an indubitable access to the nature of reality, and that we have found (and it seems highly unlikely that we ever will find) an intellectually responsible way of distinguishing true from false beliefs. The skeptics, therefore, chose to live without philosophy, that is, without the true knowledge of the nature of reality (and moral value), and found that they could achieve the philosopher's tranquility by living by appearances (and the conventions of their social group). In this way, they thought, the natural needs of a cognitive being could be met without the unnecessary and arbitrary dogmatic assertions of doctrinaire philosophy.

Whether Epicurus had anticipated this skeptical development, or whether this skepticism developed in important respects in opposition to Epicurean dogma, we need not decide. The truth is probably a combination of the two. But what is of value to us here is what Epicurus proposes as the criterion of truth, and what he takes truth to be. This becomes especially significant when seen against the backdrop of skepticism, which was only just developing in his day.

---

[15] cf. P.H. 2.20.

It is clear that Epicurus did not want to go in the direction indicated by the developing philosophical skepticism[16] but believed that knowledge of the nature of things was essential for the peace of mind essential to the good life. Yet knowledge and truth were becoming ever more problematical. Epicurus therefore looked for a sound foundation for knowledge in what he called criteria of truth, a procedure which was to become quite fashionable in his day and the subsequent centuries. Non-philosophers, whether naively in everyday life or most seriously and reflectively in, for example, a trial, take the testimony of an eye witness to be the very paradigm of the sort of thing we base sound judgements on. 'When in doubt, take a good look' is a sound principle on which to operate in practical life, a principle which can be applied naively or intelligently, a principle which we can learn to apply better with thought and the experience of difficult cases. If you want to cross a street you take a look to see if there are any cars coming, and you literally stake your life on the look you take. Of course, you know that you can be fooled sometimes and you don't believe everything you see when watching a magician because he is an expert at fooling you and that is why it is entertaining to watch him. And sometimes you take a look in poor conditions and aren't sure. Is that a coiled rope in the dark or is that a snake? Before you get too close, if you must, it is advisable to take a second look or poke it with a long stick if you have one and so forth. One might argue, of course, that such procedures of testing are not in principle infallible, that there is always room for error and that any opinion formed in such a way will always only be probable. That may be true, but there

---

[16]Long and Sedley claim that "the primacy of epistemology in [Epicureanism], and its foundation in sense-perception, can be viewed as a determined effort to reject just such sceptical challenges as the paralysing Pyrrhonian thesis 'neither our sensations nor our opinions tell us truths or falsehoods'." (The Hellenistic Philosophers, Cambridge University Press 1987, Vol. 1, p. 22.) cf. M 7.22.

comes a point at which the remaining doubt is no longer a reasonable doubt and you have formed a judgement on which you will stake your life. Such judgements all, or at least almost all, depend upon sense information about the world in which we live, and to allow the theoretical possibility of error to undermine our reliance on the senses would be practically disastrous.[17] Epicurus then saw the best chance for a philosophically defensible criterion of truth to lie in making the senses not only practically necessary, but theoretically acceptable as well.

## The Truth of Sensations

To make the senses theoretically acceptable he could not simply begin with them in the way we use them practically, that is by being selective and giving a criterial role to some sensory presentations and not to others. For that would require a further, more fundamental criterion of selection, and Epicurus saw that there was none. So he opted for what seems to be a philosophically extravagant position, namely that every sensation fulfills the criterial function and, he thought, that it could do so only by itself being true. It is important to understand this astonishing claim that all sensations are true.[18] Epicurus worked with a theoretical understanding of the mechanics of sensation inherited from Empedocles and Democritus in which objects in the world give off a constant

---

[17]cf. Lucr. 4. 507-510.

[18]The claim that all sensations are true does not occur as such in what we have left of Epicurus' writings. But it is reliably attributed to him by a number of ancient sources. (For a listing of the ancient attributions see Gisela Striker, "Epicurus on the Truth of Sense-Impressions", Archiv für Geschichte der Philosophie, 59 (1977), pp. 125-142; and C.C.W. Taylor, "All Perceptions are True", Doubt and Dogmatism, edited by Malcolm Schofield, Myles Burnyeat, and Jonathan Barnes, Oxford: Clarendon Press 1980, esp. pp. 105-106). The claim is, however, clearly made by Lucretius at 4.499.

stream of effluences that cause sensation when they act upon our sense organs. Sensation is true in the first place by being a passive natural response to contact with an effluent, and in the second place by being an accurate representation of the effluent.[19]

Let us first consider the notion of an accurate representation of the effluent. There are at least three kinds of effluents: light, sound and odour. They are known to be different because they behave differently. Light travels faster than sound which travels faster than odour, and they have corresponding ranges. Light reflects inverted from mirrors, sound gives an echo off cliffs, and odour does neither. Light will pass through glass, but not through a wooden door or over garden walls, but sound can be heard through closed doors and over garden walls, and so on.[20] Epicurus seems to reserve the word 'image' (eidōlon) for the sensible effluences of light, preferring simply to speak of particles in the cases of sound and odour.[21] All three of these effluences are very fine atomic structures given off by objects and able to act upon our sense organs. The senses, then, do not respond differently to the same effluent such that we have sense specific responses to effluents that account for the difference between sight and hearing and smell. Rather there are different effluents naturally able to act upon different

---

[19]The passivity of sensation is stressed at D.L. 10.31, M 7.210 and M 8.9. For the relation of accurate representation see, for example: "Epicurus said that all sensations are true and that every presentation arises from a real object, and is just as the thing which stimulates the sensation". (M 8.63). The real object in question here is the visual image, the stream of eidōla, as the discussion, immediately following in Sextus, of Orestes and the furies makes clear. Also cf. M 8.9. In his discussion of sensation in the Letter to Herodotus, Epicurus repeatedly claims that the images resemble the objects that give them off (Hdt. 49, 50, 51) but does not mention a relation of resemblance between the images and the visual presentation they cause in us.

[20]See e.g. Lucr. 4. 595-614, as well as other places in his discussion of sensation in Book 4.

[21]Ep. Hdt. 46a - 53.

senses. Thus eidōla, i.e. visible images, are effluences which can act upon the sense of sight but not the sense of hearing or smell. And similarly, the senses of taste and touch seem not to function in response to effluences, but taste seems to respond to parts of the tasted object that are mechanically extracted by chewing, for example,[22] and, although both Epicurus and Lucretius say very little about touch, this seems to be a response to an object itself rather than to any effluences. In addition to sensation through sense organs, the mind itself is capable of sensation not mediated by any of the organs of sense[23] and we shall have to consider this in due course. For the present, however, the point that needs making here can be made if we restrict ourselves to the sense of sight about which Epicurus and Lucretius say the most anyway.

A sensation, then, is true by being an accurate representation of a stream of eidōla, a visible image, analogous to the way in which an image on a movie screen is an accurate representation of the film frames being projected upon it. The accuracy is at least a structural one. That a sensation or, better, an object of sensory awareness is an accurate representation of a stream of eidōla means that it is a structural replica of them. This need not mean that they look the same, if only because of the difficulty of secondary properties. The image which acts upon the sense of sight is a fine atomic structure,[24] and, since individual atoms have no colour,[25] there is the difficulty how a structure of such atoms can be coloured. Epicurus' problem with secondary properties is exactly the problem we still have

---

[22]Lucr. 4. 617 ff.

[23]cf. Lucr. 4. 722 ff.

[24]Ep. Hdt. 46a ff.; Lucr. 4. 110 ff.

[25]Ep. Hdt. 54.; Lucr. 2. 737.

today. Either we can say that we see a certain part of an object to be red because red light enters our eyes from that part, and Epicurus sometimes indicates that he finds that a perfectly acceptable way of speaking by himself speaking of coloured images.[26] But then as now one might object that light rays themselves are not coloured but rather have a certain frequency which, when it acts upon the nerves responsible for sight, causes us to see red (by unexplainable miracle). Just so one might argue that Epicurus' eidōla are not themselves coloured, but have certain structural features which cause us to perceive secondary properties as a natural response.[27] There is also the difficulty that the stream of eidōla is not an object we can look at independent of the sensation it produces in us, and so we cannot compare the two for similarity. Perhaps the best way to understand the phenomenal object as a structural replica of the eidōla is to say that there is a one-to-one correlation of properties such that property X in the eidōla is productive of property Y in the object. Thus, for example, to say that an image is red is to say that it has a property which is productive of redness in the sensory object, and so on for all properties.[28] If above we suggested the relation between images on a film strip and the image on a screen onto which the film is being projected as an appropriate analogue of the relation of replication between eidōla and phenomena, we might now suggest instead, as less question-begging, the relation between the magnetic imprint on a video tape and the image it produces

---

[26]Ep. Hdt. 49.

[27]For an argument that secondary properties should be so understood in the Epicurean theory of perception, see C.C.W. Taylor, 'All Perceptions are True', in Malcolm Schofield, Myles Burnyeat, and Jonathan Barnes ed., Doubt and Dogmatism, Oxford: Clarendon Press, 1980, pp. 121 - 122.

[28]This way of correlating properties of eidōla with properties of sensory objects is suggested by Don Fowler, "Sceptics and Epicureans", Oxford Studies in Ancient Philosophy, Vol. 2, 1984, p. 262.

on a television screen. The televised image is a structural replica of the magnetic imprint without the suggestion that the properties of the magnetic imprint look like the properties of the image on the screen. Rather, there is only the relation of production. Now, we can have access to images on a film strip and the magnetic imprint on a video tape other than playing them on their proper equipment. In this way we can say that the images on a film strip not only produce images on a screen, but also resemble them, while those on a video tape only produce images on a television screen without resembling them. But we have no independent access to eidōla, so while we can say that phenomenal objects are their structural replicas, we cannot say whether they also resemble them and, if so, how much.

So far our discussion of the truth of sensations has a rather disappointing result because, so far as they are structural replicas of images, their truth seems to be restricted to images, while what we want is truth about the things in the world among which we live and about which we care. The problem is how to get beyond eidōla. Let us consider how Epicurus attempts to resolve this difficulty, and it may be appropriate to remind ourselves that Epicurus' problem of the existence of gods is just a special case of his problem of the existence of anything and eventually depends on a satisfactory solution of the larger problem.

## From Sensation to Existence

There are problems in getting from the sensation of images to knowledge of objects in the external world, the first of which is that images don't always arrive at the sense organ in the condition in which they left the object that gave them off. Edges may wear off, which is said to account for our seeing distant square towers to appear to be round.[29]  The medium through which they travel may distort their shapes, which is said to account for our seeing straight oars as bent under water.[30] Also images may hook up with other images in transit and so produce an experience of objects which don't exist as portrayed.  Centaurs, for example, are said to be the result of a collision and hooking up of man and horse images.[31] And not only may images misrepresent the world of their causal origin in this and other ways, but not all images are caused by objects since some may generate spontaneously and so represent nothing either accurately or inaccurately.[32]  It seems clear that such problems prevent the transition from images to objects being made with any reliability by sensation itself.  One might think that a peculiarly symbiotic relationship between sight and touch could provide an avenue for such a transition.  Can not the shape of an object seen to be square be confirmed by touching it, for example?  Lucretius thinks that this shows that "touch and sight are moved by a similar cause",[33] but does not go on to develop this thought.  We know that he took the cause of sight to be images, but he does not tell us whether he thinks that touch has an intermediary as well or whether it is stimulated directly by the object.  However he might have developed this thought, it is clear that if we accept that the senses can confirm each other we cannot deny that they can refute each other, and the thesis that the senses cannot

---

[29]Lucr. 4. 353.

[30]Lucr. 4. 436.

[31]Lucr. 4. 732-748.

[32]Ep. Hdt. 48; Lucr. 4. 129-135.

[33]Lucr. 4. 232-233.

refute each other is central to Epicurean epistemology.[34] It seems safe to say, therefore, that Lucretius would not have availed himself of the possible avenue for transition from images to objects which a juxtaposition of the senses of sight and touch indicates at first glance, and it seems equally safe to say that Epicurus had not already done so. The avenue for such a transition must lie elsewhere, and the clue is given by reminding ourselves that the process of perception does not naturally stop with sensations, but goes on to the formation of preconceptions, basic concepts called prolēpseis by Epicurus.

When in perception we see the shape of an object we also think that shape.[35] As cognitive beings we as naturally think as we see. In fact the two always go together. We not only see a shape, but see it, for example, as an apple or a tree or a person or as something unfamiliar and seen for the first time. This thinking that accompanies sensation has two stages. The first stage is as entirely natural, involuntary, and passive as sensation itself. It is the process by which preconceptions are formed, or by which a sensation is recognized to be of an object of which we already have a preconception. Because of the naturalness and passivity of this stage, truth is preserved here, and falsehood cannot enter until the second stage, which is a process of confirming or disconfirming, comparing or contrasting, making judgements and forming opinions.[36] The first stage accompanies sensation by natural necessity simply because we are by nature cognitive beings. A mental operation of thought must accompany sensation for

---

[34]D.L. 10.32; Lucr. 4. 486-499.

[35]Ep. Hdt. 49.

[36]Ep. Hdt. 51.

"the eyes cannot recognize the nature of things".[37] The eyes alone will only see shapes and colours, it requires a mental operation to see these shapes and colours as an apple. This first and most basic mental operation is the one by which preconceptions are formed and applied. It is because of this operation that we not only see, but see objects. And it is also a natural given that we see these objects not only as reidentifiable constants of subjective experience, but as existing objects in an extramentally real world. Every human being naturally sees such a world through the normal operation of his cognitive function.

Even if this were right, if through the normal functioning of my cognitive nature I experience an objective world of things, there is, of course, still a problem about the truth of that experience, and we must see what that problem is in order to understand Epicurus' concept of truth. If by the claim that truth is preserved through the first two stages of normal cognition Epicurus had meant that the world of objects that we experience at this stage exactly corresponds to a world of objects which exists extramentally and independent of our experience of it, a world we cannot experience directly but which we can infer to exist from the experienced world which is the mental effect and representative of the extramentally real one, then Epicurus would have held a clearly indefensible philosophical position which the argument given so far does not even begin to establish.

We should guard against thinking that Epicurus had not seen the problem. The problem was not unheard of in Epicurus' day. The Cyrenaics had already seen it and, in consequence of finding no solution had retreated into a skepticism of

---

[37]Lucr. 4. 385.

subjective experience. Plutarch describes the Cyrenaics as a school who:

> "placing all experiences of impressions within themselves, thought the evidence derived from them as insufficient warrant for certainty about reality and withdrew as in a siege from the world about them and shut themselves up in their responses,--admitting that external objects 'appear', but refusing to venture further and pronounce the word 'are'."[38]

We have no reason to think that Epicurus was not well enough acquainted with Cyrenaic thought to be aware of the difficulty they had of moving from phenomenal experience to extramental reality. Nor should we think that Epicurus may have seen that the Cyrenaics had this problem but was unaware that his philosophy must respond to that problem, for it really is quite obvious. Plutarch, for example, has seen it[39], and he does not excell Epicurus in philosophical ability.

We would do well to suppose that Epicurus had seen the problem and that his epistemology was meant to solve it. It does so, I shall argue, by providing a procedural theory of truth which finds a proper place for truth understood as correspondence, and by identifying the things in the extramental world among which we live and about which we care as phenomena.

## A Procedural Theory of Truth

We should remind ourselves at this point that above[40] we had said that sensation is true in two ways, first, by being a passive natural response to contact

---

[38]Col. 1120 c-d.

[39]Col. 1121 a-e. The problem is also pointed out as quite obvious by two recent commentators: C.C.W. Taylor, 'All Perceptions are True', in Malcolm Schofield, Myles Burnyeat, Jonathan Barnes, eds., Doubt and Dogmatism, Oxford: The Clarendon Press, 1980; Don Fowler, "Sceptics and Epicureans", (a discussion of M. Gigante, Scetticismo e Epicureismo, Naples 1981) in Oxford Studies in Ancient Philosophy, Vol. 2, 1984, p. 265.

[40]In the section titled "The Truth of Sensations".

with an effluent and, second, by being an accurate representation of the effluent. We have considered the second of these. It is time we considered the first.

Sensations and preconceptions are natural responses because they are produced by the normal functioning of my cognitive nature. This function is not something I have learned, it is not a convention or custom of my cultural group but unhistorically and cross-culturally natural. It is not something I have learned to do and now engage in well or badly any more than I have learned how to digest my food or circulate my blood. It is passive because it happens without any conscious intention, it is not planned but something that happens beyond my volitional control or rational guidance.[41] To speak of sensations and preconceptions as true means that they are naturally produced, arrived at by means of the normal functioning of my cognitive nature. This conception of truth is not a correspondence concept. Truth is not here a property of sensations and concepts which they have in virtue of corresponding with an extramental reality they represent. Rather, truth is here a procedural concept. Sensations and preconceptions are true because produced by an appropriate procedure, the normal functioning of my cognitive nature. The notion of truth as correspondence is subsequent and derived, that is, it reduces on analysis to a procedural rule. We naturally experience the world and its furniture as an extramental reality, that is, as existing outside our bodies and brains. And if I believe that there are five apples in your basket, and wonder whether my belief is true, the obvious thing to do is to look into your basket to see whether there are five apples there. If I find five apples there then my belief is confirmed, it is true, and it seems perfectly appropriate to say that it is true because there really are five apples there, that is,

---

[41]D.L. 10.31.

because my belief corresponds with reality; or that my belief is false because taking a look into the basket showed that there were four apples only, and my belief was disconfirmed, it failed to correspond with the extramental reality.

In the case of sensations and preconceptions, the procedure that establishes truth is a natural process rather than a deliberate act. Their truth is self-evident, for nothing more evident could support their evidence. And their truth is criterial, for the truth of opinions and beliefs depends upon sensations and preconceptions. This dependence is twofold. First, the procedure by which the truth of opinions is established would not be possible without sensations and preconceptions. They are, as it were, the raw material of this procedure. And, second, matters of belief or opinion derive the degree to which they are evident from the self-evident sensations and preconceptions on which they depend.

The procedure of establishing the truth of an opinion is a procedure of attestation and contestation, and non-attestation and non-contestation.[42] It is an infallible procedure in the sense that, given the Epicurean procedural understanding of truth, this procedure necessarily establishes truth and falsehood. It is not infallible, of course, in the sense that an opinion shown to be true, i.e. attested and not contested, by this procedure may not upon further investigation be shown to be false. Let me explain. Suppose I wish to confirm my belief that there are five apples in my basket. I take a look, see apples, count them, close the basket and go to the picnic. When I get there I take out the contents of my basket and find that I have four apples and a ball of yarn. My belief turned out to be false, that is, it was contested in a further application of the procedure. What can

---

[42]cf. M 7. 211-16.

I do but resolve to look more carefully next time? And, even if I do, it is still possible that next time I may arrive at the picnic with wax copies, for example, if there is a practical joker in our group. In none of this is there a problem with my senses, but the error is a consequence of hasty inference. Apples and balls of yarn look alike in the dark corner of a basket under four apples, and good wax copies look very much like the originals they are copying. Throughout this there was no difficulty with the first two stages of cognition. My sensations equally applied to apples and to the objects they turned out to be and there never was a problem of not knowing what an apple was. And throughout all of this it makes perfectly good sense to speak of truth as though it were a matter of correspondence between my belief and the real state of affairs in my basket. But the notion of correspondence itself is derived from and intelligible only within the procedure outlined. This is true even of the correspondence between the sensation and the image, the eidōla. Epicurean arguments for the existence and nature of images which mediate between objects and sense organs are an application of the truth-establishing procedure. The correspondence between the visual presentation and the object is a procedural given from the start, since I have sensory access to the object to confirm my beliefs.

My sensory access to objects never involves the senses only but always also the thinking mind which supplies the prolēpsis, the basic concept of what I am sensing. It is this preconception which gives to my experience the character of objectivity, the character of being experience of something about which my experience may be more or less accurate and complete. It is because I have a preconception of an apple that I can say that I sense an apple well or badly, clearly or unclearly. This greater or lesser accuracy is explained, if it is, by the theory of eidōla. This theory may be a more or less successful theory about certain features of perception, such as that we can perceive at a distance, that we can perceive clearly or unclearly, that we can see things in mirrors and hear voices through doors, and so forth, but it is not a theory to show that we perceive existent objects. Rather it presupposes that we perceive existent objects. This is established and must be understood within a procedural understanding of truth. But I have evidence that my sensory access to objects is mediated by a stream of images,[43]and it is at this point that truth comes to be understood as correspondence within the procedural theory, that is, the notion of correspondence is basically a procedural rule.

Might a skeptic not object at this point that, even if he grants that we have by nature a perceptual apparatus which provides us with experience, and that we can exercise care in the procedure of attestation and contestation and so arrive at opinions about the world we live in that allow us to cope in that world, could it not nevertheless be the case that our opinions were merely true of appearances, of phenomena, and not of the underlying reality? That is, could not what an Epicurean claims to be true be really false after all, because it failed to reveal the real nature of things?

There are two things an Epicurean could say in reply to such a skeptical charge. The skeptics despair of our ability to know the real nature of things and try to be content with what seems to be all we can have: acquaintance with appearances. And so, in the language becoming fashionable in the Hellenistic period, we might

---

[43]Lucr. 4. 54 ff.

say that the skeptic's criterion is the appearance, the phenomenon.[44]  The first thing an Epicurean might say is that in this respect he is not so very different from the skeptics, for it is not inappropriate to say that the criterion of the Epicureans is also the phenomenon.[45]  But in another respect there is an important difference. For Epicurus the problem of truth is whether our beliefs and claims, the propositions we hold and assert about reality, are true of reality, of the way things are outside our beliefs and assertions, of the world of things about which we have beliefs and to which we refer in our assertions.  This world of things, however, is observable, it is the world that is revealed in perception.  It is here that the notion of truth as correspondence has its proper locus, it is here where truth and falsehood are established in relation to correspondence with reality.[46]  But the skeptic might insist that not only our beliefs need to correspond with reality in order to be true, but our perception must also.  That is, only if the phenomena of perception correspond to the reality that appears in those phenomena could we say that any claim to true knowledge could be sustained.  Put this way the problem is insoluble.  Not even the atomic theory itself can do that because the atomic theory itself is derived from observed phenomena and thus dependent upon perception, and because the phenomena of observation don't directly reveal atomic structures anyway.  But this insoluble problem of the skeptics may well be regarded as a pseudo problem by the Epicureans, for it is plainly a case of taking a

---

[44]See, for example, Sextus' discussion of the criterion of skepticism, Ch. XI of the Outlines of Pyrrhonism.

[45]Diogenes Laertius does so explicitly at D.L. 9.106.

[46]This is why Epicurus said that "true means that which is as it is said to be, and false that which is not as it is said to be." (M 8.9). The correspondence is between "what is said to be", i.e. the claim or an assertion and "what is", i.e. the object of observation, the real state of affairs in the world outside of me. The notion of "what is said to be" must not be understood as equivalent to "what is seen to be", as Cyril Bailey does on p. 255 of The Greek Atomists and Epicurus.

demand which is legitimately made in one context, the context of verifying beliefs by observations, and making that demand in another context as well, the context of verifying observations by checking them against something in principle beyond cognitive access. An Epicurean might regard this as a pseudo problem for two reasons. First he might ask why a skeptic thinks that the demand of correspondence, which is legitimate in the case of beliefs and the phenomena of observation, is also legitimate in the case of the phenomena of observation and a purported underlying reality. A real skeptic, of course, would shrug his shoulders and point out that it is inconsistent with his skepticism to make such claims. The second reason why an Epicurean might think the skeptical problem to be a pseudo problem is more characteristically Epicurean. A world which is in principle beyond our experience, even if it is in some sense real, does not concern us. It does not concern us because it is in no sense either good or bad. It cannot affect the quality of human life in any way, either positively or negatively, because it is quite divorced from the possibility either of pleasure or of pain, for these are possible only in experience. Epicurus conceived of philosophy as "an activity which secures the happy life by arguments and discussion".[47] A problem, therefore, which is quite irrelevant to human well-being, is not properly a philosophical problem.

There is a further procedure in the process of confirming or disconfirming beliefs which we must note now: confirmation or disconfirmation by other people. I can confirm my belief that there is someone in the kitchen by taking a look or by asking someone who just came from the kitchen. The testimony of an eye witness is confirmed by the corroborating testimony of another witness, and if

---

[47]M 9.169.

all witnesses to an event agree about what they saw, we have better evidence than if we had only the account of one person and not of the others. We accept evidence of this kind before we become philosophers and Epicurus thought that this kind of procedure was good enough to be admissible in philosophy as well. Thus we accept that there are solid bodies in our world because we have sense experience of them, but this belief is made even more secure by the universal corroboration of others.[48] Sometimes we have reason to think that we cannot depend on our own experience and at such times it may be entirely appropriate to consult others. I may, for example, not be sure whether something I remember having done in the company of certain people really happened or whether I dreamt it. What these people say about it is surely relevant and normally decisive. If MacBeth had had serious doubts about the dagger before him, doubts which persisted after looking again more carefully, it would not have been irrelevant (though disastrous to the play) to call other people in to have a look as well. Orestes saw the Furies and had a preconception of Furies, for he knew what Furies were as distinct from, say, Muses. His mistake was an error of reasoning in believing them to be real solid bodies,[49] an error that could have been avoided by checking with other people. This confirming procedure of corroboration is, of course, crucial in the case of the gods.

---

[48]Ep. Hdt. 39.

[49]M. 8. 63-64.

## The Existence of the Gods

We have already mentioned that, under certain circumstances, the natural process of sensation may by-pass the senses according to Epicurus, and images may act directly on the mind to cause experience.[50] It is the fineness of the texture of such images that accounts for their by-passing the senses and acting directly on the mind, according to Lucretius,[51] and such images cause the experience of dreams and visions. Most of what we experience in this way is worthless, the random organization into nonsense imagery of mid-air collisions of images; some of what we so experience may serve to fill out myths and other stories with fictitious creatures like centaurs,[52] and so on. But if the mind remains alert and does not jump to unwarranted conclusions, this kind of experience should present no serious difficulty for our understanding of the world, for it is usually just a matter of distinguishing dream from reality which we can do quite well, even if we can't always explain just how we do it. Often there are clues that the creatures we see are not real because their concepts are contradictory or because such things are naturally impossible, as Lucretius argues in the case of centaurs.[53] Or we find that certain experiences are entirely private, uncorroborated by others when we would expect such corroboration, and such experiences we come to regard as dreams or imagination. The experiences are real enough, but the objects of such experiences we do not include among the solid objects of the real world, at least not without some special explanation.

---

[50]D.L. 10-31; Lucr. 4. 324-331.

[51]Ibid.

[52]Lucr. 4. 732.

[53]Lucr. 5. 878-974.

Our experience of gods is of that kind, but it has the special feature of being universally corroborated. The first two stages of our experience of gods, sensation and preconception, are entirely natural and prior to all cultural influence; and the third part, confirmation and disconfirmation, shows two features, first, universal confirmation of the existence of gods and second, the most bizarre array of culturally produced conceptions of the nature of the gods.[54] The truth in our belief in the gods is preserved through the first two stages and the first part of the third stage as well, according to Epicurus. Up to this stage we have evidence for the existence and nature of the gods which the critical philosophers can accept as clear and persuasive.[55] It is only after that, in the cultural and religious elaboration of the conception of the divine, that unacceptable nonsense is produced.

## The Indifference of the Gods

Whether Epicurus believed that it is important for the good life to have a right understanding of and appropriate attitude toward the gods because the gods really existed, or whether he believed this because the wrong understanding and inappropriate attitude were so harmful in themselves is hard to say. But it is clear that he thought that the right understanding and attitude were ethically of the first importance. The first part of that right understanding, that the gods exist, we have just discussed. There remains the second part, the nature of the gods. Much can

---

[54]N.D. 1. 42-44; Lucr. 5. 1161 - 1193.

[55]Ep. Men. 123. It should be clear that I am explaining Epicurus' argument here rather than defending its acceptability to today's philosophers, for our experience of gods is not the same as the experience Epicurus appears to draw on.

be said about Epicurus' view of the nature of the gods. We shall limit ourselves
here to the nature of the gods so far as it is ethically relevant in the present section
and briefly consider the more purely theoretical part of the theory in the next
section.

The first and, ethically speaking, most important point to understand about the
divine nature is that god is a living being who is imperishable and blessed. This
conception of god is both the beginning of a right understanding of god and of the
appropriate relationship of human and divine beings that is a necessary part of the
good life, and it is also the most basic expression for the idea of god common to
all humanity before religious doctrine, cultural education, and mistaken inferences
multiply that idea into the variety of gods found in religious traditions the world
over. That is, Epicurus takes this to be the formula which expresses our
preconception of divinity. The second step is to admit nothing into our
elaboration of the idea of god which is incompatible with the key attributes of
blessedness and imperishability.[56] This might have been a difficult idea for many
Greeks who took their gods literally and seriously. What, for example, can one
do with the idea of Prometheus having his liver hacked? It might be easy enough
to keep him alive in your story because he was a god, but how can you fail to
cloud his blessed happiness? Or, more to the point for present concerns, could a
Christian accept such an idea and continue to regard the crucifixion with its full
religious meaning? St. Thomas, for example, trying to understand how Christ's
suffering was compatible with his divinity admits to begin with that the
crucifixion was real, and that "there is no doubt that Christ suffered real pain",[57]

---

[56]Ep. Men. 123.

[57]S.T. 3A.15.5.

and that "as Christ could have real pain, so he could have real sadness".[58] But since he is no ordinary man this sadness cannot pervade his entire being. "What is ruled out in Christ is a full-blown emotion of sadness. But he did have the beginnings of sadness, as a passing feeling".[59] Finally, however, Christ's divinity must be given its full due, and it must be admitted that "the higher part [of Christ's soul] enjoyed perfect bliss all the while he was suffering [on the cross]."[60] Epicurus does seem to have put his finger on an inviolable part of the idea of divinity, for even the idea of a god in agony can never simply be that, it seems, but must somehow be understood in such as way as not to compromise the perfect bliss of divinity. It is of interest to note that St. Thomas' discussion is connected with similar discussions in Hellenistic philosophy. He has learned from those discussions and goes so far as to compare Christ with the Stoic sage[61] bearing misfortune. We shall return to this problem later when we try to understand the extreme claim that the Epicurean sage can maintain his tranquil happiness even under torture.

For the present we need to see how the basic idea of divinity identified by Epicurus functions as an ethical idea. Epicurus' own doctrinal summary is terse and to the point: "That which is blessed and imperishable neither suffers nor inflicts trouble, and therefore is affected neither by anger nor by favour. For all such things are marks of weakness".[62] The way this basic idea of divinity

---

[58]S.T. 3a.15.6.

[59]S.T. 3a.15.6.

[60]S.T. 3a.46.8.

[61]S.T. 3a.46.6, #2.

[62]K.D. 1.

functions as an ethical idea from the start is by severing all relations of reward and punishment. Such relations do not exist because they are incompatible with the idea of a blessed being that has no weakness and thus is perfectly secure in its blessedness, that never suffers trouble or worry or want or anger but regards all with perfectly tranquil bliss. The belief that the gods in any way take part in human affairs for either good or ill is incompatible with the natural preconception of divinity. It is rather a later addition of "false suppositions", a projection upon the gods of certain human virtues.[63] "For trouble, concern, anger and favour are incompatible with blessedness, but have their origin in weakness, fear, and dependence on neighbours",[64] and once this is understood "no fears of those above menace us".[65] The effect of the most basic understanding of divinity is to remove our fear of the gods.

This removal of fear, however, is bought at the price of the hope for reward, since the same argument removes both. This is as it should be, for an Epicurean life is marked by the maximum possible degree of self-sufficiency, as we shall see, and the accomplished Epicurean does not await the favour of either the gods or Lady Luck. Indeed, he would probably reject such favour if it were offered in this life. And he does not expect a reward in the next life, since there will be no next life for a mortal human being in which to receive such a reward, as we shall see in the next chapter.

The argument which infers divine non-involvement in human affairs from

---

divine blessedness is a conceptual argument. Such arguments, when sound, are logically very powerful, but in practical affairs they tend to be only a beginning. One would like to have their truth substantiated by empirical evidence drawn, if possible, from real life and practical experience. Of course, it was not difficult for Epicurus to provide such evidence, for then as now natural events and human affairs do not bear witness to the divine presence, but rather the reverse. Lactantius reports that Epicurus argued for the absence of divine intervention in our world by pointing out that there is evil in our world, which would not be so if god involved himself in its affairs. He quotes Epicurus:

> "God either wants to eliminate bad things [mala] and cannot, or can but does not want to, or neither wishes to nor can, or both wants to and can. If he wants to and cannot, then he is weak--and this does not apply to god. If he can but does not want to, then he is spiteful--which is equally foreign to god's nature. If he neither wants to nor can, he is both weak and spiteful and so not a god. If he wants to and can, which is the only thing fitting for a god, where then do bad things come from? Or why does he not eliminate them?[66]

Lactantius comments:

> "I know that most of the philosophers who defend [divine] providence are commonly shaken by this argument and against their wills are almost driven to admit that god does not care, which is exactly what Epicurus is looking for."[67]

Lactantius does not pursue the details of the Epicurean argument, but it is plainly aimed not at the existence of god, but at divine involvement in the world. Plainly Epicurus takes it to be part of the basic common understanding of god that god will not tolerate evil in his presence, that in his world, in his sphere of concern, as it were, in which he lives his divinity in serene bliss, there is no evil. The fact of evil in our world therefore proves that god has nothing to do with our world, that he does not care but is indifferent to our troubles which do not trouble

[66]Lactantius, De Ira Dei, 13, 20-22; US. 374; Brad Inwood and L.P. Gerson, Hellenistic Philosophy, Indianapolis and Cambridge: Hackett Publishing Co., 1988, p. 64.

[67]Ibid.

him, and that our world is therefore not a providential one. There are other arguments as well against divine involvement with our world, that is, against providence. The whole thrust of Epicurean physics, as of today's natural science, is to show that a natural causal explanation can be given for every event, and that attempts to give teleological explanations "are back to front, due to distorted reasoning".[68] The ethical relevance of this is to understand that the world in which we live is not divinely designed to cater to human wishes, it is too faulty for that;[69] but neither is it a hostile place of terror, for it will support life, and the good life is possible in it if we understand its laws and the nature of the human good. Lucretius gives a description of the world as a natural wilderness in which we can live but which certainly has not been designed with us in mind since so much of it is either useless or hostile to human life.[70] This account could easily be supplemented by our knowledge of the earth as a partly green speck in unimaginably vast space, cold , dark and empty, except for the rare occurrence of mindless fusion furnaces and spent slag heaps. In such a world we have to learn to live alone and be as self-sufficient as castaways on a desert island. The gods are neither with us nor against us, they neither created a world in the past for our good, nor involve themselves in the present operation of nature or the affairs of men.

The gods are utterly indifferent to us but, thought Epicurus, we should not be indifferent to them. For a start, while one would hardly think it worth a god's while to contemplate human beings, the contemplation of the gods provides a

---

[68]Lucr. 4. 832-833.

[69]cf. Lucr. 2.181; 5.199.

[70]cf. Lucr. 5.200 ff.

human being with "the greatest feeling of pleasure".[71] The contemplation of god, without ulterior motive and for no other reason than the pure contemplation itself was, if Cicero can be trusted, thought to be highly pleasurable and worth doing for its own sake. This point is reminiscent of similar points found in contemplative mystical traditions of all times and places, but we shall not pursue this lead since the point is not developed anywhere else in the extant Epicurean literature. But it is worth considering here what an Epicurean was contemplating when he contemplated god. Just what did Epicurus take the gods to be?

## The Nature of the Gods

That is a difficult question. The textual evidence is obscure, and there is no generally accepted interpretation of these difficult texts. The central text in most interpretations is Cicero[72] who prefaces his report with the warning that Epicurus' discoveries are "too acute, and his words to subtle, to be appreciated by just anyone" for they are about "hidden and profoundly obscure things". Certainly we can't expect anything easy or obvious after a warning like that, but should be prepared for something so difficult that Cicero had reservations about whether he himself understood what he was reporting. Though the gods are said to be of human shape and very beautiful,[73] they are not solid bodies, as are human beings, but "quasi-body", and they do not have blood but "quasi-blood".[74] They are

---

[71]N.D. 1.49.

[72]N.D. 1.49; 1.105; 1.109.

[73]N.D. 1.46-7.

[74]N.D. 1.49.

unlike the objects of our daily experience in that they have "neither the kind of solidity nor the numerical distinctness of those things".[75] The scholium to the first principal doctrine, however, claims that Epicurus allows that some gods have numerical identity and are thus numerically distinct from other gods. The reason why the gods, though alive, are not solid bodies like other living things is that they seem to be constituted by a constant stream of similar images flowing to a focal point from the infinite surrounding atoms, and a god is precisely the form of such a focal point kept in being by the constant stream of images. Scholarly interpretations of what to make of this fall roughly into two types. Some understand the gods as extramentally objective beings who lead their lives in a most uneventful locale not in any world but in the space between worlds. This reading places great weight on Cicero's report of first century Epicureans' designation of the dwelling place of the gods as the intermundial spaces,[76] and on Lucretius' denial that the "holy abode of the gods exists in any part of the world",[77] but rather is in a place in which there is no rain, no snow, no frost, but only cloudless air full of light.[78] And some understand the gods as not having an existence independent of human minds which conceive them. In this interpretation it is still acknowledged that the stream of images that maintains the gods is as extramentally objective as the images of any other object, for like these images it is made of atoms of extramental origin. But it is the human mind that supplies the formal focus organizing the stream of images into the stable being of

---

[75]Ibid.

[76]N.D. 1.18; De fin. 2.75; De Div. 2.40.

[77]Lucr. 5. 146-147.

[78]Lucr. 3.19-22.

a god on basically the same principles as concept formation or the production of creatures of the imagination from the supply of extramental atomic images of things.

Our proper concern here is the ethical relevance of Epicurean theology, and the metaphysics of the divine nature can only occupy us in passing, therefore. In order to arrive at a satisfying understanding of the theoretical theological issue which may fruitfully be connected with ethical considerations it will be useful to consider two recent interpretations of this material, one from each of the two strands just identified.

John Rist insists on extramentally objective ontological status for Epicurus' gods. The gods that have no numerical identity he understands as generic deities with nothing to distinguish them from other deities of the same type, such as the Graces. In addition to that, however, there are in this interpretation particular gods numerically distinct from all others, such as Zeus and Apollo.[79] What makes Rist particularly interesting is that, unlike most other interpreters who understand the gods to be extramentally objective, he is aware of the other strand of interpretation and explicitly argues for its rejection. He appeals to Cicero's important report that knowledge of the gods is given us by nature herself,[80] a point which he believes "renders impossible the theory...that the gods are identical with the images of the gods", and is "even more destructive" of the theory that the gods are "merely the projections of human ideals".[81] An interpretation which

---

[79]John Rist, Epicurus: An Introduction, Cambridge University Press, 1972, appendix E.

[80]N.D. 1.45.

[81]Rist, op. cit., p. 140, n.4.

would deny the extramental objectivity of the gods must not only do justice to the textual evidence, but have a convincing account of what Rist considered the fatal flaw of any such interpretation. The recent work of Long and Sedley does just that.

Long and Sedley argue[82] that the philosophically satisfying interpretation that is also best supported by the most authoritative textual evidence is to understand the gods as human thought constructs. The supply of similar images required for there to be gods is as objectively real and extramental as any other images, but it is the human mind that focuses these streams into a form and, by converging in our minds, they become gods. This process is simply the standard process of concept formation as it is described in Epicurean psychology. The gods, then, are essentially products of the imagination, but what distinguishes gods from other products of the imagination, such as giants, is that we produce the gods by our very natures. The human mind is so constituted by nature that involuntarily and universally human minds produce gods from the inexhaustible supply of images. The objective source of these images is especially favoured specimens of human beings which "by transition" we simplify and intensify into gods. The gods, then, are instinctive thought constructs produced by an innate and normal function of the human mind, that makes our knowledge of them natural and common to all mankind. The gods are imperishable because as concepts they are everlasting. They are eternal paradigmatic concepts rather like Platonic Forms. And as living beings we imaginatively endow them with imperishability as the ultimate in longevity. The primary Epicurean understanding of gods, therefore, is not as

---

[82]A.A. Long and D.N. Sedley, Hellenistic Philosophers, Cambridge University Press, 1987, Vol. 1, pp. 144-149.

numerically distinct solid bodies, but as a paradigmatic concept of god present in human minds by their natural constitution. Long and Sedley realize however that because of the scholium to the first principal doctrine, their interpretation must leave room for numerically distinct gods. They suggest two interpretations of this. One is a rather limp attempt to understand this in terms of the deification of Epicurean sages.[83] But the other[84] is much more interesting. The concept of god occurs in each human mind not only as a theoretical item in our cognitive stock like a fact to be noted with disinterested objectivity, but it is a projection of an ethical ideal and so, practical from the start. The idea of god is from the start the idea of a being to revere and to emulate. It is a concept that occurs in all human minds by nature, a concept that occurs in the minds of particular human individuals who are members of particular societies and cultural groups, who have regional views of moral excellence and a more or less well developed identity as an individual. Thus the idea of god is, practically speaking, universally true by giving us cognitive insight into our natural goal, the good for us so far as we are human. But none of us is merely a human being but always an individual within some cultural group, and so our goal and good may take on particular features. It is this which may distort the natural concept of god with the false beliefs of particular religions and with the projection of undesirable individual characteristics upon the gods.[85] But the fact that the idea of god always occurs in individual human beings also allows for the possibility of an appropriate extension of the universal human god relationship into an individual

[83]Long and Sedley, op. cit., p. 148.

[84]Long and Sedley, op. cit., p. 146.

[85]Ep. Men. 124.

and private form of reverence and emulation and a vision of the good with features peculiar to unique individuals. Thus Long and Sedley interpret the puzzling passage near the end of the Letter to Menoeceus[86] as being about a self-image which constitutes a person's ethical goal of which that person's god is the paradigm. This interpretation is problematical and we shall return to it in a later place. For the present we must pursue the more general ethical relevance of the Epicurean understanding of the gods.

## The Ethical Relevance of the Gods

When Cicero's Velleius described to Balbus the Stoic how the gods live[87]he makes perfect bliss the keynote. We cannot conceive a god as troubled or burdened or unhappy. But this entails that we cannot think of a god as other than at his ease, for otherwise he could not be happy. Real happiness is not possible for anyone entangled in serious affairs and occupations or engaged in toilsome labour. Quite simply, onerous work cannot be part of the divine life. We must think of the gods as idle, as taking delight purely in being themselves.

If we can accept, as seems reasonable, the interpretation of the nature of the gods as instinctive thought constructs, produced not in some arbitrary way, but by an innate and normal function of the human mind, then we can understand both their utter indifference to human affairs and how they are the supreme embodiment of our own natural good.

---

[86]Ep. Men. 135.

[87]N.D. 1. 51-52.

The gods are not in any sense other beings from whom we can expect anything, either good or bad, nor do they expect anything from us. This is their utter indifference. They take no more active part in our lives than do characters of fiction. But as fictions we project by our very nature, rather than by some playful urge to story-telling, we have in them a projected embodiment of our own natural good. The ethical relevance of the description of the divine life is not so much that it is an account of how the gods live, but that it is also an account of the blessed life as such, of a state the gods possess and human beings strive for. Happiness is the same for gods and for human beings and the essence of happiness, says Velleius, is peace of mind and leisure. But if happiness is the human good, then we must not look for the essence of man in labour. A human being compelled to work is not fully human, but rather a kind of domesticated animal, perverted by social convention in face of real or imagined need. To understand Epicurean ethics, it is necessary to conceive a human being not as an instrument of any kind, but as a self-complete or completeable end.

The gods are in perfect and eternal possession of the good because they are gods. The good is the same for gods and human beings and gods possess this good by nature, but human beings do not. Human beings can come to understand the good and strive for it, and they can come to realize it in their lives. The gods are ethically relevant to us in that they embody an image of our natural good. To understand this good, however, requires more than an image and we must philosophically develop the idea of the good in subsequent chapters. But there is another important difference between gods and human beings which we must consider first. Man, unlike the gods, is mortal. Does that not change everything?

# Chapter Three

# Death

Cicero's description of divine happiness indicates leisure as the most important ingredient. But there is more. Lucretius points out another important feature. Human beings believed the gods to be supremely happy "because the fear of death troubled none of them".[88]

Human beings, however, know that they must die and, if a good life is to be possible for them, it must also be a mortal one. Must not the knowledge of my mortality undermine the quality of my life unless I find an effective way of coping with mortality? If I would live philosophically rather than thoughtlessly then my coping must not only be effective, but also intellectually responsible. Epicurean ethics includes a philosophical way of coping with our mortality which is still eminently worth understanding today. The essence of it is captured in the formula that "when we exist death is not present, and when death is present we do not exist."[89]

There is good reason for thinking that the formula, and so the basic argument, is not original with Epicurus but that it goes back at least to the fifth century, to

---

[88]Lucr. 5. 1180.

[89]Ep. Men. 125.

Prodicus the melancholy sage of Ceos.[90]   But if Epicurus found it, he also
developed it. Whatever its origin, one can still hear a Parmenidean echo in it, and
it is instructive to hear this echo, for it highlights the important modification
Epicurus made in the metaphysical thesis about the nothingness of death in order
to develop it into an ethical thesis.

Death is conceived by Epicurus as our utter extinction, as unqualified non-
existence. Put in a Parmenidean way the Epicurean thesis would read:  death is
nothing because we cannot be dead. The dead do not exist and therefore cannot
be anything, even dead. Quite literally there is no one who is dead. If being dead
is a state or condition, then no one can ever be in that state or condition.

But Epicurus is not interested in whether metaphysical propositions which
suffer from reference failure can be meaningful or not, or whether reference to a
past event or entity is successful reference.   Or, to put it more cautiously,
Epicurus is not interested in this (or any other) issue as long as it is merely
theoretical, that is, without practical import.  To give the discussion of death
practical import he changes the thesis 'we cannot be dead' into 'we cannot
experience death' and 'death is nothing' into 'death is nothing to us'.

Epicurus is concerned to turn a metaphysical thesis into an ethical thesis. As an
ethical thesis it must not only be theoretically sound, that is, true, but also
practically sound, that is, contribute to the good life.  As an ethical doctrine the

---

[90]The pseudo-Platonic dialogue Axiochus ascribes such an argument to Prodicus at 369B.
Though the dialogue is probably Hellenistic, and so the argument may have been taken from
Epicurus, there is reason to think that it faithfully represents Prodicus on this point.  For an
argument to this effect see Theodor Gomperz, Greek Thinkers, New York: Humanities Press,
1964, Vol. I, p. 583.  Also there is evidence that Epicurus had read Prodicus since according to
Philodemus he criticized Prodicus in Book XII of On Nature.  (Philodemus on Piety, 112.5-12 =
Us 87.)

Epicurean discussion of death is in the first place addressed to those who fear that they may survive their last breath and so be available for divine punishment. These Epicurus assures that the dead cannot suffer. And in the second place the Epicurean discussion of death is addressed to those who fear that they may not survive their last breath. These he subjects to the therapeutic removal of the desire for immortality. And in the third place it is addressed to those who wonder whether a brief mortal life can ever be worth living. These he shows that a mortal life can be as intrinsically worth living as the immortal life of a god.

## We Are Mortal

Those who fear death because they fear a painful afterlife are assured by Epicurus that there is no afterlife at all and, therefore, no painful one. There is no afterlife because no soul capable of an afterlife survives the death of the body. There are no arguments for this position among the remains of Epicurus' writings. Even the passage in the Letter to Herodotus[91] hardly amounts to more than the claim that the soul disperses upon the death of the body and cannot even be imagined to retain sensory awareness. But surely there were such arguments in the text which is now lost, and the battery of arguments for the mortality of the soul given by Lucretius[92] is probably a fairly orthodox report of many of them.

The important strain of arguments in the more than two dozen given by Lucretius aims at showing that the soul behaves in every significant respect like an organ of the body. Like the other bodily organs it shows signs of heredity, of

---

[91]Ep. Hdt. 65-67.

[92]Lucr. 3. 417-829.

being the offspring of particular parents, which it would not, he thinks, if it were an immortal entity inhabiting this body for a while. Its lack of memory of life before association with this body is evidence that it did not pre-exist this body. Souls show a normal development over a lifetime in step with the development of the body. The souls of the very young are infantile, the mature have mature souls, and the souls of the old are worn out and failing with age. Souls get sick like the body and sick souls often can be cured by medicine, as can sick bodies. The soul is essentially like any other physical organ functioning in association with the body and sharing its fate.

The conception of the mechanics of death which is operating here is the dispersal of atoms. The body and the soul, each a configuration of atoms, separate at death, and each breaks up into its constituent atoms which disperse and probably become constituent atoms of other compound objects. This, of course, leaves at least the theoretical possibility that all the atoms of which I am now composed may reassemble to form a structurally identical human being sometime in the infinite future. Lucretius denies that this human being would be personally identical with me because there would be no continuity of memory to identify that human being with me. And so Lucretius thinks that it is quite possible that the configuration of atoms which I am has occurred before, but that I am not at all concerned about those "selves which I have been before" because the intervening stoppage of life has erased all memory.[93]

One difficulty with this last argument is that memory in the materialist understanding of human beings must be reducible to atomic structure. Absence of

---

[93]Lucr. 3. 847-861.

memory, then, would be evidence that the two people are not structurally identical, for on this understanding of human beings we would expect memory to go with structure such that two structurally identical people would have at least the same apparent memories. Another difficulty is that Lucretius gives us no reason to think that an intervening stoppage of life and atomic dispersal necessarily erases memory, so that it still remains possible that besides the kinds of look-alikes Lucretius evidently has in mind, there may appear a person whose memory is continuous with mine. I suppose that Lucretius does not consider this last a serious possibility because of the general apparent lack of memory continuity which he finds everywhere, and does not discuss it for that reason.

In general Lucretius' arguments are powerful and express a very reasonable judgement on the fate of human beings, given the available evidence. There can be no doubt that they are better than Plato's arguments for the opposite conclusion in, for example, the Phaedo. But they are strongly suggestive rather than rationally conclusive and, as we shall see below, there is reason to think that Epicurus himself so assessed their strength. It is quite possible to continue to fear an afterlife after having gone over the arguments against it and, to people who do, Epicurus has two more things to say. The first is that it is not in the nature of the gods to hurt anyone, as we have seen in the previous chapter, because it would be inconsistent with their untroubled blessedness.[94] If you can't get the thought of an afterlife out of your mind, then perhaps you can appreciate the concept of the divine nature well enough to realize that the gods will concern themselves with you in your afterlife no more than they concern themselves with you in your present life, that is, not at all. And the second thing Epicurus has to say to people

---

[94]K.D. 1; Ep. Men. 124.

who may continue to fear an afterlife is that the stories about the afflictions suffered by the dead are not knowledge of something happening elsewhere at all, but are projections of the evils of the present world, that is, tales of the afterworld have a perfectly reasonable this-worldly explanation.[95]

The important thing, however, if you would live by philosophy, is to realize that the weight of the evidence shows that people cease to exist at death, that death is non-existence, that it is the utter absence of sensation and consciousness, that we cannot experience death. All good or evil, however, is felt or experienced good or evil. Death is therefore neither good nor evil but completely indifferent, that is, it is nothing to us. And because death itself is not painful, the anticipation of death is not (rationally) painful either. The philosophically acquired belief in the indifference of death can thus become an ethical attitude which promotes the good life. We shall have to return to this point below.

## The Desire for Immortality

It is possible, of course, that the anguish of some people at the thought of death is dispelled by the firm conviction that it won't hurt. But some people are anguished at being mortal. The very thought that their existence will have an end occasions deep sadness. Such people have trouble coping with their finitude, they want not to give up life but to survive, they have a desire for immortality.

Lucretius has some advice for such people: pat phrases of pacification that were current then as now, phrases which point out that for the orderly balance of nature one generation has to go to make room for the next, that we are tenants

---

[95]Lucr. 3. 978-1023.

not owners, tourists not residents in the world.[96] "Come now", he says to an old man, "yield to your years: thus it must be".[97] Memmius, to whom this exhortation is addressed, might well point out that he is well aware that thus it must be, and that it is precisely this which occasions his lament. He doesn't want it to be thus. He wants immortality.

Lucretius' pat phrases are probably orthodox and to be found somewhere in the writings of Epicurus that haven't survived. But Epicurus can do better than this, even if we draw only on what still remains of his work. To a person consumed by the desire for immortality and pained by the thought of his mortality he doesn't hold out hope by trying to make the case for immortality, as did Plato, but, realizing that such a person needs more than rational persuasion, he offers therapeutic philosophy.

The idea that philosophy is not entirely a theoretical enterprise but has a practical component is, of course, not new with Epicurus. Nor is it a new Epicurean idea that this practical component is more than good advice based on experience, but is therapeutic philosophy aiming at a healing transformation of the soul. Epicurus did not invent therapeutic philosophy. It was well established before his time and continued far beyond it.[98] What is new with Epicurus,

---

[96]Lucr. 3. 963-979.

[97]Lucr. 3. 962.

[98]"The analogy between logos and medical therapy is one of the oldest and best entrenched traditions concerning logos in all of Greek culture. From Homer on, we encounter, frequently and prominently, the central idea of the Epicurean position: that logos is to illness of the soul as medical treatment is to illness of the body". Martha Nussbaum, "Therapeutic Arguments: Epicurus and Aristotle", in Malcolm Schofield and Gisela Striker ed., The Norms of Nature, Cambridge University Press, 1986, p. 52. See also the references given there to this medical analogy in writers from Homer to Aristotle. For the continuation of the idea beyond the time of Epicurus see for example, Sextus Empiricus, P.H. III, 280-182; and Plotinus, first Ennead, II, 4: 28-29: "Knowledge, if we cannot act on it at all, is foreign to us".

however, is the idea that all philosophy is in principle therapeutic.[99] Because of this subsumption of theoretical philosophy under practical philosophy, and the formulation of practical philosophy in terms of the guiding metaphor of medical therapy, Epicurus, then as now, incurred the ire of those who felt that this tainted the purity without which theoretical philosophy deteriorates into something less than rational.[100] But this is a misunderstanding. If we are going to do justice to Epicurus, therefore, we must be clear about the idea of Epicurean therapeutic philosophy.

The first thing to understand is that therapeutic philosophy remains philosophy at all times and throughout, that is, it is rational discourse which aims at understanding based on evidence and argument, and which reflects on the first principles of that activity. There may have been variation in teaching techniques at different Epicurean centres from Turkey to Italy and during the centuries of Epicureanism's existence as a major philosophical school of antiquity, indeed it would be surprising if there had not been. And there may have been variation in teaching techniques in the same school, depending on which teacher was teaching, and in the techniques of the same teacher depending on the topic being taught and the pupil to whom it was being taught. And these techniques may have included everything from rote recitation of the principal doctrines, to the acquisition of a basic familiarity with the outlines of Epicurean philosophy by the study of epitomes like the extant letters, and beyond that to the detailed study and justification of first principles and fundamental philosophical doctrines along with

---

[99]cf. Ep. Pyth. 85; Ep. Men. 122; K.D. 11; S.V. 54; Sextus Empiricus, M 7.169 = Us 219; S.V. 221.

[100]e.g. Martha Nussbaum, op. cit., p. 43, "What all argument is, in this [Epicurean] community, is therapy...purgation and drugging".

the critical discussion and refutation of conflicting philosophical doctrines and methods. There may even have been some impatience with rival philosophical schools and the dismissive gestures and name-calling that are often associated with such attitudes. I doubt that any of today's philosophy departments is a stranger to this kind of thing. And it is the kind of thing that can be exaggerated by a renegade who gains the ear of detractors.[101] All of this is, I'm afraid, human all too human. But it should not blind us to the fact that Epicurean therapeutic philosophy remains philosophy true to the basic canons of truth, evidence, argument, and reasoned response and justification.

And a second thing to understand is that therapeutic philosophy does not make understanding a goal to be aimed at for its own sake, but for the sake of living well. Because therapeutic philosophy is practical it must relate to practice in such a way that what has been theoretically understood can be put into practice. Any truth that is theoretically pure in the sense of being in principle indifferent to practice, if there is such a thing, is thought by Epicurus to be fit only for pompous academic posturing, and he will have none of that in philosophy. The therapeutic language in which Epicurus expressed this practical function of philosophy, besides being a familiar idiom to his contemporaries, probably had some methodological advantages which we need not pursue here. But it also had some disadvantages in that it could produce theoretical misunderstanding, the most important of which, as well shall see in a following chapter, was the misunderstanding that Epicurus thought pleasure to be the absence of pain.

---

[101]For a reasoned attempt to put much of the blame for detracting gossip about Epicurus on Metrodorus's brother Timocrates, see David Sedley, "Epicurus and his Professional Rivals", in Jean Bollack and André Laks ed., Etudes sur l'epicurisme antique, (Lille 1976), pp. 120 - 159.

The subsumption of theoretical philosophy under practical philosophy makes theoretical philosophy itself instrumental in our pursuit of the good life. There are people who see in this a perversion of philosophy.[102] It is true that Epicurean philosophy means to be instrumentally valuable in producing the good life for those who understand it and can put it into practice. But it does not follow from this that it has only instrumental value, like a pill or drug which is not itself pleasant but has a desirable effect, nor is it true that Epicurus thought of philosophy in this way. In fact he expressly denies that the value of philosophy is merely instrumental and insists that it is intrinsically valuable. He says, for example, that philosophy differs from other pursuits in that, while with other pursuits the reward comes only at the end, with philosophy the very pursuit of knowledge is itself rewarding.[103] In the letter to Herodotus he claims that he finds his own peace chiefly in being occupied in investigating nature, that the mainstay of his own happiness is doing natural philosophy.[104] Lucretius echoes this by referring to philosophy as "delightful toil".[105] Besides, to take a pill to propel me into bliss or have it happen through some other circumstance would be seen by Epicurus as essentially an intervention of fate and external circumstances in the quality of my life, which he would reject because the good life can have its proper value for me only if I achieve it properly myself. For Epicurus, rightly or wrongly, that meant by philosophy and prudent forethought, not by luck.[106] Nor

---

[102]For a recent example of someone who thinks this and makes the specific charges we are about to discuss, see Martha Nussbaum, op. cit.

[103]S.V. 27.

[104]Ep. Hdt. 37.

[105]Lucr. 3. 419.

[106]Ep. Men. 135.

61

must we think that an Epicurean, because he pursues philosophy as fundamentally practical and subsumes theory under practice, will lack the proper respect for the standard virtues of rational discourse. It is clear from a reading of Epicurus that he is as concerned as any philosopher that what he says be true, that his arguments be valid, and his terms clear. Yet there is something to this charge. Epicurus wants more from rational discourse than truth, validity and clarity, and does not respect these for their own sakes. He is as aware as any of us that there are indefinitely many uninteresting true propositions and valid arguments free from the blemish of unclarity, and that there are heaps of perfectly consistent trivia not worth knowing. Truth, validity, clarity and consistency don't deserve respect for themselves alone, but only for their value when combined with something else that makes the particular rational discourse worth engaging in. He is also aware, of course, that philosophy can become a cult language of academics and of those who must pretend to education and culture, and he thinks of that with the disdain it deserves.[107] We must be careful to choose the right attitude to Epicurus. It would be an inappropriate extravagance to hail him as the saviour of mankind with Lucretius,[108] but it is appropriate and worth our philosophical while to listen carefully and critically to Epicurus the philosopher.

To people then, who are troubled by their desire for immortality, Epicurus offers therapeutic philosophy. Before we can fully understand what he does with this particular desire, we must have a brief look at what he does with desire in general.

---

[107]cf. S.V. 29.

[108]Lucr. 1. 62-79.

The two main terms in the Epicurean classification of desires[109] are 'natural' and 'necessary'. All necessary desires are natural as well, and some unnecessary desires are also natural and some are not. The basic distinction between necessary and unnecessary desires is that a desire is necessary if its non-satisfaction brings pain, and it is unnecessary if its non-satisfaction does not bring pain.[110] The pain Epicurus has in mind here is natural pain or pain somehow implicit in the nature of the desire. If the pain occasioned by the non-satisfaction of a desire is not natural but due to "empty opinion", that is, if the pain can be prevented or removed in some other way than by satisfying the desire, by, for example, changing your mind or seeing the situation in a new way, then the desire is not necessary even though it may still be natural.[111]

The kind of desire we're interested in here is the kind that is natural but not necessary, for the desire for immortality seems to be one of those. The key text is Principal Doctrine 30.

> Whenever intense passion is present in natural desires which do not lead to pain if they are unfulfilled, these have their origin in empty opinion; and the reason for their persistence is not their own nature but the empty opinion of the person.

These natural but unnecessary desires are the important target of Epicurean therapeutic philosophy. The natural and necessary desires, such as the desire for food or air, must be satisfied. The desires that are neither natural nor necessary, such as the desire for fame and statues, can be controlled even by a novice. But the unneccesary desires that are also natural are a potential source of deep trouble because they have natural roots, and some can be powerful enough to ruin your

---

[109]For the classification of desires see especially Ep. Men. 127; K.D. 29.

[110]K.D. 26.

[111]K.D. 30.

life.  Let's consider an example of erotic love.  Suppose you meet someone with whom you become deeply infatuated, or even call it falling in love if you like. And suppose also that this love is not possible for some reason or other, perhaps because it is not returned or because the person dies or some such thing.  The pain of unrequited love is real, no doubt, but it is in an important sense self-inflicted. Suppose that the object of your infatuation, for whom you had fallen at first and somewhat remote sight, turned out to be a cleverly designed department store mannequin.  You would, I think, be cured of your infatuation pretty quickly and feel rather foolish to boot.  The hungry man, on the other hand, who found that the food the automat had given him was not real but artificial, would not lose his hunger over the discovery.  Or suppose again that the object of your love held up beyond the first or second look, even past a few embraces, but then you discovered, like Tom Jones or Oedipus, that she was your mother.  Again, in most cases, that would make an important difference, yet nothing has changed other than your mind or the way you see the situation.  Or suppose it turns out that the object of your desire is unavailable for some other reason, she is a nun, for example, or married, or dies, or some such reason.  The pain can be removed in a way other than by satisfying the desire because it is in important sense self-inflicted, due to "empty opinion".  With such desires it is important to know that we can cope and not allow their non-satisfaction to spoil our lives.

The desire for immortality is such a desire.  True, Epicurus nowhere in the remaining fragments actually identifies the desire for immortality as a non-necessary natural desire, but neither does he deny it, nor do we have a list of such desires from which the desire for immortality is conspicuously absent.  The idea, however, it not difficult to accept.  It is natural for any living being to want to survive, to want to live and not to die. Death, "leaving the sweet light of life", has not become a cause of lamentation only in the context of civilized conventions, but has been so since the beginning.[112] Not to want to die is, of course, not precisely the same as to want to live forever, although the desire for an indefinitely prolonged life is surely a consequence of the desire not to die. That is why Epicureans aim their arguments not only at the fear of death but also at the desirability of an indefinitely prolonged life.[113] The desire for immortality is a natural desire, certainly if understood as in the first place the desire not to die. But the desire for immortality brings no pain if it is not satisfied because death is not experienceable. It is therefore a desire which is natural and unnecessary. It is a desire which, if it brings pain at all, brings pain only in the anticipation of its non-satisfaction, and this pain is not natural in the required sense but self-inflicted. The object of the desire is unattainable. If, therefore, the desire contributes to spoiling your life it must be seen as an illness calling for a cure. Epicurean therapeutic philosophy supplies the cure, first, by producing cogent arguments for mortality, second, by exposing the desire for what it is and, third, by asking the patient to make the new belief that death is nothing to us more than a matter of theoretical assent, but to give it practical moment by making it a habitual attitude. "Become accustomed to the belief that death is nothing to us," Epicurus advises, and you will find that "it takes away the desire for immortality".[114]

This "becoming accustomed" may, of course, not be an easy matter. One may

---

[112]Lucr. 5.988-9. Though Lucretius thinks that death was no more a problem then than now.

[113]eg. Lucr. 3.1080-94.

[114]Ep. Men. 124.

65

have to dig deeply and call on a well developed sense of autarchy in order to bring it off. Indeed, even then, its expression has more of defiance in it than tranquil philosophical insight. Listen, for example, to Epicurus' chief disciple, Metrodorus:

> I have anticipated you, fortune, and entrenched myself against all your secret attacks. And we will not give ourselves up as captives to you or to any other circumstance; but when it is time for us to go, spitting contempt on life and on those who here vainly cling to it, we will leave life crying aloud in a glorious triumph song that we have lived well.[115]

Epicurus never promised that he could get you to like it, just to cure the desire for immortality and help you to face the melancholy fact of mortality. Epicurus himself puts the matter with more tranquility than Metrodorus: "When we come to the end we must be happy and content".[116] You must remember that "you are of mortal nature",[117] "that we are born once and cannot be born twice, but for all time must be no more",[118] "that the draught swallowed by all of us at birth is a draught of death".[119] A little melancholy always remains.

One might think that Epicurus had missed an important ingredient in our fear of death, that his treatment of the topic is therefore fundamentally flawed since he tackles only a poor shadow of the real thing. For example, David Furley writes:

> It seems to me that the essential element in a rational fear of death is the fear that our desires and intentions are unreal, in the sense that they have no possibility of fulfillment...I am suggesting that the fear of death is the fear that there are no more possibilities, and that Epicurus's argument does not succeed in making out that this is irrational, because it is a fear concerned with our

---

[115]S.V. 47.

[116]S.V. 48; Epicurus seems to have managed it: cf. his letter to Idomeneus, D.L. 10.22.

[117]S.V. 10.

[118]S.V. 14.

[119]S.V. 30 (Metrodorus).

66

present state, not about our future (or timeless) state.[120]

David Furley has identified a very real fear here, but it is not the fear of death. We do, of course, take an interest in the fulfillment of our hopes, intentions and plans, and view the prospect of their non-fulfillment with misgivings(for the lesser ones) or fear (for the major ones). These kinds of things may, of course, be interrupted by events other than death, by bankruptcy, for example, or by an earthquake. Make a list of your important projects, of the kinds of things Furley is likely to have had in mind. It seems incredible that if an insurance company could somehow guarantee their completion in the event of death they would have relieved you of your fear of death. True, they surely would have taken a burden off your mind, but it was a worry over and above your fear of death. In fact it might well have been a worry that preoccupied you to the extent that you were distracted from your fear of death and, now that this worry has been removed, you might well find yourself for the first time facing your death without distraction and feel the fear of it in its purity. Or, on the other hand, if you already knew the fear of death and ran across a particularly persuasive account of some "near-death experience",[121] or even had one yourself, you might end up no longer fearing death, though you might still worry about (and even fear) the non-fulfillment of your projects. It is a standard part of the account of those who have had a "near-death experience" that they no longer fear death. No mention is made of the fulfillment or non-fulfillment of present possibilities for good reason: such possibilities are a different matter, irrelevant to (or, at most, only incidentally

---

[120]David Furley, "Nothing to us?", in Malcolm Schofield and Gisela Striker ed., The Norms of Nature: Studies in Hellenistic Ethics, Cambridge University Press, 1986, p. 90.

[121]For a good account of such experiences see, for example, Raymond A. Moody Jr., Life After Life, Mockingbird Books, Atlanta, 1975.

relevant to) the fear of death. Those fears, therefore, must be held quite distinct from the fear of death, and we cannot fault Epicurus for not having dealt with them while his concern was the fear of death.

There is a related point that one sometimes hears made in criticism of Epicurus' discussion of death, namely that our deepest desire is not just for life but for a complete life, and that our fear of death is properly the fear of a premature death.[122] It is true that the fear of a premature death is a real fear, and our lamenting a friend's premature death has a special poignancy given it by the prematurity of his death. But again, the fear of a premature death is significantly different from the fear of death. Epicurus is not concerned with any special features of death, he is not concerned with death so far as it may be premature, or violent or painful, etc., but he is concerned simply with our mortality, with the fact that we must die and be no more. The elderly notoriously revive their interest in religion when there is no longer a question of the prematurity of death. They are fanning their hope of immortality, as did Socrates, simply in face of their mortality. Epicurus argues that this hope of immortality is an unjustified and irrational hope, and the point of his discussion of death is to show how we can face our mortality, how we can live a lucidly mortal life, without resorting to the irrational hope of immortality. That discussion is only clouded by bringing special features of some people's deaths, such as prematurity, into the discussion.

---

[122]eg. Gisela Striker, "Commentary on Mitsis' 'Epicurus on Death and the Duration of Life'", Proceedings of the Boston Area Colloquium for Ancient Philosophy, 4, 323-328, 1988. I don't think that Striker would disagree with my position here for she writes: "It seems to me that [Epicurus'] argument might have some merit if it were meant to address the fear of mortality, but it will not serve to establish that it makes no difference whether we have a very short or a very long life, simply because a very short life could not possibly be complete....I am inclined to think that all the Epicurean arguments were meant to show is that we should not ruin our lives worrying about being mortal" pp. 327-8.

We must briefly consider here that Epicurus was aware of the quality of his arguments for mortality, that they were strongly suggestive but fell short of inescapable proof, and that Epicurus himself was not fully convinced, either theoretically or practically, of his own utter extinction after the present life. There is, in addition to the quality of the arguments for mortality, another Epicurean doctrine to be taken into account here, the doctrine that statements about the future are neither true nor false.[123] He thought he needed this doctrine to preserve human freedom in face of the challenge to it of arguments like Aristotle's Sea Battle Argument.[124] Even a theoretical doctrine like this comes to have ethical import for Epicurus, however. After his discussion of the doctrine that death is nothing to us in the Letter to Menoeceus he adds a curious paragraph which, were it not so obviously the last point in his discussion of death, might go unnoticed as a piece of good advice about the precariousness of our best laid plans.

> We must remember that the future is neither wholly ours nor wholly not ours, so that neither must we count on it as quite certain to come nor despair of it as quite certain not to come.[125]

We needn't think that Epicurus, because he thought that statements about the future were neither true nor false, also thought that we were entirely ignorant about the future. Of two contradictory statements about the future we may not be able to say which is true and which is false because neither one is true or false, but we can still say, with Aristotle, that "one may indeed be more likely to be true

---

[123]cf. Cicero, De fato 21; 37; Academica 2.97 = Us 376.

[124]De interpretatione 9.

[125]Ep. Men. 127.

than the other".[126]   Epicurus, like Aristotle, would deny actual truth and falsehood to statements about the future, but allow them probable truth and falsehood.  And probable truth and falsehood can be established by argument from evidence.  On balance he saw the evidence for extinction to be much greater than the evidence for survival, but he also realized that it didn't amount to certainty.  So the practical advice, that it is foolish absolutely to count on or to despair of the future, need not finds its limit even here.  The reminder to Menoeceus is entirely appropriate.

But even if there is some chance of survival, for the philosopher with the evidence available to Epicurus it is too slim a chance to sacrifice your life to.  It is not enough to undermine the rationality of an enlightened carpe diem attitude to life.  The point is not to let the hope of survival renew the flirtation with immortality if it is likely to spoil your present life.  Sometimes a simple piece of good advice is no worse for being simple: "we should not spoil what we have by desiring what we have not".[127]

## A Mortal Life Can Be Good

The doctrine that death is nothing to us, practically expressed, is an attitude of tranquil indifference to death.  It is easy for people who don't understand Epicureanism to misinterpret this as an indifference to life.  This misunderstanding was already widespread enough in the ancient world for Sextus Empiricus, no friend of Epicureanism, to see fit to correct it.

Epicurus did not assert that "death is nothing to us" in the sense that to be

---

[126]De interpretatione, 9, 19a37.

[127]S.V. 35.

alive or not is a matter of indifference; for it is far preferable to be alive because the good belongs to the sentient.[128]

Death may be a matter of indifference to an Epicurean, but there is no doubt that existence, life at your lucid best, is desirable.[129] But this raises a new question: how can death be nothing to us if it means giving up a good? If I have the choice between living and dying, between something that is good and something that is neither good nor bad, then the obvious thing to choose is the good. It should be clear that, given the choice between continued existence on the one hand, and being extinguished, even if painlessly, on the other, I would not be indifferent to the choice. And it would be quite reasonable for me not to be so indifferent.

We must understand that Epicurus agrees with this fully. The reason is that life, certainly the good life, is desirable, and when choosing between a desirable good and something neither good nor bad, it is reasonable to chose the good. But given this, we must also understand what Epicurus takes to be unreasonable.

Epicurus' point is that in fact life and death are not a matter of choice. Life is to be enjoyed, and death is nothing. It is reasonable to prefer life to death. But it is unreasonable to let the thought, the anticipation of death spoil the enjoyment of life. Epicurean ethics must combine the views that life is intrinsically desirable and that death is nothing to us. The combination of the desire for life and the indifference to death is made possible by the doctrine of the nature of death and its inevitability, and the consequent removal of the desire for immortality as an

[128]M. 1.285.

[129]cf. Ep. Men. 126.

unnecessary desire which is futile and, therefore, irrational.

Epicurus shows little patience with people who see their lives as a kind of consumer good to be taken to that great complaint department in the sky if it fails to satisfy. "He is a little man in all respects", says Epicurus, "who has many good reasons for quitting life".[130] There is some irony in the notion of many good reasons, of course. One problem with the mentality of such a "little man" is that he believes in some form of providence and expects some agency other than himself to be concerned about his welfare. But reality is utterly unprovidential and if we are interested in shaping our beliefs with evidence we'll give up the idea.[131] Instead we must come to understand reality as a natural wilderness in which we are alone but in which it is possible to have a garden. With the help of philosophy it is possible to live a good life, a life intrinsically worth living. Indeed, this practical point is the purpose and value of philosophy. The basic requirements of life are usually easy to come by and, once that is provided for, the Epicurean can produce for himself a life which "might rival even Zeus in happiness."[132] The Epicurean aims to be self-sufficient, at being a self-made man responsible for his own life. This attitude is so strong that, under some circumstances at least, an Epicurean would prefer that his own deliberate plans should fail, rather than that they should succeed owing to luck.[133] An Epicurean realizes that he cannot fully control his life any more than he can control the weather, that despite his prudent philosophical lifestyle there may be bouts of bad

---

[130]S.V. 38.

[131]cf. Lucr. 2. 180-181; 5. 195-199.

[132]S.V. 33.

[133]Ep. Men. 135.

fortune. But he has learned to hang in there, he knows that things pass, and can maintain his basic happiness through periods of painful misfortune. Indeed, the accomplished Epicurean sage was said to be able to maintain it even under torture.[134]

But there must be hope that things will change again. Even an Epicurean sage would not regard a life of great pain as worth hanging on to if there were no prospect of change. With this we come upon the last role of death in Epicurean philosophy. It is possible for a self-sufficient Epicurean, who has no Socratic reservations about suicide, to choose death. This, of course, is perfectly reasonable, given that the only life worth living is an intrinsically valuable one and that life is in no way an instrument for earning advantage in an afterlife. The written remains of Epicurus contain only a rejection of suicide,[135] but such passages basically insist that neither old age nor the host of petty problems that beset little people are sufficient reason for quitting life. This is quite compatible with the view that extravagant bad fortune may make death look attractive. Nietzsche's observation that "the thought of suicide is a powerful comfort: it helps one through many a dreadful night",[136] is not incompatible with Epicureanism.

True, Epicurus never advocated suicide in writing. But great philosophers also teach by example. Epicurus' disease had progressed to the point where he was in constant pain. He was seventy-two years old and "suffered pains such as bring

---

[134]D.L. 10.118.

[135]cf. Ep. Men. 126; S.V. 38.

[136]Friedrich Nietzsche, Beyond Good and Evil, IV, 157.

men to their last day"[137] with no hope of relief. He wrote his will, got into a bathtub filled with hot water, drank a cup of wine which had been prepared for him, asked his friends to remember his teaching, and died.[138]

[137]From a letter preserved by Philodemus. S.V. 36.

[138]D.L. 10.15. Stilpo too, when old and sick, drank wine "to hasten his end" D.L. 2.121.

# Chapter Four

# The Good

## Work or Pleasure

Human mortality seems not to be an obstacle to the good life. Epicurus believes that he has found a way of coping with death that allows human beings to enjoy lives which rival those of the gods in quality. There is no great difficulty in imagining what such a life might be, at least in rough outline and with allowances for individual preferences. Homer speaks for a great many of us when his Odysseus gives the following description:

> There is no boon in life more sweet, I say,
> than when a summer joy holds all the realm,
> and banqueters sit listening to a harper
> in a great hall, by rows of tables heaped
> with bread and roast meat, while a steward goes
> to dip up wine and brim your cups again.
> Here is the flower of life, it seems to me![139]

This is a charming picture, but the difficulty is rather obvious. Perhaps the gods can sustain such pleasures indefinitely but not human beings. For us scenes like the one described by Odysseus are weekend and holiday interludes in lives taken up for the most part with work. Such things may come without effort to the gods, but in the human world someone has to work to provide such pleasures. The gods don't have to work for a living, but human beings do. Any philosophical account of the good life must face the problem of work.

---

[139]Odyssey IX, 5.

This problem is deeper than it seems at first. It is not just a matter of money not growing on trees, but seems to be a matter of human nature itself. Suppose that no one had to work to provide Odysseus and his fellows with their banquet, how long could they sustain it? A banquet after long hardship is one thing, but life turned into an uninterrupted banquet is quite another. Rest after long labour is quite different from chronic idleness. One brings an appetite to the occasional banquet which the regular banqueter no longer knows, and the sleep which the regular banqueter finds at night cannot compare to the sleep that follows an active day. And if we now suppose that the banqueters were not soldiers back from the field, but had lived in idleness supplied with every want and fancy from childhood, we would surely have nothing that anyone could describe as the flower of life. Spoiled, bored, fat and feeble these banqueters would be, without merit as human beings and probably incapable of real pleasure. There is some reason for thinking that man is a labouring animal not by circumstance, but by nature.

This issue was not unknown to the Greeks of the time of Epicurus. Xenophon[140] relates a passage from a work of Prodicus in which the question is whether the good life for a human being is essentially a life of labour or of pleasure. Prodicus had probably been Socrates' teacher[141], so Xenophon's having Socrates tell the story as he remembers having heard it from Prodicus is quite appropriate. And Socrates tells the story to Aristippus, one of his own followers who founded, or at least was the inspiration for the later founding of, the Cyrenaic school of hedonism. The story is meant to oppose hedonism.

---

[140]Memorabilia II, 1, 21 ff.

[141]cf. Meno 96d.

The story relates how the young Hercules lay down in a solitary spot to ponder what course he was to follow in life. The choice was between a life of work and a life of pleasure, which two life styles are personified as two goddesses who find the young Hercules and try to influence his choice. They are called Virtue (aretē) and Vice (kakia), although Vice insists that only her enemies call her that while her friends call her Happiness. Virtue is a well-bred lady of modest gaze and noble bearing. Vice is a painted tart with bold eyes, plump and soft and provocatively dressed. The virtuous beauty walked by Hercules wrapped in modest purity, but the tart capered up to him to offer him advice. She offered him a life of ease and pleasure, free from hardship and trouble, filled with sensuous delights. If he chose her way, she assured him, he would never have to work and, if his funds ever ran low, she would show him how to make use of other people to support his luxurious life style. At this point, of course, Virtue breaks her modest silence. The truth is, she points out, that the gods give nothing good and fair to humans unless they work for it. Learn to work with diligence therefore, she counsels, and you will have a happy life.

We need not ask just how faithful Xenophon's version of the story is to the original of Prodicus, nor how fair a portrait of Aristippus' hedonism we have here.[142] The point is that the two main options of living identified in ancient Greece even before the time of Epicurus were the life of virtue and work on the one hand, and the life of pleasure and ease on the other. Post-Socratic

---

[142]On the first point we should note that on beginning and ending the story, Socrates reminds us that he is giving an approximate version from memory, and no other versions have survived with which this one can be compared. On the second point we should remind ourselves that Xenophon and Aristippus were fellow pupils of Socrates and that Xenophon had never liked and always disapproved of Aristippus. cf. D.L. 2.65. Also, Aristippus had a daughter whom he named Aretē, like the virtuous goddess in the story, and who was a talented philosopher.

philosophers tried, on the whole, to give critical and principled expression to one or other of them in philosophical ethics.

Epicurus rejected the life of work and the virtues of service as inappropriate for human beings and instead made pleasure the foundation of his ethics. That sounds straightforward enough, but is in fact far from obvious. Epicurus' theory of pleasure is more subtle and complex than it appears at first acquaintance, and its place as the foundation of his ethics is well thought out.

## The Good: A Platonic Notion

The following three chapters are devoted to Epicurus' theory of pleasure. The next chapter, number five, is devoted to the problem of the nature of pleasure and pain, and the following one, number six, to the important distinction between kinetic and katastematic pleasure. In the present chapter we shall concentrate on Epicurus' identification of pleasure as the good. The idea of speaking of such a thing as the good is, of course, not original with Epicurus but is a Platonic notion subsequently much discussed in the Lyceum. It will be useful, therefore, to indicate its Platonic origin and the direction in which it was modified by the Peripatetics because it will give an idea of the background against which Epicurus formulated his problem and its solution. The concept of pleasure at our disposal in the present chapter will, of course, not yet be the philosophically developed concept of Epicurus. To work out that concept will be the task of the next two chapters. In the present chapter we can only work with a rudimentary, generally familiar concept of pleasure, but it will be adequate to our discussion of Epicurus' identification of pleasure as the good.

'The good' is a Platonic notion still current as a philosophical term at the time of Epicurus and thereafter. Cicero's Epicurean spokesman describes the notion

and Epicurus' position on it as follows:

> We are investigating what is the final and ultimate good, which as all philosophers agree must be of such a kind that it is the end to which everything is the means, but it is not itself the means to anything. Epicurus situates this in pleasure.[143]

Taking the good to be pleasure is, of course, quite un-Platonic. Plato's own understanding of the good, against the background of which Epicurus was still writing even half a century later, is quite obscure, an increasingly abstract object of pure theory less and less connected with human affairs. At Republic 505e he describes the good as

> a thing that every soul pursues as the end of all her actions, dimly divining its existence, but perplexed and unable to grasp its nature with ... clearness and assurance.

It is possible that in the inner circle of the Academy he sought to resolve this perplexity in the language of mathematics. In his old age, perhaps owing to political pressure,[144] he gave a public lecture on the good which seems to have been a pedagogical fiasco. Aristotle used to tell the story of that lecture to his own pupils one of whom, Aristoxenus, is our source for the following account.

> Everyone came expecting to learn something about those recognized human goods such as wealth, health, strength, and in general some wonderful happiness; but when it became plain that his discussion was about mathematics and numbers and geometry and astronomy and finally that Good is One, I think it seemed to them utterly unexpected and strange. Thereupon some of them despised the matter and others condemned it.[145]

Aristoxenus remarks that the lesson to be learned from this is that a speaker

---

[143]De fin. 1.29.

[144]see Konrad Gaiser, "Plato's enigmatic lecture 'On the Good'", Phronesis, Vol. 25 (1980), pp. 5-37.

[145]Aristoxenus, Elementa harmonica II, 30.

should begin with a summary of his lecture, so that people can leave before they get as upset with their disappointment as Plato's audience evidently did. Perhaps he is right, but the problem is deeper than that. If there really is a single intrinsic good at which our lives aim and which imparts value to everything we do and strive for, then we can expect at least a sense of recognition when someone tells us about it. Not only did Plato's concept of the good seem to people to be unrecognizable as anything that played or ought to play a central role in their lives, but also the mathematical language of his discussion seemed to divest it of practical relevance to the ethical life. Perhaps it is not surprising that ordinary Athenians were more puzzled than enlightened by their unprepared exposure to the lofty speculations of Plato, but the difficulty may well have been in the discussion itself, for a similar puzzlement seems to have been there in the inner circle of the Academy as well. Aristotle indicates this in what is left of his treatise 'On the Good'. "One must remain conscious of being human", he writes, "not only in happiness, but also in argumentation."[146]

## Pleasure: A Familiar Good

Aristotle began the move of humanizing the good again by conceiving it as the supreme intrinsically valuable thing for human beings: happiness. But Aristotle conceived the human being ethically as the citizen, which is why he can say that the good is the same for the individual and the state, but that nevertheless the good of the state is manifestly a greater and more perfect good, both to attain and to preserve.[147] This relation between the good for the individual and the state is

---

[146]W.D. Ross, Aristotelis fragmenta Selecta, Oxford, 1955, p. 113.

[147]E.N. 1094b.

preserved and reversed by Epicurus. For Aristotle the good for the individual was the good for the citizen. Happiness was a life devoted to civic virtue, that is the pursuit of the good of the state, except for a few bookish types who pursued a life of contemplation.[148] For Epicurus, however, the state is a compact of individuals acting in their own interest. The good of the state is the good of its constituent individuals, because the state is nothing more than a group of individuals brought together in the agreement to bring about and preserve the conditions under which individuals may realize the good life. The good, Epicurus thought, had to be something immediately recognizable and something to which a human being related by nature as an individual prior to any social conventions. Averse as he was to the kind of life recommended by the Cyrenaics, he thought that they were quite right about at least this: the good is pleasure. Epicurus' important disagreement with the Cyrenaics about the nature of pleasure we shall have to discuss in a later chapter. For the present let's note that pleasure is in no sense an object of mathematics and that it is not something which can be enjoyed by a state except indirectly through its members. It is the human individual who feels pleasure. Pleasure is immediately obvious and naturally valued and practically pursued long before it becomes a perplexing object of theory. However difficult the philosophical discussion of the good may become, Epicurus wants never to lose sight of two points. First, the good is the good for the human individual. And second, theoretical perplexity must have a firm footing in a familiar and natural human experience. Let's have a look at some Epicurean texts connecting the good with pleasure.

In the Letter to Menoeceus Epicurus writes that "we recognize pleasure as the

---

[148]E.N. 10, 7 and 8.

good which is primary and congenital."[149] The description 'primary and congenital' is evidently important, for it occurs again prominently in the sentence following its first occurrence, with the word here translated as congenital (suggenikon) being replaced by a synonym (sumphuton) to emphasize its descriptive importance and prevent its becoming a pat formula. We should not read 'primary' (prōton) to mean 'earliest' or 'first in time', for then we would have Epicurus simply making the same point again with 'congenital'. Rather we should understand Epicurus to be pointing out that pleasure is recognized as primary among goods, that Epicureans recognize pleasure as not just a good but as the good. And to call pleasure the congenital good points out that the recognition of the goodness of pleasure is contemporaneous with life itself, that it is naturally given from birth and not the fruit of later education. Epicurus has two kinds of arguments for the view that pleasure is the good, the first of which has been called a cradle argument,[150] and the second is a conceptual argument.

## The Cradle Argument

It is instructive to see Epicurus' cradle argument as a modification of an argument of Eudoxus.[151] Aristotle reports that

Eudoxus thought pleasure was the good because he saw all things, both

---

[149]Ep. Men. 129.

[150]e.g. Jacques Brunschwig, "The cradle argument in Epicureanism and Stoicism," in Malcolm Schofield and Gisela Striker ed., The Norms of Nature: Studies in Hellenistic Ethics, Cambridge University Press, 1986, p. 113-144.

[151]Eudoxus was a hedonist with whose views we can safely assume that Epicurus was familiar, if only because they were famous and the sort of thing Epicurus would have been interested in. Eudoxus was about twenty years younger than Plato, had probably been admitted to the Academy for a while where he may have provided the occasion for Plato's Philebus. He also had another argument for pleasure's being the good than the one being considered here. It is reported by Aristotle at E.N. 1101 b 27-31.

rational and irrational, aiming at it, and because in all things that which is the object of choice is what is excellent, and that which is most the object of choice the greatest good; thus the fact that all things moved towards the same object indicated that this was for all things the chief good (for each thing, he argued, finds its own good, as it finds its own nourishment); and that which is good for all things and at which all aim was the good.[152]

The modifications that need to be made are not difficult to see. To begin with it is an overstatement to claim that all living beings aim at pleasure as their good, for there is good reason to think that this is not true of some human beings. Certainly not all philosophers agreed that pleasure was the good, as Aristotle had already noted. "Some say pleasure is the good" he writes, "while others, on the contrary, say it is thoroughly bad."[153] And the story from Xenophon about Hercules' meeting with the goddesses plainly indicates that alternatives to pleasure as the foremost good of ethics were recommended by some people, at least. And Epicurus must have been aware that Plato and his successor in the Academy, Speusippus, denied that pleasure is the good, and that the Cynics and the Stoics did so as well.

Epicurus then does not claim that all sentient beings pursue pleasure as their chief good, for it may be true that some do not, but rather claims that all sentient beings begin by pursuing pleasure, and do so from birth until they change, if they do. The germ of this modification is already given in the argument of Eudoxus. He had argued that each thing finds its good as it finds its nourishment, and presumably he meant that this happens from birth. What Epicurus does with this material to generate his cradle argument is to retain the claim that all sentient beings pursue pleasure at the start, to find a way of condoning this chief good for

---

[152]E.N. 1172 b 9-15.

[153]E.N. 1172 a 28-29.

the entire life of the sentient being and not just its beginning, and to find a way of rejecting any change to another conception of the good. The original choice of pleasure as the good he condones as "the innocent and sound judgment of nature itself."[154] The good thus selected is the natural good for the sentient being by its very nature, and for this reason it is unaffected in principle by a circumstance such as age. If pleasure is the natural good of a human being because it is human, rather than because it is old or young, rich or poor, wise or stupid, etc., then pleasure is the chief good for the whole life of a human being and not just its early childhood. Any change in the conception of the good must therefore be understood as a change brought about by education and convention which, if it fosters what is unnatural, must be rejected as corruption.[155] Just as it is possible for convention and fashionable social pressure to recommend a diet which is nutritionally inadequate, so our natural impulses may be perverted in other areas as well.

More needs to be said here, of course. Some of it we cannot say until we have understood Epicurus' theory of pleasure in its full detail and sophistication. At present we are working with quite a rudimentary conception of pleasure, but even with only such a rudimentary concept at our disposal some things that need saying can be said.

The first point is both anachronistic and important. It is anachronistic because only in some decades of the present century have philosophers been spooked by the so-called naturalistic fallacy, and it is important because we're not only

---

[154]De fin. 1.30; cf. D.L. 10.137.

[155]Ibid; cf. Sextus Empiricus, P.H. 3.194.

interested in what Epicurus thought but also in whether he was right. Epicureanism is a species of ethical naturalism which has in recent decades been thought fallaciously to derive ethical norms from natural facts. But Epicurus is quite clear about his view that the normative nature of pleasure is not something inferred or derived from sensation (or anything else). Rather he insists that the normative nature of pleasure is as primitively given in our experience as "the heat of fire, the whiteness of snow and the sweetness of honey."[156] Human beings are not equipped with a cognitive faculty which only records factual information about the world we live in, but are equiprimordially evaluating beings to whom it matters how things are. The judgment 'X is so' is no more primitive than the judgment 'X should (not) be so', both are equally given in experience, and neither is derived or inferred from the other, validly or fallaciously. We shall in due course have to discuss the role of the feelings of pleasure and pain as criteria of the ethical life. This discussion will in outline parallel the discussion of the role of sensations as epistemological criteria. Just as every sensation is true, so every feeling of pleasure is good (and of pain bad). And just as not every sensation is to be believed, not every pleasure is to be chosen (or pain avoided). But for the present we can simply note that in Epicureanism values are not inferred from facts at all and therefore, a fortiori, not fallaciously.

The main alternative to the good life of pleasure in the Greek mind of the time, if we can believe Prodicus' Hercules story, was the life of virtue. Any philosopher who made virtue the focus of his ethics would, of course, object to ethical naturalism in any form since virtues are not natural norms. Aristotle had already realized this and said so in the Nicomachean Ethics: "it is plain than none of the

---

[156]De fin. 1.30.

moral virtues arises in us by nature." Rather, "moral virtue comes about as a result of habit" and "nothing that exists by nature can form a habit contrary to nature."[157] We have only the natural capacity for moral virtue, thought Aristotle, a capacity which can be made actual by moral training. Moral training is of course given, or at least initiated, by others, and this points to an important difference between an ethics of pleasure and an ethics of virtue. Virtue is an object of praise and pleasure is not, as Eudoxus had already noticed and thought significant.[158] The good of pleasure ethics is the good of enjoyment, the good as judged by me. The good of virtue ethics is the good of praise, the good as judged by another. The choice between pleasure and virtue is, initially at least, the choice between a self-regarding and an other-regarding evaluation of life. It is easy to see that I may want the good life of other people to be a virtuous life because it clearly is in my interest that other people be honest and kind and industrious and just and obedient and modest and so on. I am as inclined as anyone to praise virtue in other people,

---

[157]E.N. 1103 a 16-20. One might think that the Stoics held the virtues to be natural norms, but this is quite problematic. According to Cleanthes we are not born virtuous but have a natural tendency to virtue (Stobaeus 2.65, 8) and, since virtue can be taught (D.L. 7.91), we may become virtuous through education. Despite this involvement of education in making us virtuous, one might argue that in the Stoic view the virtues are nevertheless natural rather than conventional. Chrysippus, for example, held that "justice...exists by nature and not by convention" (D.L. 7.128), and since there was a tendency on the part of the Stoics to unify and even to identify the virtues (cf. Long and Sedley Vol. I, 61 B-F), it should follow that if justice is natural rather than conventional, all the virtues must be so. This is problematical, however, for at least two reasons. First, the Stoic view on virtue is complex and not entirely uniform, and Long and Sedley (Vol. II. p. 508) are quite right to point out that a thorough study of the Stoic doctrine on virtue has yet to be written. Second, while we might admit that an infant boy has a natural tendency both to virtue and to a beard, and even if we can admit that both the eventual virtue and the eventual beard are natural rather than conventional, they surely are not natural in the same sense. So, if we can agree that the Stoics held that the virtues were natural norms, it remains problematical what they meant by that. It is hard to see how they could be rooted in human nature since education is needed to make us virtuous and nevertheless very few if any of us ever succeed in becoming virtuous Stoic sages. And if their source is divine nature-at-large, one wonders whether we will have natural norms in anything other than name, rather than a theory of the divine origin of the foundation of ethics.

[158]E.N. 1101 b 27-31.

and people do take pleasure in being praised. We may recall that the "good" goddess reminds the young Hercules that hearing yourself praised is "the sweetest of all sounds."[159] An Epicurean would feel wounded in his human individuality by being asked to make the desire for praise, which is neither natural nor necessary, the springboard of his ethical life. Eudoxus has a good point, and Aristotle agrees, in his contention that being the object of praise rules out that virtue can be the good but can only be a good. Whatever we finally decide on as the good (Eudoxus picked pleasure and Aristotle happiness) would not be an object of praise itself, but rather would motivate the praise of lesser goods for it is finally the source and justification of their goodness.

Plato argues in the Philebus[160] that pleasure cannot be the good since a pleasant life becomes better when you add wisdom and worse when you take it away. He concedes that pleasure is a necessary ingredient of the good life, but insists that it is not sufficient. This indicates a mistake we must be careful to avoid and would do well to point out already now even though we're still working with a rudimentary conception of pleasure. Pleasure is not an ingredient in the pleasant life such that we can remove all the other ingredients and have pleasure left over as the last one. We cannot, for example, take the pleasure of eating an ice cream cone or of sailing on a fine summer day, and remove the ice cream or the whole complex of sailing on a fine day, and have the pleasure of eating or sailing left over as an ingredient of those experiences. The pleasure of eating ice cream is not a sensation of pleasure in addition to the sensation of eating ice cream and separable from it, because it is not properly a sensation at all but what Epicurus

---

[159]Xenophon, Memorabilia, 2.2.31.

[160]60 b-e.

calls a feeling. Sensations are cognitive, feelings evaluative, though they are both elements of experience. The pleasure of eating ice cream is the experience of eating ice cream as pleasurable. It is an evaluation of the set of sensations and the activity of eating ice cream, an evaluation you can't have left over if you remove the object being evaluated, any more than a Cheshire cat can depart and leave its grin. Try to imagine the pleasure of sailing on a fine summer day without imagining the sailing and the weather. If Plato, therefore, asks us to remove wisdom from a pleasant life we must imagine something other than wisdom there to be found pleasant, to be evaluated. And Plato may well be right that we find that we can't evaluate it as highly, that it is diminished in goodness. But surely pleasure is not an ingredient in the pleasant life like wisdom and they can't be compared without important alterations to the way the story is told.

## The Conceptual Argument

We must reserve a closer look at pleasure for our discussion of the Epicurean theory of the nature of pleasure. For the present we can consider Epicurus' second argument for his conclusion that pleasure is the good, his conceptual argument. Epicurus wrote in his book On the End:

> I know not how to conceive the good, apart from the pleasures of taste, the pleasures of sex, the pleasures of hearing and the pleasures of beautiful form.

This passage is quoted both by Diogenes Laertius and by Athenaeus,[161] except that the final words are quoted more fully by Athenaeus who indicates that the pleasures of beautiful form are kinetic pleasures of sight. One wonders why the sense of smell is left out in this list. It may be that Epicurus had had more than

---

[161]D.L. 10.6; Athenaeus 12.546e = Us 67.

enough of the perfumed Cyrenaics[162] when he wrote this and wanted on no account to be confused with them. However that may be, Epicurus is here giving a list of sensuous pleasures and pointing out that the good cannot be conceived apart from these pleasures. This is, of course, not the claim that sensuous pleasures are the good, but rather that if we try to conceive the good as entirely unlike these pleasures we find ourselves unable to form a conception with any content. If we say that the good is nothing like these pleasures, that is, that the good is not a pleasure at all, then we are left with an empty word. Epicurus' point is that the good is not an obscure and unfamiliar thing of which only a few philosophers have theoretical adumbrations, but the most common, the most familiar guide to behaviour with which every sentient being is equipped at birth. It does not follow from this that our pleasures and our behaviour must remain infantile if they are to remain natural, but it does follow that further sophistication is a development of the basic state. Shortly after the above quotation, Athenaeus quotes the following one. "The pleasure of the stomach is the beginning and root of all good, and it is to this that wisdom and over-refinement actually refer."[163] We begin to develop the idea of the good with reference to early and basic pleasures, and even later and more sophisticated goods are refined versions of the basic good and have their origin there. This is true of any later good, whether it be a good approved of by Epicureans such as wisdom (ta sopha), or a good Epicureans do not approve of such as an excessively refined life style (ta peritta). So far as such a life is pleasant it is good, and Epicureans disapprove of it, when they do, for a different reason. It is true that an Epicurean life does not pursue the

---

[162]The Cyrenaics had a reputation for the liberal use of perfume. Cf. D.L. 2.76; Lucian, Philosphies for Sale, 12.

[163]Athenaeus 12.546f = Us. 409.

pleasure of the stomach as its chief good. No kinetic pleasure can claim that place, as we shall see. But the pleasure of the stomach, and other basic pleasures, cannot be disregarded entirely, for they are pleasures derived from the satisfaction of a natural and necessary desire, the non-satisfaction of which brings pain. The good life is not possible unless basic needs are met. "The flesh's cry is not to be hungry or thirsty or cold. For one who is in these states [of not being hungry, thirsty or cold] and expects to remain so could rival even Zeus in happiness."[164] Note here that Epicurus does not claim that not being hungry, thirsty or cold is all there is to the good life. The absence of hunger thirst and cold is necessary but not sufficient for the good life. Many people who don't suffer from hunger thirst and cold, and have every reason to think that they are safe from them for the rest of their lives, are nevertheless miserable. In particular, misery seems to be as frequent among the rich as among the poor. But Epicurus certainly has this point: while we're still scrapping for the basics, while our efforts are still directed at and our energy used up in the struggle for mere survival we're hardly capable of a humanly good life.

## Pleasure as the Good

To say that pleasure is the good is to say that it is not a good among others, and it is to say that every pleasure is good, not empirically or as a matter of fact, but analytically, in the same way that every sensation is true. And just as not every sensation is to be believed because a further process of attestation and non-attestation must often justify belief, so not every pleasure is to be pursued or chosen because a prudential calculation of consequences may justify avoiding

---

[164]S.V. 33.

particular ones. But in itself every pleasure is good, that is, every object of pleasure, where pleasure has an object, is a good when and so far as it gives pleasure. It is its relation to an object, which so far as it gives pleasure is a good, which makes it more natural to speak of pleasure as a good rather than the good. But if there were an objectless pleasure, then it might be more natural to speak of this as the good. We shall see, when we can discuss kinetic and katastematic pleasure in detail, that katastematic pleasure is essentially objectless and that when Epicurus designated pleasure as the good he had katastematic pleasure in mind. This may explain that when he speaks of conceiving the good and of the genesis of our idea of the good he uses familiar everyday kinetic pleasures as his examples. But when he speaks of the nature of the good his example is a katastematic pleasure. Plutarch cites the following quotation:

> Unsurpassable joy is produced by comparison with a great evil which one has escaped; and this is the nature of the good, if one applies [one's intellect] properly and then takes a firm stand, but does not stroll around babbling emptily about the good.[165]

We might note in passing that this fragment shows a good deal of impatience with philosophical discussion which only generates perplexity. It is likely that the use of the word 'peripatē' in the fragment indicates that the impatience is directed at the Lyceum. It is possible that the discussion of the nature of the good had become ongoing and subtle in the Lyceum, subtle to the point where despite its theoretical brilliance it became practically encumbering, and that this provided the occasion for Epicurus' remark. But there is also a strong echo here of Aristotle's impatience with Plato's treatment of the good, that is, Plato may well be the real target of this fragment. Epicurus' claim is that we become directly aware of the

---

[165]Plutarch, Non posse 1091 a = Us. 423.

nature of the good in an experience, the experience of the escape from a great evil. It isn't difficult to imagine situations Epicurus might have had in mind. To the examples Lucretius gives at the beginning of Book II we could add the following example, as well as many others. Think of having a biopsy done of a tumour the X-ray machine had discovered in your liver, and being told that it is benign. There is an element here of Louis Armstrong's famous response to the lady who asked him what jazz was: if you have to ask you'll never know. Philosophical inquiry into the nature of the good must be based on a pre-philosophical acquaintance with it, otherwise it will remain a case of "babbling emptily about the good."

Epicurus' giving examples of kinetic pleasure when his concern is with the conception of the good, and giving examples of katastematic pleasure when his concern is with the nature of the good should not confuse us however, as it seems to have confused Cicero[166] because he misunderstood the Epicurean doctrine of the nature of pleasure. Cicero's misunderstanding is a rather common one, however, and a full understanding of the Epicurean doctrine that pleasure is the good will have to await our clearing up the Ciceronian misunderstanding in the next chapter as well as a full discussion of the nature of pleasure.

## Pain as the Bad

What remains to concern us in the present chapter is that pleasure has a mate, namely, pain. Just as pleasure is the good, pain is (if I may be allowed the expression) the bad. But there is an important difference between pleasure and

---

[166]cf. De fin. 2.29-32.

pain that we must briefly consider because it seems to disrupt the neat opposition Epicurus wants to work with. He denies that either pleasure or pain is a sensation (aisthēsis) and instead calls each a feeling (pathos). To my knowledge no one has ever claimed that pleasure is a specific sensation, but there is good evidence that there is a specific pain sensation called nociception.[167] But this sensation is not at all a simple matter. The complexity has to do both with the sensation itself and the fact that there are pains which do not involve that sensation at all. The evidence does not bear out the simple view of pain sensation,[168] the view that pain is a sensation subserved by a direct neural transmission line to a pain centre in the brain from specialized neurons whose stimulation is a necessary and sufficient condition for the sensation of pain, a simple sensation that varies only in intensity. Instead the sensation of pain is a complex of experiences with a large range of variation in quality describable by adjectives like splitting, gnawing, wrenching, stinging, searing, throbbing, sharp, dull, aching, stabbing and so on. Further, pain is a "highly personal, variable experience which is influenced by cultural learning, the meaning of the situation, attention, and other cognitive activities,"[169] and "the old concept of a 'pain centre' is obviously nonsense. Many areas of the brain are involved in pain processes and they interact extensively."[170]

---

[167]For a good, if somewhat dated, account of the history of and evidence for the claim that there is a specific pain sensation see Edward R. Perl, "Is Pain a Specific Sensation?", Journal of Psychiatric Research, 1971, Vol. 8, pp. 273-287.

[168]For a criticism of the so-called "specificity theory" of pain see Ronald Melzack and Patrick D. Wall, The Challenge of Pain, New York: Basic Books, 1983.

[169]Melzack and Wall, op. cit., p. 99.

[170]Melzack and Wall, op. cit., p. 151.

Complex as pain sensations are, however, it makes sense to distinguish those sensations from our dislike of them,[171] such that it is possible to ask whether we can have the sensation without disliking it.[172] We shall argue in the next chapter that the distinction is possible and that the Epicurean concept of pain refers, as a technical term, to the evaluation rather than the sensation. This evaluation extends beyond nociception to pains which are not sensations at all, to grief for example, and to other unpleasant experiences which are not happily called pains in English, experiences such as fear and boredom, or even unpleasant smells and tastes. The Epicurean distinction between pleasure and pain might best be captured in English by the distinction between pleasant and unpleasant, but we shall stay with the traditional terms as we develop them in the next chapter.

It may appear at this point that, if we interpret pleasure and pain as evaluations of something, it will be the thing being evaluated which is either good or bad rather than the evaluation, pleasure or pain, itself. This, it seems, would preclude pleasure and pain from being either good or bad and thus surely not the good or the bad, quite apart from whether other contenders for the position, such as virtue and vice, are more appropriately called the good and the bad. This is another issue to which we shall have to address ourselves after the fuller discussion of pleasure and pain in the next chapter.

---

[171]R.M. Hare argues for this distinction in "Pain and Evil", proceedings of the Aristotelian Society, N.S., supplementary volume 38, 1964, pp. 91-106.

[172]Richard J. Hall argues that we can in "Are Pains Necessarily Unpleasant?", Philosophy and Phenomenological Research, Vol. XLIX, No. 4, June 1989, pp. 643-659.

# Chapter Five

# Pleasure and Pain

The function of medicine is to restore health by removing sickness. If you ask a physician what he thinks health is, you will probably receive the reply that health is the natural state of an organism free from all sickness and deformity. This is not so much because he thinks that health is in its nature something negative, a mere absence of something, but because his professional involvement with people is with their diseases and injuries, which are the things to which he addresses himself directly in treatment. In such a practical situation it is not surprising that the defect, the illness or injury, comes to be seen as something positively present to which to relate, and that the restored healthy condition comes to be seen as the state in which there is nothing further for the physician to relate to, nothing to be treated anymore, a state which from the practical perspective of the physician is characterized by the absence of illness. One could, of course, just as easily think of health as the positive state of an organism and of illness as the negative state of the loss of health. But this would not be a useful way of looking at sick people who come to the physician for treatment. He cannot think of himself as having a commodity called health which he can inject into patients for a fee, because that is not how he works. Rather, he diagnoses the patient to find the problem, then treats the patient to remove the problem, and the patient's health is restored without any additional contribution by the physician. This is essentially the way medicine has been practiced from well before the time of Epicurus to the present day.

As we saw in the third chapter, Epicurus conceived of philosophy on the model of medical therapy and, guided by this therapeutic metaphor, he conceived of philosophy as the activity which produced a good life for people by removing obstacles to it such as fear, ignorance, harmful opinions and desires and the like. The key concept in what characterizes the good life was pleasure, and the key concept in what characterizes the bad life was pain. Conceived on the medical model, Epicurean philosophy sought to remove pain and restore pleasure. That Epicureans tended to speak of pain as the positive thing to be treated and removed, and of pleasure as the negative thing, as the absence of pain, is hardly surprising. Just as it is useful for a physician to approach a situation in which he is to practice his profession as one in which illness is the positive thing to be removed and health a state characterized by the absence of illness, so it was useful for the Epicurean practitioner to think of pain as the positive thing to be removed and of pleasure as the state characterized by the absence of pain, a state which no longer required his philosophical intervention.

But this practical way of seeing the situation must not be translated into a theoretical doctrine of the nature of pleasure and pain because it would generate misunderstanding of the theoretical foundation of Epicurean ethics and introduce confusion into important elaborations of the theory which build on that foundation. Unfortunately, though perhaps predictably, such misunderstanding did occur and can be documented in the writings of critics and commentators from the time of Epicurus to the present day. The heart of the misunderstanding is the view that Epicurus took pleasure to be negative in its nature, that an adequate conceptual expression of the nature of pleasure was to characterize it as the absence of pain. Our first task in the present chapter must be briefly to document this misunderstanding and then to show that it is a misunderstanding. The importance of removing this misunderstanding will become apparent as we develop the theory of pleasure and pain.

## Pleasure and the Absence of Pain

Despite Epicurus' well known aversion to giving definitions he is criticized by some contemporary Cyrenaics for defining pleasure as the absence of pain, a condition which they thought more accurately described death than pleasure.[173] But the most widely read critic of Epicureanism who builds much of his criticism on this misunderstanding is Cicero. He wrote that "Epicurus holds the highest pleasure [to] be to feel no pain",[174] and that "the greatest pleasure ... is that which is experienced as a result of the complete removal of pain."[175] True, he is writing about the greatest pleasure, not any pleasure whatever, but when he finally argues against Epicurus he generalizes quite readily and argues essentially that 'pleasure' does not mean the same as 'freedom from pain'.[176] Plutarch had a similar view. He thought that among Epicurus' many mistakes was the one of "attaching the pleasurable life to painlessness."[177]

This misunderstanding is not confined to antiquity but is more or less the going view today as well. John Rist holds essentially the same view as Cicero: "The

---

[173] As reported by Clement of Alexandria in his Stromateis 2.21, 179, 36 = Us 451

[174] De fin. 1.39

[175] De fin. 1.37

[176] De fin. 2.9

[177] Non posse 1088b; cf. Col. 1123a

highest pleasure is the absence of pain",[178] except that he adds that "it is certain that for Epicurus"[179] this is so. In their recent book Gosling and Taylor repeat the criticism of the Cyrenaics: "pleasure is defined as the absence of pain".[180]

When a philosopher is as widely misunderstood as this there surely is some reason. In the case of Epicurus the basic reason was probably the medical metaphor which guided his philosophical practice. But this is further complicated by his effort to distinguish his philosophy from Cyrenaic hedonism, an effort which sometimes led him to formulate his own hedonistic principles in ways easily misunderstood by inattentive people. For example, in the widely available letter to Menoeceus he writes:

> So when we say that pleasure is the end, we do not mean the pleasures of the dissipated and those that consist in having a good time, as some out of ignorance and disagreement or refusal to understand suppose we do, but freedom from pain in the body and from disturbance in the soul.[181]

Epicurus is not defining pleasure here. He is responding to a criticism of his doctrine which tends to identify his hedonism with Cyrenaic hedonism. And he responds by distinguishing between two kinds of pleasure. First, the pleasures of the dissipated, the pleasures of drinking and parties, of enjoying boys and women, of luxurious and extravagant dinners. He does not deny that these are pleasures. In fact, he calls them pleasures. And from these he distinguishes, second, freedom

---

[178]John M. Rist, Epicurus: An Introduction, Cambridge University Press, 1977, pp. 100-1; the same point had already been made in his "Pleasure: 360-300 B.C.", Phoenix, Vol 26 (1974), No. 2.

[179]John M. Rist, Epicurus, p. 109.

[180]J.C.B. Gosling and C.C.W. Taylor, The Greeks on Pleasure, Oxford: Clarendon Press, 1982, p. 347. They qualify the notion of absence of pain to include consciousness in order to rule out the objection that death is not a pleasure.

[181]Ep. Men. 131.

from pain in the body and disturbance in the mind. If this really is a distinction, and Epicurus plainly thinks that it is, then the description of the second kind of pleasure does not apply to the first kind. It cannot, therefore, count as a definition of pleasure, nor could Epicurus be thought to be giving one.

Rather, what he _is_ doing here is explaining the Epicurean doctrine that pleasure is the end, or, at least, clarifying a misunderstanding about the doctrine. He points out that this doctrine does not commit Epicureans to the pursuit of the pleasures of dissipated profligates and, in general, it does not commit Epicureans to any pleasure merely because it is a pleasure. The pleasures of dissipation are rejected, not because they fail to be pleasures, but because they don't produce a pleasant life. The pleasant life, rather, is produced by "sober reasoning which searches out the reasons for every choice and avoidance and drives out the opinions which are the source of the greatest turmoil for human souls."[182] The pleasant life is produced by choosing a style of life, by choosing a pattern of things to be done and not done based on pleasure and pain as criteria of choice and avoidance. The reference to "freedom from pain in the body and disturbance in the soul" is an indication of the basic style of an Epicurean life, given here especially to distinguish it from the style of a Cyrenaic life. But it surely is not a definition of pleasure.

Further, in the same letter to Menoeceus, shortly before the passage we have been considering, Epicurus speaks of pain as the absence of pleasure. He writes: "the time when we need pleasure is when we are in pain from the absence of

---

[182]Ep. Men. 132.

pleasure."[183] No one would say that if he were about to define pleasure as the absence of pain, or even if he thought that the conception of pleasure as generally the absence of pain were somehow an important doctrine in his philosophy. In another place Epicurus writes: "the time when we need pleasure is when we are in pain from the absence of pleasure; but when we are not feeling such pain, though we are in a condition of sensation, we have no need of pleasure."[184] The first part of this passage repeats the passage in the letter to Menoeceus, which indicates that the formulation is not an accident but orthodox. But something is added here which is also a continuation of the passage in the letter in somewhat different words. The reason why we have no need of pleasure when we are in a condition of conscious painlessness, is that this is a condition in which pleasure is not absent, and in such a state we do not need pleasure since we already have it. And the reason why pleasure is not absent in such a condition is that pain, according to this passage, is the absence of pleasure. Non-pain will therefore be the non-absence of pleasure. That we have no need of pleasure in such a condition, however, does not mean that we are not capable of further pleasure. We must, of course, not jump to the conclusion that Epicurus defines pain as the absence of pleasure. That would be as unwarranted a misunderstanding as the opposite mistake. It might be helpful to mention at this point that Lucretius treats pleasure and pain as two distinct feelings caused by different kinds of atoms.

---

[183]Ep. Men. 128. The sentences immediately preceding the one just quoted read: "For this is what we aim at in all our actions--to be free from pain and anxiety. Once we have got this, all the soul's tumult is released, since the creature cannot go as if in pursuit of something it needs and search for any second thing as the means of maximizing the good of the soul and the body". The medical analogy referred to at the beginning of this chapter is quite plain in this passage. Aim to remove pain and, since there is no neutral state between pleasure and pain, you will find that pleasure has taken its place. This is not to be construed as a definition of the nature of pleasure as the absence of pain, however, as is made quite plain by the following sentence.

[184]Us. 422 (quoting Stobaeus).

Smooth ones cause pleasure and rough ones cause pain.[185]  This is probably orthodox Epicureanism, and it is not compatible with the definition of either pleasure or pain as the absence of the other.

It is tempting to think of desire as a painful state and of the pleasure of gratifying desire as the removal of that pain. And if one puts too much emphasis on an ancient commentator's scholium to Principal Doctrine 29 one may be tempted to think that Epicurus had such a view of desire. That scholium speaks of "desires which bring relief from pain",[186] which is a bit awkward, of course, since presumably it is not the desire but its satisfaction which would bring relief from pain. But Epicurus never speaks of desire in the way this commentator does. Rather he speaks of desires which bring pain if not satisfied and desires which do not bring pain if not satisfied.[187] That is, for Epicurus pain (like pleasure) follows upon desire, but is neither identical nor contemporary with it, at least in the early stages. Given the desire, we can choose to satisfy it if we can, which brings pleasure; or we can choose not to satisfy it, which will bring pain if it is a necessary desire. Pleasure is not conceived here as the absence of pain, nor as the removal of pain, but as its alternative. Pleasure is thought of as incompatible with pain (in the same place and respect) however, and is therefore also its absence incidentally; and pain is the absence of pleasure, also incidentally. So, while it is true that Epicurus speaks of pleasure as the absence of pain, and of pain as the absence of pleasure, this must not be misunderstood as a definition of the nature of either one but rather as expressing their incompatibility as alternatives.

---

[185]Lucr. 2.398-443; cf. Ep. Hdt. 55.

[186]D.L. 10.149.

[187]K.D. 26, 30.

# The Limit of Pleasure

There are some Epicurean texts dealing with the notion of the limit of pleasure which may also be thought to support the misunderstanding that pleasure is the absence of pain in its nature rather than incidentally because of their mutual incompatibility. For example, the third principal doctrine:

> The removal of all pain is the limit of the magnitude of pleasures. Wherever pleasure is present, as long as it is there, pain or distress or their combination is absent.

This does not say that pleasure is the removal of pain in the sense that pleasure is experienced whenever some pain is being removed and is precisely the experience of this removal, nothing more and nothing less. It says that pleasure and pain are incompatible, that we cannot feel both at once in the same place and in the same respect. If you are feeling pleasure in some part of the body (or mind) you cannot also be feeling pain in that part. So, to feel pleasure in all parts and respects is to be in a state in which there is no room for pain, it is the removal of all pain or the consequence of such removal, and this is the limit of the magnitude of pleasures.

This notion of the limit of pleasures is spoken of in three distinct senses in Epicurean texts. There is, first, the extensive limit. In this sense the limit of pleasure is reached when all areas in which pleasure is possible, both physical and mental, are covered, a state in which there is pleasure everywhere and pain nowhere. This evidently is the sense of "the limit of the magnitude of pleasures" in the third principal doctrine quoted above.

But there is also, second, an intensive limit. A particular pleasure may be more or less intense, and so each has a greatest intensity which is its intensive limit. In Epicureanism the prudent deliberation on courses of action involves calculating pleasures and pains,[188] such that a pleasure is rejected if it will bring a greater pain later, or a pain may be accepted if it leads to greater pleasure than avoiding it would. This calculation need not be confined to particular pleasures and pains, but may also be carried out in consideration of the overall hedonic state of the person. For example, the fourth principal doctrine speaks of "pain which just exceeds the pleasure in the flesh." This may be understood extensively (the area in which there is pain is slightly more extensive than the area in which there is pleasure), or it may be understood intensively (the pain is slightly more intense, in sum, than the pleasure, as might be the case with a toothache), or it may, of course, be understood as involving both, that is, some combination of the extension and intensity of pain. Epicurus speaks of degrees of intensity in particular pleasures in the ninth principal doctrine.[189]

> If every pleasure were intensified and were present, both in time and in the whole compound [body and soul] or in the most important parts of our nature, then pleasures would never differ from one another.

Epicurus is here concerned with the difference between pleasures at their most intense, and, so that the focus can remain on the issue of their intensity, he eliminates considerations of extension by giving the pleasures to be compared maximum extension or, at least equal extension, both in time and organismic area. He is speaking of a plurality of pleasures, the various particular pleasures of which we are capable, which are to be compared, and the puzzle is that in order to compare two things they must in some sense be different, while he finds the

---

[188]cf. Ep. Men. 129.

[189]For difficulties with the text of KD9 see Gosling and Taylor, op. cit., pp. 377-82.

comparison to show that they are not different. The puzzle is, however, not very difficult at all. Let us take two particular pleasures, say gustatory pleasure and sexual pleasure, and give them equal intensity and extension. They would, obviously, retain their qualitative difference, that is no one would confuse them or be unable to tell them apart. It would be silly for Epicurus to deny that, and I take it to be an acceptable principle of interpretation to save the philosopher you are interpreting from silliness, where possible. The difference he must have had in mind is the important ethical difference of choiceworthiness in the pleasure and pain calculus. His point is that two particular pleasures which are equally intense and extensive, both in duration and organismic area, do not differ ethically, that is, as pleasures they are equally good, so that if one is going to make different ethical judgments about them it must be on other grounds. Our proper concern at this point, however, is not yet the ethical goodness of different pleasures, but simply intensity as one sense in which there can be a limit of pleasure.

There is yet a third sense in which we can understand Epicurus to speak of the limit of pleasure, and that is its variability. Even once the limit of extension and intensity is reached, variation is still possible. The eighteenth principal doctrine states that

> The pleasure in the flesh does not increase when once the pain due to need has been removed, but it is only varied.

This passage is not about pleasure in general and it does not say that all pleasure results in the removal of pain due to need where it reaches its limit. The reference to pain due to need makes it clear that Epicurus is here talking about necessary desires, desires, that is, which bring pain if they are not satisfied. The pleasure at issue here, then, is the pleasure of satisfying necessary desires such as the desire for food. When the desire for food has been neglected to the point where your hunger has progressed beyond the natural invitation to dinner and is becoming painful (the pain due to need of food), then to eat will remove this pain and it will be a pleasure. But it is a pleasure only up to a point. When you are full it is no longer pleasant to eat, the "pleasure in the flesh" is not increased beyond that. But it can be varied. This variation can take two forms. Either the means used to produce the pleasure can be varied, that is, do it with different food next time. But when you're full, you're full. Or you could still produce some additional pleasure unrelated to the pain of non-satisfaction: you can usually still enjoy dessert after you're full, it doesn't require hunger or pain due to need. This is strictly a matter of variety rather than amount at this point, either of extensional or intensive limits.

## Pleasure and Pain are Evaluations

The first conclusion in our attempt to understand the account given of pleasure and pain in Epicurean philosophy is that the widely held belief that Epicurus took pleasure to be something negative in its nature, an absence of pain, is a misunderstanding, but that, rather, pleasure and pain are equally positive experiences, incompatible with each other and, therefore, reciprocal alternatives. And our second conclusion was that a consideration of the Epicurean notion of the limit of pleasure does not support that common misunderstanding, but is best understood on our interpretation of pleasure and pain. These two conclusions now make it possible to begin to develop the Epicurean theory of the nature of pleasure and pain.

Epicurus distinguishes pleasure and pain from sense perception not as he would distinguish an object of sensation like an apple or a song or a game of chess, that is, not as he would distinguish between a conscious act and its object, but as he would distinguish one conscious act from another. Pleasure and pain are not in the first place objects of conscious acts but, rather, are themselves conscious acts. Acts of sense perception he calls sensations (aisthēseis), pleasure and pain he calls feelings (pathē).

The English word 'feeling' covers rather more than it should. The word is not meant here as one might use it in 'I have lost feeling in my toes', or 'I have a feeling that today is my lucky day' or 'I don't feel well' or 'How do you feel about Sunday shopping' for example. But rather it indicates a passive state of consciousness in which what happens is like an event which befalls a person, a conscious act, in this case, which is carried out without deliberate control and purpose rather like seeing when the eyes are open or hearing when there is a sound. What distinguishes acts of feeling from acts of sensation is not their natural passivity, for they are exactly alike in that respect, but that sensations are in their nature cognitive while feelings are in their nature evaluative. If I am eating ice cream or listening to music then it is through sense perception that I am informed about the ice cream or the music. And if I find this eating or listening a pleasure then I am not having a further sense experience like sweet strawberry or piano arpeggio, but rather am evaluating my sense experience. If I am tasting something and enjoying it then this enjoying is not a further taste sensation added to the others, but a different act of consciousness altogether, an act evaluating the cognitive acts rather than a further cognitive act.

The case of pain is more complicated than the case of pleasure for two reasons. First, pain behaves more like a special sense than does pleasure and, second, if we are going to understand pleasure as the positive evaluative feeling then its mate, the negative evaluative feeling, covers more than pain but extends to the whole range of the unpleasant.

As we have seen in the previous chapter, there is a well established but less well understood pain sensation called nociception with specialized receptors called nociceptors. Nociception seems to be a neural warning system signalling tissue damage and the threat of tissue damage. Thus if you puncture the skin with a pin causing actual tissue damage you don't only feel through the tactile sense that and where your skin has been punctured, you are also given a stab of pain by a different neural mechanism. Or if you touch something hot you are also warned with a surge of pain that you are running the risk of tissue damage. Nociception, of course, makes good evolutionary sense since it makes the avoidance of harm much more efficient than would be the case if the neurology of pain were exactly like the neurology of pleasure such that the evaluation of sensation would have to give rise to a decision to act before avoidance behaviour could be initiated. This is dramatically illustrated by people whose nociceptive neurology is defective to the degree that they are "pain blind."[190] Such people, despite normal intelligence and sensory functions in other respects, are a positive hazard to themselves and run a very high risk of repeated and serious tissue damage. One would expect evolution to reject the pain blind from the gene pool, despite the fact that nociception is a less perfect neural mechanism than it might be. Notoriously very serious tissue damage like cancer is undetected by nociception until it is far too late. And also one wonders about the survival value of toothache and similar pains in primitive tribes who were unable to respond to tooth decay effectively. Even so,

---

[190]Richard A. Sternbach, Pain: A Psychophysiological Analysis, New York Academic Press, 1968 Ch. VII.

nociception makes evolutionary sense. Of course, in a human body the feelings of pleasure and pain both require a neural basis or, in Epicurean language, a substructure of soul atoms and their appropriate movements. The fact that the neural structure is not the same for pleasure and pain but that the neurology of pain, or rather of some kinds of pain, is similar to the neurology of sensation, need not confuse the Epicurean distinction between cognitive sensation and evaluative feeling.

To the extent that there is a specific nociceptive sensation, there is a cognitive element in pain sensation, so that nociception is both cognitive and evaluative. Richard Hare[191] has argued that this introduces an ambiguity into the word 'pain', which in one of its senses refers to the distinct sensation and in the other sense refers to the dislike of that sensation, although in normal use it usually refers to both. Thus it is logically possible to distinguish two senses of pain namely the bare sensation, which he calls 'pain', and the evaluation of that sensation, which he calls 'pain'$_1$. And, he argues, it is also practically possible to make that distinction, that is, it is possible to experience pain, give it one's full attention, and not to dislike it, not to suffer from it. Substantially the same point was argued for again more recently by Richard J. Hall.[192] He also limits his discussion to the pain of nociception and argues that the pain sensation can be distinguished from its unpleasantness. "The unpleasantness of pain sensations consists in their being disliked. The dislike of a pain sensation is a separate mental state, separate, that is, from the sensation." So, while pains are unpleasant, "that

---

[191]R.M. Hare, "Pain and Evil", Proceedings of the Aristotelian Society, supp. vol. 38, 1964, pp. 91-106.

[192]Richard J. Hall, "Are Pains Necessarily Unpleasant?" Philosophy and Phenomenological Research. Vol. XLIX, No. 4, June 1989, pp. 643-59.

unpleasantness is not a phenomenal quality of pains."[193]  Hall cites an experience in a dentist's office where, under nitrous oxide, he had dental work done and felt the same sensations as he did during untreated drilling except that this time it did not hurt, that is, was not unpleasant. And he points out that there is a narcotic drug, fenatyl, which seems to have the opposite effect of being able to reduce the pain sensations without reducing their unpleasantness. The upshot of all this is that pains are not necessarily unpleasant because we are experiencing two distinct mental states, a cognitive one and an evaluative one, which may be logically and practically distinguished. Also we must note here that nociception is only a species of pain. Apart from quasi-physical pains like phantom limb pains, which are fairly common in amputees, or the pain of certain kinds of epileptic seizures which originate in the brain and give the feeling of pain in parts of the body without nociceptive stimulation, there is also the whole range of mental pains such as the experiences of fear or failure or the many things which bring grief to our kind.

Because of the distinction, both logical and practical, between pain sensations and their negative evaluation it is true that not all pains are unpleasant. But it is also true that not everything unpleasant is a pain. The whole range of things we can find pleasant is matched by the range of things we can find unpleasant, and that exceeds the range of painful things. The proper opposition in our account of the Epicurean doctrine of the feelings as fundamentally evaluative in their nature is the opposition between positive and negative evaluation, between pleasant and unpleasant. The use of the English word 'pain' introduces some terminological difficulty. There are a number of Greek words which are normally translated as

[193]Richard J. Hall, op. cit., p. 646.

'pain'. Epicurus does not range across these words but almost exclusively uses one of them, algēdōn. This is one of the family of words derived from the root of the verb algeo which equally applies to feeling physical and mental pain, it can mean to suffer, to grieve, even to be ill, or to suffer hardship. The noun algēdōn also ranges over physical pain to mental pain, grief and distress. Epicurus was in general more concerned with mental pains and pleasures than with bodily pains and pleasures.[194] It seems quite appropriate, then, to understand the Epicurean notion of the negative evaluative feeling not on a narrow conception of pain sensations, but rather as the evaluative dislike of such sensations and to all kinds of pain beyond such sensations and, indeed, beyond even that to the whole range of the unpleasant. We shall henceforth use the word 'pain' as a technical term with that extensive range.

Pleasure and pain, then, are two primitive conscious acts, equiprimordial with sensation and evaluative in nature. We don't from time to time evaluate as well as sense depending on accidental circumstance, but evaluate by the very nature of consciousness. This gives us a clue about how to understand a puzzling Epicurean doctrine. It is not a very prominent doctrine in Epicurean literature, but appears to have been prominent enough to be thought worth noting by Cicero who tells us through Torquatus, his Epicurean spokesman, that "Epicurus did not accept the existence of anything between pleasure and pain."[195] The issue is not particularly new. Plato had already discussed it[196] and noted that there was some difficulty in the notion of a neutral state between pleasure and pain since to people suffering

---

[194]D.L. 10.137.

[195]De fin. 1.38.

[196]Republic 583c - 584a.

pain this mental state appears to be pleasurable, and to people enjoying positive delight the neutral state appears to be painful. But he sets this difficulty aside as an illusion of perspective which does not justify rejecting the notion of the neutral state. And Plato surely has this point: the rejection of a neutral state between pleasure and pain seems strongly counter-intuitive. If we can trust Cicero on this point however, and Epicurus really did deny the existence of a neutral state between pleasure and pain, not as a passing remark in some conversation, but as a basic doctrinal tenet, then we can also readily see what he would have meant by it, both practically and theoretically.

Practically speaking the denial of the neutral state can be understood on the medical model of philosophy with which Epicureans worked. The conception of a neutral state between sickness and health does not make practical medical sense. As a practitioner the physician has no use for the idea of such a neutral state because his whole practice is aimed at removing illness. If someone came to a physician claiming to be in the neutral state between sickness and health, insisting that the physician not set about removing illness, for there was none to remove, but instead set about giving him health, for there was none of that either, the physician might humour such a patient for a fee and prescribe vitamins or exercise or a holiday, but he would not accept the patient's description as a theoretically sound understanding on which to base future practice. The Epicurean practitioner understood his own philosophical practice on the medical model and extended the notions of sickness and health to the more inclusive notions of pain and pleasure. And just as, practically speaking, there is no use for the idea of a neutral state between sickness and health, so there is no use for the neutral state between pain and pleasure. If this is counter-intuitive it is because the common sense understanding of a neutral state, which we all think we can find in daily experience, is limited to the common sense conceptions of kinetic pleasure and pain. Plato in the passage referred to above is plainly working with the idea of kinetic pleasure and pain only,[197] as did the Cyrenaics who also accepted the neutral state. The Epicurean, however, would insist that his understanding becomes plain if we include the notion of katastematic pleasure as well. This would not mean much to us at this point because we have not yet discussed kinetic and katastematic pleasure, and must therefore leave the practical point here without developing it any further.

But the Epicurean denial of the neutral state has also a deeper theoretical meaning. One sometimes, when reading Cicero, gets the impression that he was writing with Epicurean textbooks to hand which he was paraphrasing and from which he extracted occasional quotations without always understanding them. Just so here. In the context in which he informs us that Epicurus rejects the neutral state between pleasure and pain he also has Torquatus remark that "anyone aware of his own condition must either have pleasure or pain."[198] This must not be understood as the claim that everything we do must either be a pleasure or a pain, for Epicurus is quite aware that the value of some acts is purely instrumental; nor as the claim that every part of our bodies must either be in pain or feeling pleasure, for the falsehood of that is too obvious to anyone who cares to check his own body parts, say the palate or the genitals, or the toes or the back of the head; nor as the claim that sensuous pleasures always supervene on either existing pleasures or pains, for surely there are unexpected pleasant smells or

[197]Ibid. 583e.

[198]De fin. 1.38; cf De fin. 2.12-13.

sights or sounds, or the unexpected pain of sitting on a thumb tack or the like, where there was no awareness of either pleasure or pain in the affected part prior to the painful or pleasant surprise. Rather it means that consciousness is by nature evaluative, and that anyone who is consciously sensing or thinking and self-consciously aware of his own experience and condition, must be evaluating. And since all evaluation is understood by Epicureans as positive or negative, as pleasure or pain, anyone who is conscious must be having pleasure or pain. This should be understood not so much as a claim about the phenomenology of self-consciousness but as a theoretical claim about the nature of consciousness. Even the most evenly balanced condition between pleasure and pain is not value free. We never are pure cognitive recorders of the passing show, indifferent to our experience. Even scientific objectivity at its uninvolved and passive best is not value free, but is in fact much to be prized and praised under appropriate circumstances. And the dull indifference of everyday hum-drum life is in fact indifferent for a self-aware human being in a way it never could be for an unaware cinematographic recording machine. So, this claim applies to every human being simply by virtue of being conscious. But the claim further points to a specific Epicurean self-awareness which can be cultivated until it reaches perfection in the Epicurean sage. This, however, cannot be profitably discussed at the present stage of our development of the Epicurean understanding of pleasure and pain, and we must leave the point where it stands for now.

There is a further feature about the nature of pleasure and pain as primordial evaluative acts of consciousness which we must now consider. Consciousness is reflexive. I not only see something, but I am also aware that I see something; and I not only evaluate something, but am also aware that I evaluate something. Self-consciousness, like consciousness, is both cognitive and evaluative. That is why the awareness of pleasure, of the conscious act of positive evaluation, is itself pleasurable, why pleasure is not just the evaluation of something as good, but is itself something good. And similarly pain is not just the evaluation of something as bad, but is itself something bad. Because pleasure and pain are not only evaluations, but are themselves good and bad, they may themselves become the intended goal of our acts. Thus I may do something not so much because I naturally evaluate it as good in the first evaluative act of consciousness, but because of the reflexive evaluation of self-consciousness. Thus I may play tennis, for example, not because I believe that it is good or right for a ball to be hit over a net, but because of the pleasure it gives me; or I may avoid wearing short sleeved shirts and sandals in winter because of the pain it gives me. This is true of locatable pleasures and pains such as eating or toothaches, as well as of non-locatable pleasures and pains such as the joy of success and the pain of failure.

## Pleasure and Pain as Ethical Criteria

The reflexivity of consciousness, that I am aware not only of the object of a conscious act but also of the act itself, is of the nature of consciousness and, therefore, as it were, automatic. But self-consciousness is not automatically reflexive, for then there would be an infinite regress of conscious acts, which there is not. However human consciousness, though it is automatically self-conscious, may also reflect on itself deliberately. I may for example be enjoying something, say sugar in my coffee or a cigarette, and reflect on this and disapprove. I may find, at the level of first order wants, that I want sugar in my coffee or that I want a cigarette and, at the level of second order wants, that I do not want sugar in my coffee or a cigarette. To the natural first order approval which is my pleasure at drinking sweet coffee or smoking a cigarette, I may oppose a deliberate second order disapproval. And such disapproval can be effective, that is, I can learn to dislike what once I liked such that the very thing which once gave me pleasure now gives me pain. The same holds true for pain. To my non-deliberate first order disapproval I can oppose a deliberate second order approval, and I can learn to like what previously I disliked. All those people who have to work at quitting smoking once had to work at starting to smoke. That such change in likes and dislikes, in the spontaneous feeling of pleasure or pain, is not equally easy or difficult with all pleasures or pains goes without saying. It may also be true that some likes and dislikes can never be changed, that there are limits to the changes my freedom can make to my nature, and that such limits may not be the same for all people, and it may never be clear exactly where they are with anyone. But such demarcation of limits is not particularly important to our present concern.

Our present concern is to understand that the complexity and variability just sketched does not compromise the Epicurean view that every pleasure is good and every pain bad, and that in fact it makes it possible for pleasure and pain to function as ethical criteria.

There is no reason why pleasure is good and pain bad anymore than there is a reason why circles are round or water wet. It is analytically true and the very foundation of our understanding of good and bad, as we argued in the previous chapter. But, even though every pleasure is good and every pain is bad, they are not for that reason always to be chosen or avoided.[199] They only function as

---

[199]Ep. Men. 129.

criteria of choice and avoidance.

We have seen in our sketch of Epicurean epistemology in the second chapter how to understand the claim that every sensation is true and functions as a criterion of truth. The place of the feelings of pleasure and pain in Epicurean ethics is similar. Just as every sensation is true but not necessarily to be believed, so every pleasure is good but not necessarily to be chosen and every pain bad but not necessarily to be avoided. The truth of sensations cannot be overruled for there is nothing more basic than sensations by which to judge them. Just so the goodness of pleasure and the badness of pain cannot be overruled because there is nothing more basic by which to judge them.

The system of my beliefs about the world in which I live is derived from sensations by a procedure which considers every sensation but does not accept all of them as contributing to my knowledge of the objectively real world. Similarly the system of acts and experiences which constitutes the good life considers every feeling but does not choose or avoid every one simply because it is a pain or a pleasure. There is nothing more basic than the feelings by which to overrule their goodness or badness, but just as in the case of sensations which form the basis of a system of beliefs by a procedure there is a procedural rule which includes a requirement of consistency as a logical requirement of the possibility of belief, so the feelings form the basis of a system of acts and experiences which is derived from them by a procedure which includes a requirement of consistency as a practical requirement of action. The action in question here is the action which chooses good and avoids evil. And a consistency requirement is included as a practical requirement because there are acts which produce both good and evil, that is, bring both pleasure and pain, usually not at the same time but in temporal sequence. It is possible for there to be such acts because there is a distinction between intrinsic and instrumental good and bad.

It is possible for a certain pleasure, which qua pleasure is intrinsically good, to bring about later pain which is intrinsically bad. Anything, however, which is instrumental in bringing about something intrinsically bad is for that reason itself instrumentally bad, whether or not it is also intrinsically good or bad or indifferent. There are pleasures which are intrinsically good and instrumentally bad and pains which are intrinsically bad and instrumentally good, and such pleasures and pains are not necessarily to be chosen or avoided. They rather become the objects of prudent deliberation. To reject a pleasure, however, is not to apply a higher criterion of goodness and find that this pleasure is not good, and likewise for the badness of pain, but rather it is to reject a pleasure or a pain by the very criterion of pleasure and pain. To choose a pain is not to accept that the pain is good, but to accept that choosing the pain is good because it is instrumental in bringing later pleasure. This is what Epicurus means when he notes that "at certain times we treat the good as bad and conversely the bad as good."[200] This procedure functions with pleasure and pain as ethical criteria throughout because intrinsic good and bad functions as the criterion for judging instrumental good and bad, and the ethical life is to a very large extent the choice or avoidance of instrumental good and bad.

An ethical criterion is a characteristic by which to judge the ethical goodness of our behaviour. Our behaviour is ethical so far as it brings about intrinsic good or evil either directly or indirectly by bringing about instrumental good or evil. The

---

[200]Ep. Men. 129.

ethical criterion could therefore itself be the intrinsic good or evil, or it could be a reliable indicator of intrinsic good or evil. As we have seen, pleasure is both a natural indicator that something is good and also itself a good, and the goodness in both cases is intrinsic. The same applies to pain and badness.

What makes pleasure and pain the criteria in Epicureanism is that they are the natural indicators, and the only natural indicators. Any other criterion would either be arbitrary, or it could only be justified by the use of the natural indicators. If our moral intuitions propose something to be intrinsically good or right without any reference to pleasure or pain, we should be on our guard that we're not giving vent to an arbitrary convention.

What could this alternative intrinsic good be? A plausible alternative is virtue, but Epicurus gives an analysis of virtue in terms of pleasure and pain which we shall consider in Chapter 7 and especially Chapter 8, and if that analysis is successful then virtue is not an alternative to pleasure and pain but derived from them. Another possibility might be to treat the pronouncement of an authority as the criterion of goodness, an authority like parents, public opinion, the priest, the king, or the god of your religion. The question here is why one should obey that authority. If the answer is that refusal to obey will have painful consequences while obedience will have pleasant consequences, then we plainly have no alternative criterion. Or if obedience is given because obedience is a virtue, then this alternative is not distinct from the one just mentioned. If the answer is that obedience is given because you see that the authority's pronouncement is right, then you are pursuing a good because it is good rather than because it is underwritten by an authority. But what is this good? Is it nothing like pleasure? Epicurus is probably right that at this point we would have an empty word. But most people don't go that far, not even Plato. The usual claim is not that the intrinsic good is nothing like pleasure, but that there are pleasures which are not good. If this means that there are instrumentally bad pleasures which are to be avoided, then of course Epicurus agrees, but he would quite rightly claim that his hedonistic ethics can allow for that. To insist that some pleasures are intrinsically bad would indicate to Epicurus that an analytic truth had been misunderstood. Even the pleasure got from torturing innocent children, if some monster could derive pleasure from this, is qua pleasure, good. It is the means of producing this pleasure[201] which is evil, and the natural approval is quite rightly opposed by a deliberate disapproval.

A difficulty at this point is that we are still trying to understand the theoretical foundations of a personal ethics conceived as the pursuit of the good life by a human individual, and that we are not yet ready to see this in a social setting which eventually we must. But we cannot do this yet because we have not yet given the full account of pleasure and pain. Epicurean ethics, either personal or social, cannot be understood without understanding katastematic and kinetic pleasure and pain. We must therefore now give an account of these two kinds of pleasure and pain.

---

[201]Ep. Men. 130.

# Chapter Six

# Kinetic and Katastematic Pleasure

Diogenes Laertius tells us that "Epicurus disagrees with the Cyrenaics on pleasure: they do not admit katastematic pleasure but only the kinetic type, whereas he accepts both types, for soul and for body."[202] The distinction between kinetic and katastematic or static pleasure is not new with Epicurus, nor is the preference for katastematic pleasure. It, or something very much like it, can already be found in Aristotle,[203] though Plato and the Cyrenaics did not recognize it and it does not loom large in Aristotle either. Whether Epicurus is to be read as reviving and giving great importance to an Aristotelian point, or whether he is essentially working out an independent insight is not of importance to us because it would not help us to understand the Epicurean distinction. We had best approach what Epicurus has to say on this matter on its own rather than try to understand it as an attempt to interpret Aristotle.

The distinction is of central importance to understanding Epicurean ethics. Diogenes Laertius lists several books of Epicurus[204] in which he works on this distinction. As we shall see, katastematic pleasure is the most important concept in Epicurean ethics and, though it is not wrong to think that Epicurus took

---

[202]D.L. 10.136.

[203]Aristotle characterizes pleasure as "the activity of the natural state" (E.N. 1153a14) and observes that "there is not only an activity of movement but an activity of immobility, and pleasure is found more in rest than in movement." (E.N. 1154b28).

[204]D.L.10.136: On Choice and Avoidance, On the End, On Lives book 1, the letter to the philosophers in Mytilene.

pleasure to be the good. Plainly it is important to a proper understanding of Epicurean ethics to get this central concept right. But it is a difficult concept and there have been divergent accounts of it in the literature of Epicurean scholarship. Before we attempt to give a reading of it here it would be appropriate and helpful to consider some recent and important interpretations.

There can be no question of exhaustive discussion of the literature on the subject, especially since recent scholarly work will always already have taken critical account of earlier work. We shall here consider only recent and important interpretations of the concept of katastematic pleasure, both to show the difficulty of the matter than can give rise to such divergent conclusions, and to learn what we can before attempting our own interpretation. Some of the discussion will have to be quite technical and detailed. But since we are here dealing with the central concept, the very nerve of Epicurean ethics, this is justified. The professional reader will, of course, want to follow the argument in detail, while the more casual reader may prefer to skip ahead to the section entitled, "Kinetic and Katastematic Pleasure".

## Two Recent Interpretations

Anthony Long and David Sedley have collaborated to produce a wonderful study of Hellenistic philosophy.[205] Their treatment of Epicurus' distinction between kinetic and katastematic pleasure, however, and in particular of the ethically central concept of katastematic pleasure is disappointing. Kinetic

---

[205]A.A. Long and D.N. Sedley, The Hellenistic Philosophers, Cambridge University Press, 1987. 2 vols. It is an excellent and most welcome study even with the flaws pointed out by John Rist in Canadian Philosophical Reviews, VII, 12, December 1987, pp. 503-4.

pleasure is interpreted as "all experience which consists in the active stimulation of enjoyable bodily feelings or states of mind."[206] This is a fine characterization of kinetic pleasure so far as it goes, but then they go on to say that Epicurus treats kinetic pleasure "either as a stage on the way to the ultimate goal of absence of pain, or as a variation of that condition when achieved."[207] An inadequate understanding of katastematic pleasure is already evident in that way of characterizing the Epicurean subordination of kinetic to katastematic pleasure. When they give an account of katastematic pleasure they describe it as "a bodily state which is 'comfortable' or suffering from no unsatisfied desire."[208] The restriction of katastematic pleasure to a bodily state must be an oversight, for if anything is clear to the point of obviousness in Epicurean texts it is that there is katastematic pleasure of the mind as well as of the body and that, in fact, the mental pleasures are the more important. We can let that unfortunate point go, therefore, and needn't worry about it.

But there is something more importantly problematical about their interpretation. They base their understanding on two texts, one from Plutarch and one from Cicero. The text from Plutarch reads: "The comfortable state of the flesh, and the confident expectation of this, contain the highest and most secure joy for those who are capable of reasoning it."[209] A peripheral point about this passage might first be noted. It may be that this passage is taken from a section of

---

[206]Long and Sedley, op. cit., p. 123.

[207]Ibid.

[208]Ibid.

[209]This is text 21N in Long and Sedley. It is from Plutarch's Non posse 1089d = Us. 68. Plutarch is quoting from Epicurus' On the End.

Epicurus' book which was aimed at Plato[210] or the Academy, and thus have had a context no longer available to us. This might recommend some caution in interpreting it, or in relying on it too heavily as an attempt to articulate doctrine rather than, perhaps, a fragment of polemic. A more important consideration is that the comfortable state of the flesh referred to here is said to be the kind of joy (chara) which Epicurus clearly identifies as a kinetic pleasure rather than a katastematic one in his book On Choice and Avoidance.[211] Also expectation of the future, like memory of the past, is, when pleasant, a kinetic pleasure. Rather than being a sure reference on which to rely for interpreting katastematic pleasure as a kind of physical stability, it seems that this text is better suited as evidence that katastematic pleasure is not the same as the comfortable state of the body.

The second text on which Long and Sedley rely in their interpretation of katastematic pleasure is from Cicero. It reads: "Quenched thirst involves katastematic pleasure, but the pleasure of the actual quenching is kinetic."[212] There is no difficulty with the second part of the passage, that the pleasure got from drinking when thirsty is kinetic pleasure, as long as we don't infer from that that all kinetic pleasure is pleasure got from satisfying desire. We are here given an important example of kinetic pleasure, no more. But the first part of the passage is problematical, for two reasons. First, it is evident from reading Cicero

---

[210]Epicurus' last phrase is tois epilogizesthai dunamenois, which may well be an allusion to Plato's tois [ou] dunamenois logizesthai (some manuscripts include 'ou', most leave it out) at Timaeus 40d where Plato speaks of the movement of celestial bodies which frighten and fill with foreboding people who can't calculate them with mathematics. cf. Norman DeWitt, Epicurus and his Philosophy, p. 234.

[211]D.L.10.136. Diogenes Laertius says that it is from Epicurus' book On Choice, but I take that to be an abbreviation.

[212]This is text 21Q in Long and Sedley. It is from De fin. 2.9.

that the concept of katastematic pleasure gives him a lot of trouble and that so far as he thinks he understands it he treats it as absence of pain. That this is an important misunderstanding we have already shown. And second, Cicero hesitates here and does not simply identify the state of not being thirsty, or the state of just having quenched your thirst (which is not quite the same as simply not being thirsty) as katastematic pleasure, but writes that it involves (habet) katastematic pleasure. He is indicating that katastematic pleasure is different from kinetic pleasure and that it is more like the feeling of having quenched your thirst than the feeling of drinking when thirsty. To base a general interpretation of kinetic pleasure as the pleasure of satisfying desire and of katastematic pleasure as the pleasure of satisfied desire on this Ciceronian reference is hasty and ill advised. There is in any case much more to be considered when trying to understand the distinction between kinetic and katastematic pleasure than Long and Sedley do.

Another recent discussion of this topic is that by Phillip Mitsis.[213] His is a major attempt, in the context of a book devoted to Epicurean ethical theory, to interpret the Epicurean understanding of pleasure and its distinction into kinetic and katastematic. Extended as this attempt is, it suffers from the basic flaw of linking pleasure and pain too closely to the satisfaction and frustration of desire. It is true that Epicurean texts frequently indicate a connection between pleasure and the satisfaction of desire and pain and the frustration of desire, if only for the obvious reason that those are among the ways that pleasure and pain come into our lives. Such texts point out that satisfaction of desire brings pleasure and that there is pain due to want, or even that meeting your basic needs is a condition of

---

[213]Phillip Mitsis, Epicurus' Ethical Theory: The Pleasures of Invulnerability, Cornell University Press, 1988.

happiness, but they don't justify the claim that Epicurus "regularly equates pleasure with the satisfaction of desire and pain with the frustration of desire",[214] nor do they justify the claim that Epicurus "also claims that all the pleasures that a rational agent should pursue presuppose an existing lack or want."[215] Such claims could, of course, be made trivially true since the only pleasure any agent could pursue is one he lacks or wants, but if we understand the claim in this way, then one doesn't need to appeal to any Epicurean text for it, nor will one succeed in making an interesting point about Epicurean ethics with it. Certainly it would not allow one to make the substantial claim about the Epicurean understanding of pleasure which Mitsis goes on to make, that "Epicurus distinguishes two varieties of pleasure: the kinetic pleasures of motion (satisfying a desire) and the katastematic pleasures of stability (having satisfied a desire)".[216] This last claim sounds very much like the Ciceronian claim we have just seen in connection with the work of Long and Sedley, except that Cicero's hesitation has been removed. The basic problem with this claim is that it implies that all pleasure presupposes a desire, which is false, both as a general claim about pleasure and as a claim about the Epicurean understanding of pleasure. It is true that Epicurus' understanding of kinetic pleasure is based on the pleasure we get from satisfying desires, though it is not confined to such pleasures, as we shall see. Mitsis also refers to the passage from Epicurus' book On the End, which we we have just seen Plutarch quoting, except that Mitsis quotes Gellius,[217] who thinks that Epicurus defines pleasure as

---

[214]Mitsis, op. cit., p. 31.

[215]Mitsis, op. cit., p. 32.

[216]Mitsis, op. cit., p. 45.

[217]Mitsis, op. cit., p. 48, n. 97; the reference is to Aulus Gellius' anthology Noctes Atticae IX.5.2, which is Us. 68 along with the Plutarch reference.

the stable condition of the flesh (<u>sarkos eustathes katastēma</u>). As we have already noted above, this condition is identified by Epicurus as a kinetic pleasure and cannot, if only for that reason, count as a definition of pleasure. The idea that we have here a definition of pleasure is in any event an addition by Gellius which probably was not meant seriously in any technical sense. We shall not comment in detail on the notion of katastematic pleasure here since that would be difficult to do briefly without simply presupposing a reading of katastematic pleasure which we have not yet given. But we might point out here that Epicurus thought that katastematic pleasure was possible under torture[218] which cannot be thought to be a stable or a comfortable condition of the flesh; and, if katastematic pleasure can be identified with happiness, then Epicurus' claim that he was happy, even blessed, near death and while in great kinetic pain,[219] also indicates that katastematic pleasure is compatible with kinetic pain and an unstable condition of the body. Such considerations, and others, should make us very hesitant to adopt the essentially Ciceronian interpretation of kinetic and katastematic pleasure in terms of satisfying and satisfied desire.

## Gosling and Taylor

Cicero should be read with caution, for when read with caution he is without doubt a valuable source of Epicurean thought. It is, of course, difficult to say just how far a commentator can be trusted once you have good reason to have reservations about his reports. But such reservations can be taken too far and it seems to me that the work of Gosling and Taylor is a case in point. In a major

---

[218]cf. D.L. 10.118.

[219]cf. D.L. 10.22.

recent interpretation[220] of the Epicurean theory of pleasure they essentially ascribe the distinction between kinetic and katastematic pleasure to Cicero, then undermine Cicero's credibility as a reliable source of authentic Epicureanism, with the effect that the distinction itself is almost eliminated.

In the fourth century there were a number of attempts to analyze pleasure as a replenishment of an organic lack or deficiency, as a process of restoration to the natural state of the organism.[221] To this view of pleasure Aristotle opposes his own analysis of pleasure as the unimpeded actualization of the natural state.[222] Gosling and Taylor interpret Epicurus' theory of pleasure as a reconciliation of these two views. They offer this not so much as a claim about Epicurus' intentions, than as a fruitful and plausible way in which Epicurus' theory can be seen. The view that pleasure is a movement of restoration is captured in Epicurus' conception of kinetic pleasure, and the Aristotelian view of unimpeded actualization is captured in the conception of katastematic pleasure. The key to the reconciliation is the insight that the two apparently opposed theories of pleasure are about two different kinds of pleasure which share the important characteristic of being cases of the awareness of proper functioning. Katastematic pleasure is the consciousness of the proper functioning of the organism, and kinetic pleasure is the consciousness of the proper functioning of an organ or part of the organism. Thus the difference between the two kinds of pleasure is preserved, but it is a difference without great importance in Epicurean hedonic

---

[220]J.C.B. Gosling and C.C.W. Taylor, The Greeks on Pleasure, Oxford, The Clarendon Press, 1982, pp. 345-413.

[221]See, for example, Plato's discussion at Philebus 53c - 55a.

[222]Book VII of E.N.

theory. Much more important is the common characteristic of proper organismic functioning, which makes both of them pleasure, and which allows both to be accommodated in a unified theory of pleasure as the consciousness of the proper functioning of the organism. The prominence of the distinction between kinetic and katastematic pleasure in Epicurean scholarship, argue Gosling and Taylor, is almost entirely due to Cicero, who can be shown to be unreliable on this point.

It should be clear that Gosling and Taylor's interpretation is a dramatic departure from the norm of Epicurean scholarship in that it rejects what had previously been a fundamental point of agreement among diverse interpretations. They are, of course, aware of that and their argument reflects this in its thoroughness and detail. But their argument is unconvincing and it is important for us to see how it fails before offering our own reading of Epicurus' theory.

There are, to begin with, some prima facie difficulties with the analysis of Epicurus' conception of pleasure as a proper functioning and, as would seem to be a necessary corollary of this, of his conception of pain as an improper functioning.

Everyone knows that there are pleasant and unpleasant memories, and everyone also knows that memory can function properly and improperly, that is, that we can sometimes remember accurately and at other times misremember. There is, however, no correlation between pleasant memories and a properly functioning memory, and between unpleasant memories and an improperly functioning memory. Memories which are pleasant are no more likely to be accurate because they are pleasant, that is, the pleasantness of a memory is no evidence for its accuracy. One might say that a pleasant memory is the memory of a pleasant event and that proper functioning of the organism should be looked for in the event being remembered rather than in the memory of it. True, pleasant memories seem all to be memories of pleasant events, but this does not prevent the pleasure of the memory being distinct from the pleasure of the past event, and it is the former that seems to be not a matter of proper functioning. Pleasant memories are not the only ones we take pleasure in, however. If I pride myself on my memory and take pleasure in recalling trivia in, say, playing Trivial Pursuit, then I take pleasure in remembering something that is not a pleasant event and would therefore not happily be called a pleasant memory. But there is pleasure in remembering all those trivia, and the ones that later turn out to be wrong, that is, cases of misremembering or improper functioning of the memory, were just as pleasant at the time as the accurate ones. This lack of correspondence between pleasure and proper functioning of memory is quite obvious really, and it is hard to see how Epicurus could have missed it if he had been developing a theory of pleasure in terms of organismic functioning, given the importance he seems to have attached to pleasant memories.[223]

Epicurus was well acquainted with the pleasures of philosophy and theoretical inquiry.[224] As was argued in the second chapter, truth was essentially a procedural concept for Epicurus including the proper functioning of the senses and the mind as an important element. If that is right, and if Gosling and Taylor are right that for Epicurus "a particular feeling of pleasure is true in that it faithfully represents the fact that a part of the organism is functioning properly",[225] then pleasure would be a criterion not just of the truth of ethical

---

[223]D.L. 10.22.

[224]Ep. Hdt. 37; S.V. 27.

[225]Gosling and Taylor, op. cit., p. 405.

beliefs, but also of the truth of the propositions of natural philosophy. But Epicurus never gives pleasure and pain a criterial role in the pursuit of theoretical truth, though he had plenty of opportunity to do so.[226] This makes it unlikely that he believed pleasure to be a reliable indicator of the proper functioning of the mind.

Despite his generally ascetic life style, Epicurus must surely have been acquainted with the pleasures of intoxication as well as with the improper functioning of the whole organism, both mind and body, characteristic of this pleasant state. The question here is not whether he approved of having a cup or two in excess from time to time, but of the relation between pleasure and proper functioning of the organism, and the pleasure of wine seems to be a pleasure of improper functioning. Had he held the theory of pleasure ascribed to him by Gosling and Taylor, he would surely have had something to say in the Symposium about the prima facie difficulty for his theory of pleasant intoxication. But the several fragments on wine which have been preserved from that work[227] indicate that he saw no problem here.

If we can accept as a corollary to the view that pleasure is the proper functioning of the organism the view that pain is its improper functioning, then we would have to account for grief and fear and other such painful or unpleasant

---

[226]K.D. 22, "We must consider both the real purpose and all the evidence of direct perception, to which we always refer the conclusions of opinion; otherwise, all will be full of doubt and confusion", has sometimes been taken to connect pleasure and our reliance on our senses (e.g. Mitsis, Epicurus' Ethical Theory, p. 41). But 'eph hēn' (to which), being feminine singular, most probably refers only to the evidence in the second part of the conjunction and not to the purpose in the first. It should therefore be read 'to which latter' rather than 'to both of which'. And even if it could be read to refer to both, that would still be a long way from making pleasure and pain epistemological criteria.

[227]By Plutarch and Philodemus (Arrighetti 21, 1-5; Us. 58, 59, 60, 64).

mental states in terms of improper functioning of the mind. But it is very difficult to see how this might be done. There are some fears induced by the wrong opinions about the gods for example, and these might be accounted for in terms of improper functioning, but there are also other fears, for example the justified fears of the presocial condition of man against which we enter into the compact not to harm or be harmed, or the fear of detection of the criminal.[228] Such fears do not indicate that the mind is functioning improperly, but rather the reverse. If anything is functioning improperly here it might be said to be social relations, but not the organism. Similarly with other painful emotions. Some kinds of grief are unjustified matters of faulty thinking, I suppose, but sometimes grief is quite appropriate and not just an indication of faulty thinking. We must still learn to cope with it, but something other than repairing a faulty mind may be called for.[229]

It is not just mental pain which provides prima facie difficulties for Epicurus as interpreted by Gosling and Taylor however, but physical pain is problematical as well. Physical pain is not only a report, as it were, of tissue damage, but also a warning that we are in danger of tissue damage. If I put my hand on the hot handle of a frying pan it hurts and I withdraw my hand quickly, before there is tissue damage. That the painful warning came in time to prevent tissue damage indicates that nociception was functioning properly. We don't, anachronistically, have to suppose that Epicurus had knowledge of the neurology of nociception to admit this point in consideration of the theory being ascribed to him by Gosling

---

[228]K.D. 35.

[229]S.V. 64, for example, bids us grieve for our dead friends (or, perhaps, share the suffering of living friends) not by lamenting but by meditating, possibly on pleasant memories of them (or, if living friends are meant, by showing thoughtful concern).

and Taylor. All we have to suppose is that he was aware that pain is sometimes a warning, and that to give this warning is the proper function of a part of the organism. But this awareness was surely available to Epicurus, for it is available to anyone who has ever been saved from harm by pain, even if it was just a case of saying uncle when wrestling with other boys while still at school. I don't know whether Epicurus knew anything of the condition of pain blindness which marks people whose nociceptive physiology is defective, but there is no reason to suppose that the condition was unheard of in his day. This condition makes it rather obvious that sometimes failure to feel pain is a case of improper functioning of an organ and pain itself is its proper functioning.

This list of prima facie difficulties with the theory of pleasure ascribed to Epicurus by Gosling and Taylor could be extended, but there is probably not much to be gained by doing so for the point being made. So let's conclude this with a couple more quick and obvious points. The distinction between pleasant and unpleasant food is not the same as the distinction between nutritious and unnutritious food. What's good for you doesn't always taste good and positively harmful stuff can be pleasant. I happen to have an intense dislike of seafood, but I don't suppose that has anything to do with the improper functioning of my palate. And one last point. There are many non-painful medical problems, cases of improper functioning of a part of the organism which are not painful. Had Epicurus held the view under discussion, we could expect him to have tried to accommodate such considerations, or for some of his critics to have raised them. But he didn't and they didn't. Such difficulties recommend that we take a critical look at Gosling and Taylor's interpretation and try to save Epicurus, if possible, from what appears prima facie to be rather a clumsy blunder.

Diogenes Laertius tells us, and I know of no reason for thinking that he may have been wrong about this or even that the point was controversial, that Epicurus disagreed with the Cyrenaics about the relative value of bodily and mental pains and pleasures. Unlike the Cyrenaics he held that mental pains were worse than bodily pains, and he also held mental pleasures to be greater than those of the body.[230] Given this, it comes as a surprise to find Gosling and Taylor arguing for the primacy of sensory pleasure in Epicureanism, for the identification of sensory pleasure with bodily pleasure, for the interpretation of mental pleasure as dependent on bodily pleasure by being no more than the thought of it, for the interpretation of ataraxia as the "confident expectation of bodily pleasure and pleasant memory of it", and for the value of ataraxia as "parasitic upon that of aponia" and of aponia as "not non-sensory" but rather "a condition of sensory pleasure."[231] Their evidence for this primacy of sensory pleasure they find, again surprisingly, in Cicero. The Ciceronian source for such an important point is surprising not only because Gosling and Taylor eventually reject Cicero as a reliable source, but also because quotations of Epicurus found in Cicero must always be taken with some caution for they are not direct quotations in Greek, as are those of Diogenes Laertius and Plutarch for example, but rather translations into Latin. Translations are always already interpretations[232] and we should keep in mind that Cicero is not a sympathetic translator. The passage in Cicero is his translation of two quotations from what is generally thought to be the Peri Telous

---

[230]D.L. 10.137.

[231]cf. Gosling and Taylor, op. cit., pp. 353, 372.

[232]The reader might care to compare four or five published translations into English of the Cicero passage in question or, for that matter, any other ancient text to see what subtle (and not so subtle) differences there are.

of Epicurus. The first is:

> For my part I cannot understand what that good is if one subtracts those pleasures perceived by taste, those from hearing and music, and those sweet movements, too, got from visual perception of shapes, or any of the other pleasures generated by any sense in the whole man. Nor can one hold that joy of mind is alone among the goods. For as I understand it the mind is in a state of joy when it has hope of all those things I have mentioned above, that nature may acquire them with complete absence of pain.

The second is:

> I have often enquired of those who were called wise what they had left among the goods if they removed those ones — unless they wanted to emit empty noises; I could learn nothing from them; if they want to boast about virtues and wisdom they will say nothing unless they mean the way by which those pleasures are achieved which I mentioned above.[233]

The context of these quotations is debate and refutation of other philosophers, probably from the Academy.[234] The first quotation is from a debate with someone who believes the good to be something which does not include sensory pleasures, something which is quite unlike sensory pleasures to the extent that the only pleasures which can be called good are mental pleasures, and sensory or bodily pleasures do not even rank among good things. Epicurus' reply to these people is that he finds this concept of the good quite unintelligible, that he cannot understand a concept of the good which would entirely exclude sensory pleasures, for whatever desirability one may attach to particular sensory pleasures (such as those of the sensualists mentioned in the letter to Menoeceus, for example) they are still pleasures and, qua pleasures, good. And he further replies that one cannot

---

[233]Both quotations are from Tusc. 3.41-2. I give Gosling and Taylor's translation. Part of the original Greek translated by Cicero is preserved by Athenaeus at 12.546e (see Bailey, p. 122 no. 10), and by D.L. 10.6.

[234]Long and Sedley (Vo. II, p. 121) remark that the second quotation "reads like anti-Stoic polemic." My reasons for thinking the Academy the more probable target is that the first quotation is part of an argument about the nature of the good, which has more of a Platonic ring than a Stoic; and the second quotation is aimed at "those who were called wise", who seem to me more probably to be found in the Academy than in the fledgling Stoa.

simply separate mental pleasures from bodily pleasures and insist that the former are the only pleasures which can be called good, for it is clear that "the mind is in a state of joy when it has hope of all those things I have mentioned". That is to say, the expectation of bodily pleasure is a mental pleasure and it would surely be inconsistent to allow that the latter is good if you are going to deny this of the former, especially if the bodily pleasure is the choiceworthy kind which sober reasoning shows not to be associated with later pain. This quotation gives no warrant at all for believing that Epicurus is "very insistent on the importance of sensory pleasure".[235] It is true that the good life is not possible if you remove sensory pleasure from it entirely since there are necessary desires whose non-satisfaction brings pain and a refusal to enjoy the sensory pleasures of eating and breathing, for example, would terminate the good life, if only because it would terminate life itself. I'm sure that Epicurus would agree with this because it is too obvious for him to have missed, and I'm also sure that this is not a point he is trying to make in the passage translated by Cicero. So, while Gosling and Taylor are quite right to point out that Epicurus does not only hold "that sensory pleasures are a good thing, but that nothing is left to the good life if you subtract them",[236] they are quite mistaken to think that he is making that claim in the Cicero passage and also quite mistaken that the primacy of sensory pleasure in Epicurean ethics can be inferred from it. Nor does this passage give reason to think that all mental pleasures are secondary and dependent upon bodily pleasures in the way that some of them obviously are. The memory of a good meal is an obvious case in point, and it is such pleasures which Epicurus refers to here to

---

[235]Gosling and Taylor, op. cit., p. 367.

[236]Ibid, p. 368.

make his point that if you are going to call the memory good you must call the meal good too. But he is certainly not claiming here that all mental pleasures are like that. Surely the pleasant memory of conversations with Idomeneus he mentions in his last letter to him was not restricted to conversations about food etc., nor is the pleasure he got from philosophy dependent upon sensory pleasures. So, not only need we not suppose on the basis of the Cicero passage, that Epicurus took all mental pleasure to depend on bodily pleasure as does the fond recollection of a good meal, but we have excellent reason to think that he did not believe this to be so.

Cicero's second quotation probably has much the same context and is about the same issue as the first one because he says that it occurs "a little lower down" in Epicurus' book than the first one and Cicero's quoting them together is good reason for thinking that they are on the same topic or, at least, that Cicero thought so. For the second quotation we have no quotation of the Greek original and must therefore rely entirely on Cicero's Latin. But that is a problem, for it is unclear in which of two crucially different ways we are to understand Epicurus' question, in particular the words quid haberent quod in bonis relinquerent. Translators are split roughly down the middle in their interpretation of those words.[237] Is Epicurus asking: If you remove sensory pleasures from the set of good things, what have you got left, that is, aren't sensory pleasures the only goods? Or is Epicurus asking: If you remove that which makes sensory pleasures good from other goods, what justification is there for still calling them good, that is, isn't what

---

[237]Gosling and Taylor (p. 368): what they had left among the goods; Long and Sedley (p. 117): what they could retain as the content of goods; Inwood and Gerson (p. 43): what they would have left [to put] in the category of goods; J.E. King (Tusculan Disputations, The Loeb Classical Library, Harvard University Press, 1966, p. 275): what content could be left in a good.

makes sensory pleasures good and what makes other goods good the same thing? The first question would be that of a person who thought and was arguing that sensory pleasures are the only good, and the second question would be that of a person who thought that sensory pleasures are good. Cicero's Latin does not clearly demand one or the other of the two readings and it is unclear what the original Greek must have been. We have just given two examples of mental goods which are not sensory goods and that is reason to think that Epicurus was not asking the first question, but the second. In the first quotation, he is arguing with someone who wants to maintain that mental pleasure is the only good and against this Epicurus argues that one cannot coherently affirm that mental pleasure is good and deny that sensory pleasure is good. In the second quotation he is arguing against people who may be denying that sensory pleasure is good because no pleasure is good, and Epicurus' argument is that whatever list of goods they have they will find that what makes them good is the same thing that makes sensory pleasure good and, in particular, if that list includes (or is restricted to) virtue and wisdom, they will find that their value is the instrumental value of producing pleasure, in particular, sensory pleasure. The issue for us here is not whether Epicurus was right or whether he may or may not have had a good argument, but whether these two quotations are evidence that Epicurus took all pleasure to be sensory or even held to the primacy of sensory pleasure in his ethics, and it is clear that they do not support that view.

Another step in Gosling and Taylor's argument to show the unimportance in Epicurean ethics of the distinction between kinetic and katastematic pleasure is their argument to the effect that "Epicurus is insistent that the senses are the criterion of truth, and in particular the criterion of goodness".[238] It is not quite

---

[238]Gosling and Taylor, op. cit., p. 368.

right to claim that Epicurus took the senses to be the criterion of truth since he took them to be a criterion of truth, preconceptions (prolēpseis) being another one. But it is quite wrong to say that Epicurus took the senses to be the criterion of goodness. Such a view quite ignores the difference between the senses (aistheseis) and the feelings (pathē), the latter being the criteria of goodness, not the former. As evidence for their view Gosling and Taylor cite three passages from Epicurus and one from Cicero which they claim confirms this view. A look at this evidence will make it quite clear that their conclusion is untenable.

The reference which may most plausibly be seen as evidence for the view that Epicurus took the senses to be criteria of goodness is Ep. Men. 124, since here Epicurus actually says that "all good and evil lie in sensation." The argument in that section of the Letter to Menoeceus is not about the criterion of goodness however, but about death. The main reason why "death is nothing to us" is that only a conscious being, a being capable of sensation, is capable of experiencing good and evil, and the dead are incapable of sensation. Epicurus' argument is that "death is nothing to us for all good and evil lie in sensation, whereas death is the absence of sensation." Sensation, according to Ep. Hdt. 63-7, is not an intrinsic property of either the body or the soul, but an accidental property of their union. As long as the union persists, that is, so long as the person remains alive, sensation never ceases. He makes it clear that what he is saying here applies both to sensation and feeling, although the discussion, for the sake of brevity of expression perhaps, is given in terms of sensation alone. But it is clear that the cessation of sensation at death is also the cessation of feeling because it is the cessation of all consciousness whatever.[239] This is how Ep. Men. 124 must be

---

[239]cf. K.D. 2.

understood. Death is nothing to us because good and evil exist only for conscious people and consciousness ceases at death. Epicurus is not careful to distinguish sensations from feelings here because there is no need for the point he is making. When however, he is talking about the criterion of goodness he is careful to make the distinction. In Gosling and Taylor's second reference to Epicurus at Ep. Men. 129, for example, he is quite clear that the standard by which every good is judged is not sensation but feeling. Their third reference, to D.L. 10.137, is puzzling. Diogenes Laertius is here reporting Epicurus' use of the cradle argument. Nothing is said about sensations being criteria of goodness, though he does say that if we are "left to our own feelings (autopathos)--we shun pain." And we mustn't think that wherever Epicurus writes about feelings we can treat that as a discussion of sensations for, when it matters, he is quite clear that they differ and that they are separate as criteria.[240]

Gosling and Taylor find "confirmation" for their view that Epicurus thought sensation to be the criterion of goodness in Cicero's De finibus. This love and hate affair they seem to be having with Cicero always surprises. They accept, indeed they argue, that Cicero's reliability as a reporter and interpreter of Epicurean doctrine is suspect and should be treated with reservation unless we can confirm what he says directly in the text of Epicurus. This should be a general principle not to be used or rejected as convenience demands. In Book I Section 9 of De finibus Cicero has his Epicurean spokesman Torquatus argue that pleasure is the good. He first gives Epicurus' cradle argument that every animal shows pain and seeks pleasure from birth on. Thus he says that the desirability of pleasure and undesirability of pain are a natural given from the start and do not

---

[240]eg. Ep. Hdt. 38, 82.

need to be proved. We perceive this desirability and undesirability as directly as we perceive that fire is hot, snow white, or honey sweet, and is in as little need of proof by argument as these are. He also reports some disagreement within his school about whether the desirability of pleasure and the undesirability of pain are quite simply matters of perception as are the heat of fire etc. All of this is entirely compatible with Epicurus distinction between sensation and feeling though it does not explicitly use that distinction. But a confirmation that sensation is the criterion of goodness, as distinct from feeling, is not to be found here.

We can now proceed directly to their discussion of the distinction between kinetic and katastematic pleasure. They divide the ancient texts usually thought to be evidence for the distinction into three groups: first, Lucretius 4.627-9 and the fragments collected by Usener numbered 408-415; second, the testimony of Cicero in De finibus and Tusculan Disputations; third, Diogenes Laertius 10.136.

Gosling and Taylor are quite right that the distinction between kinetic and katastematic pleasure is never explicitly made by Lucretius and that he has nothing to convince anyone to make the distinction who is not convinced already on other grounds. In the Usener material they focus on no. 411, a fragment from Plutarch and on no. 413, a fragment from Athenaeus. Plutarch, in writing of sensory pleasure, reports the Epicureans as saying that sensory pleasures "invite one themselves, these beautiful, smooth and gentle motions of the flesh."[241] The Epicurean argument which Plutarch is reporting in this context is that pleasure is naturally perceived as good, that we need no teacher to discover this, and that even the skeptical suspension of judgment does not prevent it, since the

---

[241]Col. 1122e = Us. 411.

evaluation is pre-deliberative and as spontaneous as sensation itself. It is true that Plutarch is not concerned with the distinction between kinetic and katastematic pleasure here, but it is also clear that he thinks of sensory pleasures as kinetic here, for he calls them motions (kinēmata) of the flesh. Gosling and Taylor's dismissal of this is most unsatisfactory. They say in response that "Epicurus would have to think of all pleasures as motions, so that this sort of passage gives no ground for supposing these pleasures to belong to the special class of kinetic pleasures."[242] This response is unsatisfactory because, while it is true that Epicurus would have to think of all pleasures as atomic motions, that kind of motion is not at issue here, and it is not true that he would have to think of all pleasures as motions of some other kind, the motion of restoration to the natural state, for example. In the fragment from Athenaeus[243] he writes that "Epicurus and his followers were fond of kinetic pleasure" and goes on to embellish on the kinds of sensory pleasures he has in mind. Whether he is fair to Epicurus here is not the point. Gosling and Taylor agree that "clearly Athenaeus considers these sensory pleasures to be kinetic",[244] and that is to our present point. Their dismissal of this Athenaeus passage is also most unsatisfactory. They charge two things against this passage, first, that it is not a quotation from any Epicurean and, second, that Athenaeus may be no more reliable than Cicero. I too have reservations about Athenaeus as a reliable interpreter of Epicureanism, so I won't object to that charge. But, while it is true that the passage under consideration is not a quotation, Athenaeus goes on almost immediately to quote from Epicurus'

---

[242]Gosling and Taylor, op. cit., p. 376.

[243]Athenaeus 12. 546e = Us. 413.

[244]Gosling and Taylor, op. cit., p. 376.

<u>Peri Telous</u> in which Epicurus speaks of a number of sensory pleasures calling them, or at least one of them, kinetic pleasures. Perhaps Gosling and Taylor missed the quotation because they were working with Usener's collection and he puts the quotation with the material from the <u>Peri Telous</u> (Us. 67) rather than with the material Gosling and Taylor were considering. I won't go into their consideration of the material from Cicero here because it is long and involved and finally inconclusive. They do find the distinction between kinetic and katastematic pleasure to be unmistakable and prominent in the Cicero material, and they are right about this, and they make a case for undermining the reliability of Cicero with which I am very sympathetic. We should not, I think, go to Cicero to find out how to read Epicurus, but rather we should go to Epicurus to find out how to read Cicero. If therefore the distinction can be attested in Epicurus we can give the proper credibility to the Cicero material as well, even if we retain reservations about how well he understood it or about how sympathetically he presented it.

Gosling and Taylor's third group of evidence, D.L. 10.136, is crucial. Three distinct things occur in this passage. There are some grammatical difficulties in it which allow some differences in reading, but these are neutral with respect to the three basic points of this passage. First, Diogenes Laertius points out a point of disagreement between Epicurus and the Cyrenaics on the question of pleasure. The Cyrenaics recognize only kinetic pleasure to be pleasure, but Epicurus recognizes, in addition, katastematic pleasure. Epicurus thinks of these as two distinct kinds of pleasure, both of which occur as mental pleasure and also as bodily pleasure. There are, then, four distinct types of pleasure in the Epicurean hedonic classification. And this is not a chance point Diogenes Laertius has fished out of some debate between Epicurus and the Cyrenaics, but, he assures us, it is a distinction to be found in several books. Further, and this is the second thing, the distinction is not an idiosyncrasy of Epicurus which did not find favour with other leading figures of the Epicurean school, but is a distinction which can also be found in the writings of leading Epicureans, two of whom he mentions together with the titles of works in which the distinction is made. And the the third thing is the affirmation that, though kinetic and katastematic pleasures are distinct types, they are nevertheless both conceived of as pleasure. The whole section is then supported with a quotation from a book by Epicurus in which he distinguishes kinetic and katastematic pleasure, and gives two examples of each. This seems, at first glance, conclusive.

It will remain conclusive at second glance as well, for Gosling and Taylor's attempt to bend this passage to their interpretation is all dust and no substance. Their strategy is to approach the passage through a grammatical awkwardness in it which allows two translations of part of it. The two translations[245] are:

> Similarly, Diogenes, too, in the seventeenth book of the Epilecta and Metrodorus in his Timocrates say as follows: 'but both kinetic and katastematic pleasure being considered pleasure.' And Epicurus in Of Choices says this: 'for ataraxia and aponia are katastematic pleasures; but joy and well-being are seen in actuality in motion (kinēsis).'

> And similarly Diogenes in the seventeenth book of Epilecta and Metrodorus in his Timocrates say the same; but with both kinetic and katastematic pleasure being apprehended by the mind. Epicurus in On Choices says as follows: 'while ataraxia and aponia are katastematic pleasures joy and well-being are seen in actuality by/in motion.'

The difference between these two translations is allowed by the grammatical awkwardness of the Greek phrase 'nooumenēs de hēdonēs tēs te kata kinēsin kai

[245]Ibid, pp. 388-390.

tēs katastēmatikēs.' The difference, as Gosling and Taylor point out, is that the first translation attributes the passage to two authors as a quotation occurring in each of their books. The second translation attributes the point to Epicurus as a further point in the account of his theory of pleasure. The remainder of the passage, however, is substantially the same across both readings. Gosling and Taylor exploit the difference in translation allowed by the grammatical awkwardness of one Greek phrase beyond anything it will bear as though it will allow very different interpretations of the entire passage, in particular as though it will allow their interpretation as equally legitimate alongside the one taken by "most commentators".

Let us see what they say about the first reading, beginning with the acceptable points. It attributes a single fragment which is not a sentence but a genitive absolute phrase to two authors. Yes, that is an awkwardness which recommends the second translation. And this is the only point they make which is about the difference between the two readings occasioned by that grammatical matter. All others are about what is essentially the same in the two readings, but presented as though they were matters of interpretation somehow related to matters of translation. They comment: "This makes Epicurus put joy and well-being down as kinetic pleasures, and would certainly entail that he is not just considering pleasures of restoration to a natural state as kinetic."[246] True, and an important point to take into consideration in understanding Epicurean kinetic pleasure. This is in no sense an objection to a peculiar reading of this passage. Next: "it would be hard to avoid a strongly negative view of katastematic pleasure." True, both ataraxia and aponia begin with a negative prefix. But that is as far as it goes, and

---

[246]This and subsequent quotations are found on pp. 388-89.

there is nothing here which makes it hard to avoid a strongly negative view of katastematic pleasure. What could it be? Gosling and Taylor don't say. "It seems that once a pleasure is experienced it becomes kinetic." What in the world could they possibly think makes it seem so? There is nothing here to suggest that all experienced pleasures (and what other kind is there?!) are kinetic. "This would raise severe difficulties for Epicurus' view that the good is given in unthinking perception, since it would seem that only kinetic pleasure is so given, while the position requires that katastematic pleasure be so known as the good." If by "unthinking perception" is meant the pre-deliberative feeling of pleasure, rather than their interpretation in terms of sensation which we have just discussed, then that way of referring to Epicurus' view is acceptable. But then the point reduces to something like: if Epicurus is here claiming that katastematic pleasure is an unexperienced pleasure then his view that the good, which is pleasure, must be experienced is in difficulty. True, but he is making no such claim and cannot reasonably be thought to be. Gosling and Taylor are raising a lot of dust without substance. Let's take just one more point: "we have to take 'chara' ('joy') and 'euphrosune' ('sense of well-being') as referring to kinetic pleasures". Yes, quite plainly we do. Gosling and Taylor find two difficulties with this. "First, Cicero regularly makes Torquatus' use the word 'gaudium' to talk of katastematic pleasure and this suggests (but does not prove) that Epicureans (a) used the natural Greek equivalent 'chara' in this way and (b) did not have a totally 'negative condition' view of katastematic pleasure." In reply to this we may note that Epicurus is quite clear that 'chara' is kinetic joy, and when he speaks of katastematic joy, Torquatus' 'gaudium', he uses the word 'gēthos'. We shall consider the significance of this later when we offer our own interpretation. And it is quite true that Epicurus did not have a totally negative view of katastematic pleasure, but this is as strongly suggested by Epicurus himself as by Cicero's use of 'gaudium', and it has nothing to do with his giving 'chara' as an example of kinetic pleasure. The second difficulty Gosling and Taylor see in our having to take 'chara' and 'euphrosunē' as referring to kinetic pleasures is that 'euphrosunē' is an unusual word for sensory pleasures. True, but that is not a difficulty. Rather it is an indication that, while all sensory pleasures may be kinetic, not all kinetic pleasures are sensory. But Gosling and Taylor, who have already persuaded themselves that Epicurus thought that all pleasures are sensory, will have difficulty seeing this indication.

We cannot continue commenting on Gosling and Taylor's work at this level of detail. Let it be said though that this detailed commentary could continue for many more pages with essentially the same results. To make it short then, the difficulties they think they find with the first interpretation of D.L.10.136 suggest to them another interpretation which is a suitably adjusted version of Bollack's.[247] This alternate interpretation is one for whose rightness they admit there is no proof from within the passage, but one to which one may be brought by "prior views" and "predilections" about what Epicurus is all about.[248] This interpretation does away with any important difference between katastematic and kinetic pleasure, interpreting them as merely the negative and positive ways of saying the same thing. Thus 'ataraxia' is merely the negative expression for 'chara', and they mean essentially the same thing. Thus 'chara' and 'ataraxia', 'euphrosunē' and 'aponia' are "four names for two conditions."[249] The

[247]Jean Bollack, Epicure, La Pensée du Plaisir, Paris, 1975.

[248]cf. Gosling and Taylor, op. cit., pp. 390-91.

[249]Ibid, p. 392.

advantages claimed for this interpretation are that it gives a positive account of katastematic pleasure which distinguishes it from apatheia, and it allows us to see that Epicurus makes perception the criterion of good. But, this alternate interpretation is not recommended by difficulties with the first interpretation for, as we have shown, these are without substance; and it is not recommended by the text of D.L.10.136, in fact, the reverse; and the claimed advantages of the alternate interpretation are problematical in that first, to call katastematic pleasure positive because it is the negative expression of something positive is highly tenuous, especially if a more plausible interpretation of its positive nature can be given and, second, that it recommends ignoring the distinction between sensations and feelings in the account of the Epicurean criterion of the good, as do Gosling and Taylor, surely is a disadvantage of this interpretation rather than an advantage.

## Rist and Merlan

There is one more cluster of interpretations of the nature and relation of kinetic and katastematic pleasure which we should look at before attempting our own. Right after the second world war C. Diano in his influential work on Epicurus[250] proposed an interpretation, based on Lucr. 4.627-9, of katastematic pleasure as the condition of the organism free from natural and necessary wants, and of kinetic pleasure as presupposing katastematic pleasure and consisting merely in the variation of it. In 1960 Philip Merlan undertook to refute Diano and offer his own interpretation of Epicurean ethics as a philosophy of joy rather than pleasure in any ordinary sense. In 1972 John Rist defended Diano against Merlan's

---

[250]C. Diano, Epicuri Ethica, Florence 1946.

objections and reaffirmed Diano's interpretation. In this dispute I am more on the side of Merlan than Diano and Rist. It will therefore be convenient to begin with the Diano/Rist view as presented by Rist and consider why it is unacceptable before we turn to Merlan to see what we can learn from him.

Rist argues that when the organism or some part of it is in a painless state then the organism or that part is in a state of katastematic pleasure, for katastematic pleasure is precisely the absence of pain. We have already shown that view to be false in our previous chapter, and mention it here only to point out that it forms the background for Rist's discussion of the present issue. Kinetic pleasure, he argues, always supervenes upon some existing katastematic pleasure, which it presupposes and only varies. For evidence of this relationship between kinetic and katastematic pleasure Rist appeals to K.D.18 and to Lucr. 4.627-9 as well as to three other sources which he believes support his theory indirectly.

K.D.18 says that "the pleasure in the flesh does not increase when once the pain of need has been removed, but is only varied." We have already discussed this doctrine in our previous chapter and will not repeat that discussion here. But it is appropriate to point out here that this doctrine gives no reason to think that the pleasure in the flesh of which it speaks is katastematic pleasure. We shall soon argue that it is not. Rist interprets the notion of varying pleasure as a tickling or soothing of the senses. As evidence for this he refers to a place in Plutarch, a place in Lucretius and two places in Cicero.[251] It is true that some version of the word occurs in these places, but in none of them is it claimed, nor is there any other indication, that a variation of katastematic pleasure is meant.

---

[251]Gargalismos (Plut., De lat. viv. 1129b), mulcat (Lucr., 2.42), permulcet (Cic., De fin. 2.31), titillaret (Cic., De fin. 1.39).

Rist also, and more emphatically, appeals to Lucr. 4.627-9, which was the basis of Diano's interpretation. Lucretius is at this point giving an explanation of how the senses work and has just turned to the sense of taste and undertakes "to explain the tongue and the palate, by which we perceive flavors." (4.615-6) We chew our food, he explains, and squeeze out substances which enter "the pores of the palate and the tortuous passages of the spongy tongue." (4.620-1) If these substances are made up of smooth bodies the taste will be pleasant, if of rough bodies the taste will be unpleasant. (4.622-6) And then comes the passage to which Diano and Rist appeal to support their theory that all kinetic pleasure supervenes on katastematic pleasure, aware that it is "the only evidence which favours it directly."[252] Lucretius writes: "the pleasure that comes from flavour does not go beyond the palate; but when it has dropped down through the throat, there is no pleasure while it is all being distributed abroad through the frame." (Lucr. 4.627-9) This means, says Rist following Diano, "that, when we eat, our palate, which is already in a state of katastematic pleasure since it experiences no pain, comes to feel the kinetic pleasure of eating. Later, when the food has passed through the mouth into the body, this kinetic pleasure ceases; then the various parts of the body are restored by the food and katastematic pleasure accompanies the restoration."[253] The part of this interpretation that the palate is in a state of katastematic pleasure because it is experiencing no pain is, of course, not given in Lucretius either directly or indirectly. It is simply the old misunderstanding, to which Rist subscribes and which we have already refuted in the previous chapter, that Epicurean pleasure is the absence of pain, which is slipped in as being so

---

[252]John Rist, Epicurus, Cambridge University Press, 1972, p. 110.

[253]Rist, op. cit., p. 110.

evident that Lucretius need not even mention it. But even if, for the sake of argument, we did not object to this here, it would still not be clear why, if there is no pain in the palate, the pleasure there must be katastematic pleasure rather than kinetic. Perhaps the reasoning was that since there is no pain in the palate there must be pleasure there (since that is what pleasure is). Eating brings kinetic pleasure to the palate, a pleasure which begins with eating and so is new to the palate, at least on the occasion of the present meal. But if the pleasure already in the palate were kinetic pleasure, then the kinetic pleasure of eating could not be new. The pleasure already there before eating begins must therefore not be kinetic but katastematic, since that is the only other kind recognized by Epicurus. This reasoning would present difficulties to understanding the pleasure of the second bite or the pleasure of having a sip of wine with your food. The pleasure of the second bite would show at least that kinetic pleasure need not be new to be pleasure, and the wine would show that kinetic pleasure can be new even if the pleasure already in the organ is kinetic pleasure as long as it is different. I assume there is no difficulty in thinking that the pleasure of the food and the wine are different. A very problematic bit of reasoning seems to underly the Diano/Rist theory at this point, reasoning which remains problematical even if the false assumption about the nature of pleasure is granted.

Rist appeals to further indirect evidence to support his theory. First he appeals to one of Epicurus' principal doctrines and to a passage from Olympidorus.[254] The point of these references is to the effect that pleasure and pain cannot be present in the same organ at the same time. And the second reference to which Rist appeals is a passage in Aetius in which it is claimed that according to

---

[254]K.D.3; Us. 421.

Epicurus feeling and sensations are in the sense organs, but that the mind, the deliberating and decision making part of the soul, is without feeling.[255] It is clear that a great deal needs to be said before these references can be seen to provide even indirect evidence for the theory that all kinetic pleasure supervenes upon and varies prior katastematic pleasure. This theory is not entirely without merit, of course. What is attractive about it is that it makes katastematic pleasure our natural state when nothing is bothering us, much as health is our natural state when we're free of disease and infirmity. But it is based on very flimsy evidence which, to bear any burden at all, relies on an unacceptable assumption. Not only is it ill supported, however, but there are good reasons for rejecting it.

The theory involves the implausible notion of localized katastematic pleasure. Some pleasures are localized and others are not. All localized pleasures, however, seem to be kinetic pleasures. This theory claims that localized kinetic pleasures supervene on katastematic pleasures in that locality and, therefore, this theory is committed to the notion of localized katastematic pleasure. This notion is implausible for at least two reasons. First, none of Epicurus' examples of katastematic pleasures, for example ataraxia and aponia, are plausibly understood this way. And second, this notion commits the theory to the incoherent notion of unfelt pleasures, i.e., unfelt feelings. Suppose we accept the theory that there is katastematic pleasure in my palate to be varied by kinetic pleasure when eating. Is this katastematic pleasure there all the time when there is no specific pain, or is it there only when actually being varied by kinetic pleasure? If the claim is that the pleasure is there all the time, then the obvious problem is that I am not aware of

---

[255] Aetius 4.23.2 (Us. 317): Epikouros kai ta pathe kai tas aistheseis en tois peponthosi topois, to de hegemonikon apathes.

this pleasure all the time, for example when writing philosophy or playing tennis. The claim that the pleasure is there all the time, then, involves the theory in the incoherent notion of unfelt pleasure. But to claim on the other hand that the pleasure is not there all the time, even when there is no pain, would require some serious modification at least of the underlying assumption that pleasure is the absence of pain. But perhaps the theory need only advocate the physical basis of katastematic pleasure, smooth and regular atomic motion, such that katastematic pleasure comes to be felt when I pay attention to this smooth motion, and is not felt when I'm doing something else. If this is what the theory advocates then in sitting down to eat there should be a noticeable progression from neither pleasure nor pain in the palate to katastematic pleasure in the palate and then to the kinetic pleasure of eating. But I cannot find the katastematic pleasure stage in my own experience. I find a pleasurable anticipation of eating, but that is a distinct kinetic pleasure as is the subsequent memory of the pleasant meal, neither of which must be confused with the alleged katastematic pleasure in the palate. If katastematic pleasure begins to be felt on the occasion of being varied by kinetic pleasure, then there ought to be an experience of it distinct from the kinetic variation. But there isn't. So, either way this theory must advocate an unfelt pleasure, which is incoherent.

The Diano/Rist theory takes its rise from Lucretius' example of eating about which it has some initial plausibility because the pleasure of eating and the pangs of hunger do not occur in the same place. But how would this theory handle other pleasures?

Let us first take the example of satisfying a natural and necessary desire. Let's say that I have cold feet, cold enough to be painful, and I know that in a Canadian winter this could become very painful and worse. The rest of me is warm enough because I'm wearing my parka. But I decide to go home to warm my feet and get a proper pair of winter boots. What a pleasure it is to warm my feet! A kinetic pleasure, which according to this theory supervenes on a katastematic pleasure. This example differs from the example of eating in two important respects. Whereas in the example of eating the pleasure is not localized in the same place as the hunger pangs, here the pain and pleasure occur in the same place. As the feet get warm they cease to be cold, and as they feel increasingly pleasant they feel decreasingly painful. And the second respect in which they differ is that in this example it is just plain nonsense to speak of a kinetic pleasure supervening upon an existing katastematic pleasure and merely varying it. Could we say that the katastematic pleasure which is being varied is not in the feet but elsewhere? Surely not, but I could also have left off my parka in addition to my winter boots and so have become cold all over, leaving no place for katastematic pleasure to be varied. And I don't suppose that anyone would want to suggest that, since there is no bodily katastematic pleasure being varied as I warm up, there must have been mental katastematic pleasure upon which the kinetic pleasure of warming up could supervene.

We might also briefly consider the pleasure of satisfying a natural but unnecessary desire:  sex. Here too the pang of desire and the pleasure of satisfaction occur in the same organ, and in that respect it differs from Lucretius' example. But there is a further feature of this example which shows the implausibility of the Diano/Rist theory and which is more obvious here than in Lucretius' example. I take it that when the pangs of the sexual urge have been removed entirely in the complete satisfaction of sexual desire, then the sex organ would in the Diano/Rist theory be in a state of full katastematic pleasure. But it is precisely in this state that the sex organ is least susceptible to the kinetic pleasure of sex. This is a curious circumstance for which I can see no explanation in this theory, and which therefore contributes to its implausibility.

Merlan's challenge that the Diano/Rist theory explain mental pleasure has some of the features of the above two examples, but Rist thought he could evade the difficulty by having part of the mind in a pacified and tranquil state enjoying katastematic pleasure, while another part was distressed by, say, the fear of death. And the pleasure of philosophic instruction which removes the fear of death supervenes upon and varies the katastematic pleasure in the tranquil part of the mind which has the further effect of pacifying the disturbed part. This is, of course, entirely a construction to save a theory for which there is no independent evidence and which involves the implausible view that the part of the mind which has the question is not the part which gets the answer, that the part which is ignorant is not the part which gets the instruction.

Rist argues that if his theory were wrong "Epicurus would have to think that in the case of mental pleasures the same organ (the mind) experiences pleasure and pain at the same time. That would involve him in a contradiction of which he could hardly have been unaware."[256] The obvious question that springs to mind is why Rist thinks that the truth of his theory would save Epicurus from this contradiction, as I suppose he does. Does not Rist portray a mind suffering from fear of the gods as a mind which, besides the pained area afflicted with this suffering, has a tranquil area enjoying katastematic pleasure ready to receive

---

[256]Rist, op. cit., p. 172.

156

instruction? Why is that not the very contradiction Rist alludes to? Nevertheless, it just isn't true that Epicurus would be involved in a contradiction if Rist's theory were wrong, because failure to accept the truth of that theory does not commit one to treating the mind as an organ which cannot experience simultaneous pleasure and pain anymore than it would commit one to treating the body in this way. One could easily admit that one part of the mind was tranquil while another part was distressed by fear of the gods. If one then said that the kinetic pleasure of instruction in Epicurean philosophy is experienced in the distressed part, analogous to the way the kinetic pleasure of warming cold feet is felt in the feet rather than some other warm part of the body, one would not involve Epicurus in a contradiction over K.D. 3 as Rist claims. One would merely be rejecting the Diano/Rist theory that kinetic pleasure always supervenes upon and varies existing katastematic pleasure, which is quite all right.

Philip Merlan's[257] study of the Epicurean concept of pleasure is on the face of it a discussion of how best to translate the word 'hēdonē', but it is also, beyond what is required to settle the translation problem, an interpretation of that concept. On the question of translation he recommends that 'hēdonē' be more often translated 'joy' rather than 'pleasure' and cites the German scholars Schadewaldt and Mewaldt as precedents. But this recommendation has found no favour and 'pleasure' remains the standard translation. The German precedent is rather unfortunate in any case, since German has no adequate single word for pleasure, which becomes obvious the moment you try to translate a few English sentences containing the word into German. You will find yourself fishing among a number

---

[257]Philip Merlan, Studies in Epicurus and Aristotle, Otto Harrassowitz, Wiesbaden, 1960. This is no. 22 of Klassisch - Philologische Studien, edited by Hans Herter and Wolfgang Schmid.

of words (Lust, Vergnügen, Behagen, Genuß, Freude etc.) trying to capture the sense of 'pleasure' in the particular sentence. Also Greek itself seems to have had the very problem that Merlan finds in English. For example, Aristotle comments about 'hēdonē' that "the bodily pleasures have appropriated the name both because we most often steer our course for them and because all men share in them; thus because they alone are familiar, men think there are no others."[258] Also we want to keep the word 'joy' to translate 'chara' and 'gēthos' which are a species of hēdonē, just as joy is a species of pleasure. And lastly, we need to retain the unity of pleasure all the way from the most earthy and physical kind to the most rare and spiritual kind. The common thread is the natural positive evaluation in all cases, which would be clouded if we adopted Merlan's suggestion.

Merlan's discussion of the Epicurean concept is insightful and valuable. The only other study with a similar interpretation which has appeared in English is that of Norman DeWitt.[259] Merlan, however, is more concerned to give his interpretation in direct opposition to that of Diano which we have just discussed.

Merlan understands the basic difference between kinetic and katastematic pleasure to be the source from which they spring. Kinetic pleasure has its source in some external stimulus, while the source of katastematic pleasure is the organism itself. This is a valuable hint, as we shall see, but it can't be maintained without some important modification because as it stands it generates difficulties which Merlan had apparently not anticipated. For example, some pleasures that

---

[258]E.N. 1153b, 33-35.

[259]Norman Wentworth DeWitt, Epicurus and his Philosophy, Minneapolis, University of Minnesota Press, 1954.

are most plausibly understood as of the kinetic sort seem rather to become katastematic on this interpretation. Pleasures such as the pleasure of exercise, dancing, masturbation, philosophical contemplation, memory and the like, which seem clearly to be kinetic pleasures, require special explanations as to why they are not katastematic, if indeed we can avoid having to think of them as katastematic on Merlan's interpretation. Also Merlan's overriding effort to read Epicurus' 'hēdonē' as 'joy' serves to muddy the important difference between the two kinds of Epicurean joy, chara and gēthos. Epicurus is quite clear that chara is a kinetic pleasure[260] and, unless we have excellent reason to think that Epicurus held this to be true only sometimes but not always, we are bound to maintain the kinetic nature of this kind of joy in our interpretation. Merlan points to a passage in Plutarch as evidence that 'chara' should not always designate kinetic joy. Plutarch writes that according to the Epicureans "the comfortable state (katastēma) of the flesh, and the confident expectation of this, contain the highest and most secure joy (chara) for those who are capable of reasoning."[261] Merlan thinks that the occurrence of the noun 'katastēma' (= state, condition) in this passage somehow helps to think of chara as katastematic. "The words 'katastēma' and 'chara' are so clearly linked", writes Merlan, "that it is very difficult to imagine that the same Epicurus should elsewhere have said of chara that it is limited to kinetic hēdonai."[262] Several things need to be noticed here. The passage speaks of two distinct kinds of pleasure either separately or in combination, namely the comfortable state of the flesh and the anticipation of this

---

[260]D.L. 10.136.

[261]Plutarch, non posse 1089d = Us. 68.

[262]Merlan, op. cit., p. 14 n. 16.

condition in the future. The comfortable condition might well be a katastematic pleasure, but the pleasures of anticipation, like those of memory, are kinetic. Also Plutarch is not quoting Epicurus but reporting the doctrine of the Epicureans, and the choice of the word 'chara' in this place is Plutarch's. Merlan's speaking of "the same Epicurus" is therefore not warranted. Even if there were a conflict between this Plutarch passage and Diogenes Laertius' quotation, we would have to give greater weight to the quotation. But there is no conflict and thus no reason to think that chara is ever anything other than kinetic joy. This conclusion is even strengthened by the Plutarch passage since this passage is produced as the best evidence against the conclusion by someone as well read in Epicurean literature as Merlan. Its feebleness makes it evidence to the contrary.

Merlan sees Epicureanism as a fundamentally optimistic philosophy, and he is surely quite right about that. In order to bring out the special character of Epicurean optimism he presents it against the background of a pessimism of similar character found in Aristotle who appeals to the authority of natural philosophers for the crucial proposition. Thus, even if Epicurus had not read Book 7 of Nicomachean Ethics, as is improbable, it is still plausible that he would have been aware of this brand of pessimism from general reading and that it might therefore have influenced him in shaping his own doctrines. A question to which Aristotle addresses himself in his discussion of pleasure is why some people prefer bodily pleasure to other kinds, and one answer is that, because of the violent nature of bodily pleasure, it is the only kind that can be enjoyed by people incapable of enjoying the gentler kinds. Such people pursue bodily pleasure even when not feeling any particular bodily pains because in the neutral state in which there is no particular pleasure or pain they find that the very act of being alive is

160

painful and they pursue bodily pleasures to mask or bring relief from the constant background pain of simply being alive. This pain is the lot of human beings by their very nature as living animals, "for the animal is always in travail."[263] Not all of us, to be sure, suffer from this pain. The young usually don't because the natural growing processes of the organism have an effect similar to intoxication which masks the burden of being alive as well as alcohol. And some of us have become so used to this pain that we become as insensitive to it as to a constant monotonous noise in our environment. But certain people with irritable temperaments, melancholics (hoi melagcholikoi), are always subject to it, even their bodies are in constant torment because of this temperament and they are given to violent desires. Such people are in constant need of relief and pursue pleasure to the point of self-indulgence and moral wrong. Note that the pessimism which finds expression here is not one of bad fortune or a world which inevitably frustrates our ambitions, rather it is a pessimism which has its source in our very natures as living beings, a pessimism which finds life itself a painful burden quite apart from particular pleasures and pains we might experience in the course of life.

Epicurus' optimism is presented by Merlan as the mirror image of this pessimism. The source of this optimism, too, is not in having found a way of satisfying all our desires and realizing our ambitions, but rather in the basic act of

---

[263]E.N. 1154b6. Aei gar ponei to zōon. Aristotle simply refers to natural scientists in general as his authority for that statement without citing anyone in particular, but one could refer to Anaxagoras as an example. Anaxagoras is reported by Theophrastus as having thought that our natural operations are painful such that even "every perception is accompanied by pain". cf. Kirk, Raven and Schofield, The Presocratic Philosophers, Cambridge University Press, 1983, #511, p. 383. Note that the word used by Aristotle for this katastematic pain is 'ponos', the negation of which, 'aponia', will become an important example of Epicurean katastematic pleasure. It should go without saying, incidentally, that whether Aristotle shared this pessimism when writing Book 7 of E.N. does not here concern us.

human existence itself. Epicurus would deny that the judgment that life is trouble is a philosophical insight, rather he would say that the opinion is a symptom of a vital distortion which needs to be fixed. Life, thought Epicurus, when untrammelled and natural is a pleasure of the highest sort.

A difficulty with Merlan's presentation of the opposition between this optimism and pessimism is that the choice between them is not a matter of philosophical truth and argument, but "the choice between them will always be rooted in some personal factor."[264] In the case of Epicurus, he speculates, this personal factor may have been his illness which produced his optimism as a "reaction and overcompensation."[265] There is no evidence, however, that the painful illness from which Epicurus suffered at the end of his life (and what other illness might Merlan have had in mind?) was with him when some forty years earlier he opened a school to teach his optimistic philosophy. Also, seeing the foundation of philosophy in some such freak of fortune runs counter to the whole tenor of Epicurean philosophy. He really thought that his philosophy rested on truth and argument, and only if we find it philosophically weak or arbitrary should we resort to psychological diagnosis. Even if the diagnosis is correct, and something other than the normally motivated search for truth motivated Epicurus, this can never count for more than a bit of gossip next to the critical philosophical evaluation of what he was motivated to produce.

Nevertheless Merlan's account of the general character of Epicurean philosophy and of the key concepts of kinetic and katastematic pleasure is valuable.

---

[264]Merlan, op. cit., p. 10.

[265]Ibid.

Katastematic pleasure in Epicurus surely is something like the pleasure of just being alive, and kinetic pleasure something like the various particular pleasures we experience in the process of living. We shall have to see now whether we can develop these concepts in a philosophically critical way from evidence in the Epicurean literature.

## Kinetic and Katastematic Pleasure

A philosopher who writes about pleasure is writing about something very familiar. The most familiar kind of pleasure is probably that of satisfying desires like hunger and thirst, a kind of pleasure that has some very familiar characteristics. It comes and goes, for example. We enjoy it when eating and drinking, it lasts for a little while and then we must wait for the return of desire before we can enjoy it again. Continued eating and drinking will cease to be pleasurable beyond a certain point. The pleasures of eating and drinking are by nature intermittent pleasures. Another familiar characteristic of this kind of pleasure is that it has an object, it is pleasure taken in eating porridge and drinking tea, for example. Eating and drinking are typical of many of our pleasures in this respect. Any pleasure got in the satisfaction of recurring desires will have the two characteristics of being intermittent and having an object. In fact it seems that all sensuous pleasures have these characteristics whether or not they are associated with a desire. If you chance upon a pleasant fragrance while passing a flowershop, for example, this pleasure is quite independent of any antecedent desire, yet it will have an object and will not normally be sustainable beyond a certain time, after which it will fade and you will have to turn your nose to another flower or let it rest for a while to renew this pleasure. These are the kinds of pleasures to which Epicurus refers when speaking about the most basic conception of the good, as we have seen already, and he calls them kinetic pleasures.[266] These are the kinds of pleasures the Cyrenaics recognized and they only recognized kinetic pleasures.[267]

Though Epicurus agreed with the Cyrenaics that pleasure was the good, there was in his mind a strong reluctance to understand the good as kinetic pleasure. To begin with there may have been no more than the provincial's disapproval of the wicked city life style. This disapproval is evident enough in the letter to Menoeceus, for example. But we would be doing Epicurus a disservice if we only saw the prudish provincial and failed to see the philosopher. Although we learn the concept of goodness in our experience of kinetic pleasure, and qua pleasure it is and always will be good, there is something intrinsically unsatisfactory in its kinetic nature. It is essentially discontinuous, for it comes and goes because of the kind of thing it is and, because it has an object, it is dependent upon its object. The availability of the object of kinetic pleasure, however, depends upon something other than ourselves. It is a matter of chance whether or not we will be able to continue a life of kinetic pleasure and, even if fortune continues to smile, that kind of life is lived at the cost of self-sufficiency and freedom, which Epicurus considered a loss of the highest order.[268] One might think that wealth can make us immune to the vagaries of fortune, but this isn't so, not only because fortune can make the rich poor again, and because it is very difficult to acquire wealth without servility to the mob and the powerful while living a life of hard

---

[266]Athenaeus 12.546e = US. 67. Actually the only one of the list of sensuous pleasures given here which is specifically called a kinetic pleasure is the pleasure of seeing a beautiful form, but it is clear enough that this one is not meant to be singled out.

[267]D.L. 2.87, 89; 10.136.

[268]We cannot discuss the virtues yet, but for the importance of self-sufficiency (autarkeia) see Ep. Men. 134-5; and for its relation to freedom see S.V. 77.

work fit only for a beast of burden,[269] but also because you may find that wealth enables you to escape the ills of the poor only to land you with the ills of the rich.[270] These ills are not confined to the work and worry of keeping your wealth but, unless you can keep busy, you may find yourself the prey of a new kind of pain: boredom.[271]

Boredom is one of the family of existential pains which it might seem anachronistic to think had figured prominently in Epicurean philosophy. But it is entirely plausible to think that he was aware of them and that his therapeutic program was directed not only at everyday kinetic pains like hunger and thirst and fear of the authorities, human and divine, but also at pains of a different kind like boredom and the fear of death. Indeed, it would not be unreasonable to think that these latter presented the greater philosophical problem.[272] What distinguishes pains like boredom, the fear of death and existential despair from kinetic pains is that with them there is not a proper object of pain or fear, as there is with hunger or toothache or the fear of dogs and the like. We have already seen in our third chapter how Epicurus exploits this objectlessness for therapeutic purposes in the case of the fear of death. In the case of boredom Lucretius points out that each person is to himself the quasi-object of his pain and so, in boredom, "each man tries to flee from himself",[273] and the cure he recommends is philosophy, not the

---

[269]cf. S.V. 57; Porphyry to Marcella 28 = Us. 480.

[270]Porphyry to Marcella 28 = Us. 479.

[271]Lucr. 3. 1053-75.

[272]cf. Wolfgang Schmid, a review of six books on Epicurus in Gnomon, Vol. 27, 1955, pp. 405-431. "Indeed, Epicureanism may be understood as an ancient philosophical attempt to overcome existential dread." (In der Tat läßt sich der Epikureismus als antiker philosophischer Versuch der Überwindung der Existenzialangst fassen), p. 417.

[273]Lucr. 3.1068.

further frenzy of distraction in excitement and the pursuit of kinetic pleasure "as if he were bringing urgent help to a house on fire."[274]

Philosophy holds the promise of understanding the nature of reality, the gods, death, and pleasure as the good. Pleasure, however, is distinguished into kinetic and katastematic, a distinction similar to the distinction found in pain. Kinetic pleasures and pains, and their objects, provide the content for the popular pre-philosophical understanding of good and evil. But a philosopher cannot remain with this understanding "for everything that the many regard as good and evil is transitory (ephēmeron)",[275] it is short-lived, ephemeral, non-continuous. Kinetic pleasure and pain can only achieve the quasi-stability of repetition, with the attendant disadvantages of giving yourself in pawn to fortune or finally falling prey to boredom like Lucretius' "man who has been bored to death at home [and] often goes forth from his great mansion" only to find more of the same.[276] Some philosophers, having seen the inadequacy of pursuing kinetic pleasure as the good, abandoned pleasure altogether and recommended something else instead, virtue for example. But Epicurus rather makes katastematic pleasure the good of his ethics because it is continuous in its nature. In the context, apparently, of distinguishing his ethics from that of philosophers who make virtue the central concept of their ethics he writes to Anaxarchus: "But I summon you to continuous pleasures (hēdonas sunecheis) and not to vain and empty virtues which have but disturbing hopes of results."[277] 'Continuous pleasures' does not

---

[274]Lucr. 3.1064.

[275]Porphyry to Marcella, 30 = Us. 489.

[276]Lucr. 3.1060-61.

[277]Plutarch, Col. 1117a = Us. 116.

mean constantly repeated pleasures, but pleasures continuous in their nature, continuous without intermission or repetition. Continuous pleasures are not kinetic, which are intermittent in their nature, but katastematic. Katastematic pleasure differs from kinetic pleasure in being continuous rather than intermittent.

Katastematic pleasure also differs from kinetic pleasure in not having an object. A prominent Epicurean example of a katastematic pleasure is ataraxia, unperturbedness or tranquility, which is a pleasure without an object. It results in the removal of an object of fear or disturbance such as the superstitious understanding of the gods or celestial phenomena or whatever else one may find deeply troubling. The removal of these objects of disturbance (tarachē) results in ataraxia, and the negative form of the word expresses the objectlessness of the state (katastēma) rather than some sort of psychological vacuum, some absence of feeling. We must be clear that ataraxia is not apatheia but a pathos of pleasure, which is a positive state despite the absence of an object, much as boredom or dread are not states of apatheia, but the negative pathos of pain without an object. But in order that it result in ataraxia, the removal of the objects of fear must have the permanence of secure knowledge to make the pleasure fully continuous. In the letter to Herodotus, after having given a list of troubling fears that are removed by the true understanding of philosophy, Epicurus writes that "ataraxia is a release from all this and involves a continuous recollection (sunechē mnēmen) of the general and most important principles."[278] Making progress in philosophy is pleasant,[279] but it eventually sets up a steady state of knowledge, a memory

---

[278]Ep. Hdt. 82.

[279]S.V. 27.

which is not an intermittent forgetting and remembering again, but a secure knowledge which is continuous (sunēches) in the same way that katastematic pleasure is continuous. The continuity of this knowledge provides, at least in part, for the continuity of ataraxia.

Another prominent example of a katastematic pleasure in Epicurean literature is aponia, literally the absence of toil and hardship (ponos). The pleasure which is the end according to Epicurus in the letter to Menoeceus is not to be described in terms of the sensuous pleasures of Athenian fun seekers, that is in terms of kinetic pleasures, but rather in terms of the absence of pain in the body and trouble in the mind (to mēte algein kata sōma mēte tarattesthai kata psuchēn).[280] This passage is reminiscent of the beginning of the passage quoted by Diogenes Laertius from the Peri Telous in which aponia and ataraxia are given as examples of katastematic pleasure.[281] In the passage from the letter to Menoeceus Epicurus' point is not so much to give an account of his doctrine as to distinguish Epicureans from another set of people who pursue pleasure and with whom they have been confused. This may account for the purely negative formulation. But in the Peri Telous he seems rather concerned to expound his own doctrine. We have already discussed ataraxia, but aponia needs discussion as well and is perhaps a little more difficult. The word used to be translated as the absence of bodily pain, but it surely means more than the negative formulation in the letter to Menoeceus passage, as most contemporary translators recognize. The group from which Epicurus means to distinguish himself in the passage from the letter to Menoeceus may well have been the Cyrenaics who recognized only kinetic pleasure and

[280]Ep. Men. 131.

[281]D.L. 10.136.

developed a kind of sybaritic technology for getting it. Diogenes Laertius gives a rather interesting account of their basic principles. He says[282] that they recognize two feelings (pathē), pain and pleasure (<u>ponon kai hēdonē</u>), both of which are kinetic, the former being a rough motion, the latter a smooth motion. It is interesting that the contrast with pleasure is <u>ponos</u> rather than the more obvious <u>algos</u> or <u>lupē</u>. Both <u>algos</u> and <u>lupē</u> are readily translatable into Latin as <u>dolor</u> or into English as pain. But <u>ponos</u> is more happily the Latin <u>labor</u> or the English toil or hardship. One suspects that Diogenes Laertius, writing long after Epicurus and Aristippus (both the elder and the younger) is giving an account of contemporary Cyrenaicism which is now being formulated in opposition to Epicurus. Choosing <u>ponos</u> as the opposite of <u>hēdonē</u> allows them to put <u>aponia</u> into the neutral state between pleasure and pain,[283] and claim that <u>aponia</u>, since it is not kinetic, is the condition of someone who is, as it were, asleep,[284] rather than the great pleasure prized so highly by the Epicureans. The Cyrenaics, I suppose, found the Epicureans boring. We must not allow their inability to appreciate Epicureanism have the last word in our understanding of Epicurean <u>aponia</u>, however. A much more valuable clue comes from another source which, to be sure, is also marked by an inability to appreciate Epicureanism. In <u>De Natura Deorum</u> Cicero has his Epicurean claim that "we for our part deem the good life to consist in tranquility of mind and entire exemption from all duties (<u>animi securitate et in omnium vacatione munerum</u>)".[285] The parallel with <u>ataraxia</u> and <u>aponia</u> is unmistakable.

---

[282]D.L. 2.87.

[283]D.L. 22.90.

[284]D.L. 2.89.

[285]<u>N.D.</u> 1.53.

The Cicero passage is part of an argument that there is no god running the world because that would be "a bondage of irksome and laborious business",[286] and no god could be conceived as subject to such labour because we must conceive the gods to be happy and part of happiness is freedom from onerous toil. Aponia, then, would be not having to do any onerous work, to be able to do what we do freely and without duress or compulsion. In fact, aponia in Epicurus means something like idleness in the best sense of the word.

For this reading we can look to a passage in Aristotle's Rhetoric.[287] Aristotle is pointing our here that to be compelled to do anything is unpleasant "for compulsion is contrary to nature." The various forms of idleness (aponia) are pleasant, he writes, owing to idleness not being "in any way compulsory." To understand what Epicurus meant by aponia, we might try to imagine the state of the gods, a state of utter physical ease, totally alive idleness, stressless health and well being. The best single word is probably 'idleness' if we understand it well. At the risk of being anachronistic let me quote something from Kierkegaard that could be a lost fragment of Epicurus (though it isn't). "Idleness as such is not the root of all evil, on the contrary, it is a truly divine life when one is not bored ... it is rather the true good."[288] Ataraxia means something very similar with a mental

---

[286]Ibid 1.52.

[287]Rhetoric, 1.11.4, 137 a; see also Aristotle's discussion of leisure (scholazein) in the Politics (1334a ff, 1337 b 30 - 1338 a7) where he argues that the end of work or business (literally the absence of leisure, ascholia) is leisure (1334a 16), that philosophy is required for leisure (1334a 24), that leisure contains pleasure and happiness and the blessed life (1338a 2-3), while business or the absence of leisure is accompanied by toil (ponou, 1337b 40). If the absence of leisure involves ponos then leisure would be a species of the absence of ponos, that is a species of aponia. The understanding of Epicurean aponia as the positive and desirable state of idleness or leisure, rather than simply the absence of bodily pain, is supported by this discussion, even if there is no evidence that Epicurus drew on it in the formulation of his concept.

[288]Soren Kierkegaard, Either/Or, (The Rotation Method), Garden City, New York, 1955, Vol. 1, p. 285.

emphasis. It is untroubledness, tranquility, life at your lucid best. So, what Epicurus means by ataraxia and aponia in the fragment from the Peri Telous quoted by Diogenes Laertius is a lucid tranquil state of pleasant idleness which, if it continues to be sustained without boredom and other species of katastematic pain[289], is the good, katastematic pleasure. This state may of course be difficult to attain for the uninitiated who when they take a break from business find that their "rest is stagnation."[290] Nor is this state incompatible with activity, for it is not the same as indolence or laziness. Epicurus himself was a very prolific writer, but he worked without duress and with pleasure.[291]

We have emphasized the elements of continuity and objectlessness suggested by the negative form of ataraxia and aponia in our interpretation of katastematic pleasure, but the notion of objectlessness needs some qualification. Katastematic pleasure cannot have an intermittently available (or unavailable) object as does kinetic pleasure. But it cannot be absolutely objectless either. It is time to remind ourselves that we had interpreted pleasure as an evaluation and that every evaluation must in some way be an evaluation of something. If katastematic pleasure, then, is truly to be a pleasure it cannot be absolutely without an object. It will be remembered that boredom had a quasi-object in Lucretius' account of it, namely the self, that is me, my existence, my life. This quasi-object is not one object among others which might come and go as the object of some kinetic

---

[289]The terminological distinction between kinetic and katastematic pain cannot be attested in the remaining Epicurean text. We simply find reference made to pain without its ever being qualified as either kinetic or katastematic. But there is no reason to think that the distinction made in pleasure does not find a parallel in pain, not only because there is no denial of the distinction in the text, but also because examples of both kinds come readily to mind.

[290]S.V. 11.

[291]Ep. Hdt. 37.

pleasure or pain, but the continuous object, the condition for the possibility of there being any other objects at all. This continuous object is also the object of katastematic pleasure, which therefore is, in its nature, the stable positive evaluation of my existence, my life. But if, as Epicurus believed, I exist as fundamentally a physical and a mental being, then my existence can be thought of as having a basic mental-physical structure, and katastematic pleasure would show such a structure as well. This structure accounts for the distinction between ataraxia and aponia which are probably best thought of as two basic elements in a single complex pleasure rather than as separate pleasures.

Note that our interpretation of katastematic pleasure makes it incompatible with katastematic pain, though not with kinetic pain. It is part of becoming an Epicurean sage to learn to develop katastematic pleasure when there is no kinetic pain, rather than the boredom and stagnation which Epicurus says befalls most people when they take a break from work or entertaining distractions. This, however, is for relative novices. The more accomplished Epicurean has also learned to sustain katastematic pleasure during bouts of kinetic pain. This would be an important accomplishment, for all of us must face and learn to cope with the slings and arrows of everyday life. Pain is an inevitable part of everyone's life, no matter how well protected or how prudently conducted, and the Epicurean sage has learned not only to endure it like a Stoic, but to experience genuine katastematic pleasure during it. Just how much kinetic pain a person could handle without clouding katastematic pleasure apparently depended on the degree of accomplishment in practical Epicureanism. Epicurus himself claimed to be happy during the last days of his life[292] which contained a lot of kinetic pain. One

[292]D.L. 10.22.

technique for coping with such pain was to generate mental kinetic pleasure with pleasant thoughts and memories,[293] but we mustn't think of this as some kind of hedonic arithmetic in which the state of a person equals the remainder after kinetic pain has been subtracted from kinetic pleasure. Such arithmetic might describe the practical philosophy of the Cyrenaics, which is why Hegesias, who thought that people were on the whole the losers in this kinetic balancing act and who also believed that there was no more to life than that, recommended suicide as the philosophically enlightened act.[294] But the Epicurean used such techniques to achieve something else. For him this was part of the technique of sustaining katastematic pleasure which he could sustain even if the kinetic balance tipped strongly in favour of kinetic pain, under torture, for example.

The question whether the philosophical sage could be happy while suffering great pain, of which situation torture was the limiting case, was not invented by Epicurus. The question was already around when Aristotle was writing the Nicomachean Ethics[295] and it was probably put to Epicurus at some point. And he answered it in the affirmative.[296] It is not that the sage won't feel pain, he'll howl with pain like the rest of us. He'll just not let this pain distract him from the katastematic pleasure he has learned to attain and, so, he'll sustain his happiness throughout the ordeal. But this kind of perfection is for sages only, I think. Cicero was appalled by this and made fun of the Epicurean on the rack,[297] but

---

[293]Ibid.

[294]D.L. 2.94-6.

[295]E.N. 1153b19; cf. Plato, Republic. II 361e.

[296]D.L. 10.118.

[297]Tusc. 5.72-82.

what else can one expect from a commentator who neither has nor pretends to have understood katastematic pleasure?  Plutarch[298] also had trouble with this situation because he could not understand how the memory of conversation with friends could be pleasant enough to outweigh the pain of torture. But, of course, it can't. Plutarch, too, was asking the wrong question. But even if we ask the right question, it still seems rather extravagant and smacks of something like philosophical one-upmanship. St. Thomas thought that Jesus had managed it on the cross, as we pointed out in our second chapter, but he also thought that Jesus was more than a human sage. In a world such as the Epicureans take this one to be, a natural accident rather than a detailed divine plan, there is of course no requirement that a philosophy be able to make everyone happy under any conceivable circumstances. So it would probably not be a serious criticism of Epicureanism if we found the torture case implausible, even if not for the wrong reasons like Cicero and Plutarch.

Not only can kinetic pain distract the novice Epicurean from katastematic pleasure, there is also the subtler challenge of kinetic pleasure. The Epicurean sage must, therefore, also learn to develop an appropriate attitude to kinetic pleasure, an attitude that is essentially a matter of learning to enjoy it without needing it. To this end Epicureans cultivated the virtue of self-sufficiency (autarkeia) and a simple life style. The reason for this was not so much that simplicity of life was intrinsically desirable, but that it was important to learn to live on little so that one could be content if ever that was all there was.[299] An expensive life style will usually require lots of work and worry to sustain, which

---

[298]Non posse 1088b.

[299]For this and the following points see Ep. Men. 130-1.

is a decided disadvantage. And there are also decided advantages to a simple and inexpensive life style, even if there are no financial difficulties to prevent a more luxurious one. For one thing, the person who is used to luxurious food regularly and in plenty will hardly ever sit down to a meal really hungry. To get any pleasure out of his meal, therefore, it will have to be rather special fare, and it is quite appropriate to say that he has come to need luxury rather than food. On the other hand the person of simple life style who eats plain fare when hungry discovers that hunger is the best cook, as the saying goes. And if he from time to time has a gourmet meal as a special treat he will enjoy it more than the person who gets such fare regularly. To put it in the words of Epicurus: "they derive the greatest pleasure from luxury who need it least ... and bread and water generate the highest pleasure whenever they are taken by someone who needs them." A simple life style thus maximizes kinetic pleasure. Further, Epicurus was aware that simple fare was better for people's health and gives more energy with which to face the necessary business of daily life, and keeping to a simple life style even if you could afford better was the sort of exercise in prudent self-control which strengthens the character so that we really cease to need luxuries and are better able to cope with the ups and downs of life. All this is good advice, aimed essentially at undermining our need for the objects of kinetic pleasure, at least for all but the simplest objects of the necessary desires for food, air, warmth and the like. The main reason for getting rid of this need is that kinetic pleasure can distract us from katastematic pleasure as much as kinetic pain, and the Epicurean sage must be able to sustain katastematic pleasure continuously. The need for the objects of kinetic pleasure is like an addiction in this, that when they are not available or when they cease to give pleasure because we have had too much of them like the wealthy man in the example from Lucretius, then something like withdrawal symptoms set in. Katastematic pains like boredom and a sense of stagnation are symptoms of something like an addiction, which is a loss of self every bit as much as the ponos of servitude. The prudent self-control of a simple life style, then, not only has advantages in terms of improving the quality of kinetic pleasure, it also has the great advantage of promoting our ability to sustain katastematic pleasure, the true Epicurean good.

That katastematic pleasure is the good, Epicurus states in a fragment preserved for us by Plutarch:

> Unsurpassable joy (anuperbleton gethos) is produced by comparison with a great evil which one has escaped; and this is the nature of the good if one applies [one's intellect] properly and takes a firm stand, but does not stroll around babbling emptily about the good.[300]

We are not interested now in the impatient gesture in this fragment. We have already discussed that in our second chapter. What interests us here is the joy of escaping a great evil. Shortly before giving us this fragment Plutarch lists examples of the sort of evil Epicurus might have had in mind from his own experience, examples such as the fury of mobs and the savagery of bandits. To have escaped an evil of that magnitude leaves one unscathed and it is difficult not to become aware of one's unscathed existence as such. This awareness is, according to Epicurus, a pleasure of the highest order if one is capable of apprehending it, a pleasure of such a high order that it deserves to be called the good. It is katastematic pleasure, the quasi-object of which is what has been there continuously the whole time, but is rarely apprehended as clearly as at such time of avoided catastrophe. We note here that katastematic pleasure too has degrees of intensity and anuperbleton gethos is Epicurus' expression for what appears to be

---

[300]Non posse 1091b = US. 423.

its highest degree of intensity.

Two things need to be remarked upon here. The first is that gēthos is not a negative expression, but a positive word meaning 'joy', a word which emphasizes the pleasurableness of katastematic pleasure rather than its objectless continuity, as do ataraxia and aponia. The other thing is that Epicurus evidently distinguishes between katastematic joy (gēthos) and kinetic joy (chara).

Both gēthos and chara are given the meaning of joy or delight by Liddell and Scott. Gēthos seems to be a fairly rare word. Liddell and Scott give only three references for it and ours is one of them. Chara, on the other hand, gets many references, and the tendency is for it to signify joy or delight in or at something, that is, chara normally takes an object. In the fragment quoted by Diogenes Laertius, Epicurus says that "joy (chara) and delight (euphrosunē) are regarded as kinetic and active."[301]Euphrosunē, which is the mate to chara here as though it were similar, means delight or cheerfulness or merriment at, for example, a banquet or a party in full swing. Chara and euphrosunē are rather puzzling examples of kinetic pleasure. Ataraxia and aponia seem to be paradigm examples of katastematic pleasures, but chara and euphrosunē seem not to be paradigmatic examples of kinetic pleasures. Had Epicurus' intention been to give such examples we would expect him to have given examples of standard sensuous pleasures. The context of the fragment is lost, however, and the best clue we have is that Diogenes Laertius quotes it in the context of distinguishing between katastematic and kinetic pleasure. It would not be unreasonable, therefore, to

[301]D.L. 1O.136

assume a similar context in Epicurus. But it does not seem likely that Epicurus is here distinguishing katastematic from kinetic pleasure by giving paradigm examples of each. Rather, he seems to be trying to prevent a misunderstanding about certain kinetic pleasures which might be mistaken for katastematic pleasures, because they are not straightforwardly sensuous pleasures. The general joy and delight one might experience at having one's way with the board of governors, or at winning a big prize, or seeing one's children do well, or having fun at the local pub and so forth, are still intermittent and objective in the way that sensuous pleasures are, and in that respect fundamentally different from katastematic pleasure. That is, Epicurus' point is probably a more subtle one than the point Diogenes Laertius is making with the quotation.

The Epicurean individual who seeks pleasure, katastematic as well as kinetic, is never fully alone, however, but conducts his life in a social setting. Before we can give a full account of the Epicurean good life, we must therefore first consider the social philosophy of Epicurus.

# Chapter Seven

# Social Philosophy: Justice and Friendship

Epicurean social philosophy is no more scientific, in the sense of aiming at knowledge for its own sake, than is Epicurean physics, astronomy or meteorology but, like them, it is thoroughly practical, seeking understanding for the sake of living well.[302] It is, however, neither utopian nor revolutionary. Although there is an element of millennialism in later Epicureanism, there is, with Epicurus and the early Epicureans, no attempt here to design an ideal society in which human beings can finally be happy, nor to discover in the workings of society the means for radical change. Rather, it is an attempt to understand the society in which the Epicurean happens to live with a view to understanding whether and how the good life is possible within it.

Epicurus tries to understand the complex set of relations and interrelations which obtain in a society in terms of relations between individuals, justice and friendship, for it is in terms of these that each individual realizes his social existence in the society of which he happens to be a member. The society itself, however, is a given for each individual, much as is the language he finds himself speaking once he is old enough to reflect on the matter. Epicurus attempts to understand this society as a human product, a historical artifact of human art, rather than as a natural formation such as the organization of social insects or as the providential design of a higher power. To understand something as a historical

---

[302]cf. Ep. Pyth. 86.

artifact, however, is to understand how and why it was made.

The most detailed account of the Epicurean explanation of the origin and development of society is found in Lucretius (5.925 ff.). It is not clear from this account whether Lucretius, or his source, thought that he was telling the true history of the development of society, that is, the account which uniquely explains the social phenomena available to present observation. Lucretius makes no attempt to produce any evidence he may have had for any of the crucial events in his story. It may well be, therefore, that he thought of it as similar to the case of celestial phenomena "which have a multiplicity of explanations consistent with things evident,"[303] so that what is required here is to give a plausible account consistent with the phenomena and with what is already known of the world through the study of natural philosophy and ethics, where it is possible to discover explanations uniquely consistent with the phenomena.[304]

Lucretius' story begins with solitary hunter gatherers who "spent their roving lives in the manner of wild beasts."[305] They had no agriculture, no fire and no clothes. Even if, as seems unlikely from Lucretius' tale, they congregated in groups, as do wolves and apes, motivated perhaps by the "natural affinity" of which Porphyry speaks,[306] each maintained his or her life in solitary fashion, hunting and gathering and mating without customs or laws or any conception of the common good.[307]

---

[303]Ep. Pyth. 87.

[304]Ep. Pyth. 86.

[305]Lucr. 5.932.

[306]De abst. 1.7.1 (Long and Sedley 22M1.)

[307]Lucr. 5.958-9.

The next stage[308] in the development of human society seems to be due to a lasting bond between some males and some females who stayed together to raise their children in a favourable location where they built a hut. By this time they had already discovered the use of fire and had learned to make clothes of animal skins. Something like the rules of family life and single marriage developed at this time, and the existence of several such units in favourable locations set the stage for further social development by giving each family neighbours. It is at this stage that a crucial point is reached in Lucretius' story. He writes:

> "Then too neighbours began to form friendships, eager not to harm one another and not to be harmed; and they gained protection for children and for the female sex, when with babyish noises and gestures they indicated that it is right for everyone to pity the weak. Yet harmony could not entirely be created; but a good and substantial number preserved their contracts honorably."[309]

This seems to be a description of the event of the social contract which in Epicurean social theory is thought to be the foundation of society. But as described here it is much richer than the bare agreement by the participating parties not to harm each other.

The contract itself has something rudimentary and tacit about it. It is made, of course, in the absence of any body of positive law, of any contractual conventions or customs, and of any language in which the terms of the agreement may be articulated and defined. Such a definite contract comes later, as we shall see. But at this point we must imagine parties to an agreement who only recently have lived the solitary life of animals and have neither the language in which to articulate nor the concepts with which to conceive a proper contract and its terms. They communicate with "babyish noises and gestures" and are, if only for that

---

[308]Lucr. 5.1011 ff.

[309]Lucr. 5. 1019-25.

reason, capable of contracts in a most attenuated sense only. Epicurus confirms this by referring to this contract as "a kind of contract (suntheke tis)".[310]

The basis of this contract, the motivation for entering into it, surprisingly is not fear or the pursuit of security so much as friendship and an eagerness not to harm or be harmed. There is no sense of disaster or impending disaster against which these people are taking precautionary measures in Lucretius' story. Rather, there is a new sense of the easing of an earlier harshness of life, a new softening of body and spirit, and a spontaneous feeling of friendliness towards neighbours, growing perhaps out of the natural affinity of which we spoke above and which is being nurtured by the new ease of settled life.

One might argue that this passage has nothing to do with friendship but that "Lucretius is describing only the foundation of justice, the basis of which is a contract for avoiding mutual harm."[311] But, of course, we cannot just ignore that Lucretius speaks of the formation of friendship between neighbours. Nor is there good reason for claiming that amicitia[312] cannot mean friendship here. Even if the word amicitia, or the rare form amicities, can be found in the literature of the Republic to refer to political alliances, it still refers there to a friendship between states beyond mere mutual non-aggression but indicates further friendly relations

---

[310]K.D. 33; Reimar Müller, Die Epikureische Gesellschaftslehre, Berlin 1972, p. 43, argues that Epicurus should not be read as intending an attenuation of the contract in K.D. 33, and his reason is that Lucretius, in the place we are at present considering, writes that many kept the contract, without any word or phrase of attenuation in the sentence. But it is clear that Lucretius, rather than inserting a single word of attenuation, as does Epicurus, gives us instead a fuller description of the sense in which this is an attenuated contract.

[311]Phillip Mitsis, Epicurus' Ethical Theory, Cornell University Press, 1988, p. 106; see also his discussion in notes 14 and 15 on that page.

[312]This holds true as well for the rare form amicities used by Lucretius here. The Oxford Latin Dictionary gives Lucr. 5.18189, our passage, as the only reference for this rare form.

such as open borders, a readiness to give aid when needed, sheltering each other's citizens and so forth. The motivation to form friendships is described by Lucretius in terms of the standard Epicurean formula for justice.[313] This is no more reason for insisting that '<u>amicitia</u>' should be understood to mean 'justice' rather than 'friendship', however, than it is to insist that the formula 'not to harm or be harmed' describes friendship rather than justice. We might rather allow that Lucretius knew perfectly well what he was doing, and that he is describing the common origin of the two basic social relations, justice and friendship, neither of which existed prior to this, and both of which came to be, unclearly distinguished, in the original agreement he is describing.

This contract is not just a matter of avoiding harm, but clearly part of the motivation for entering into it is an eagerness not to cause harm to others. This is not a concession one party makes to another in return for safety, but there is here the inception of the kind of benevolence much more characteristic of friendship than of justice. And a kind of fairness is seen to be part of justice at this stage, a fairness alien to justice conceived as mere mutual non-aggression, for it is seen to be right not to harm the weak even though they pose no threat. Appropriate behaviour toward others includes a kind of chivalry at this stage as well as a proto-benevolence which are a consequence of the kinship of justice and friendship, siblings born together in a single human act.[314]

But the social structure produced by the original contract did not last. At first,

---

[313]<u>nec laedere nec violari</u> seems to be a straightforward Latin rendering of <u>tou mē blaptein ē blaptesthai</u> (K.D. 33).

[314]The thesis of the kinship of justice and friendship is not new with Epicurus. Aristotle already noted it at E.N. 1159 b 25, though I am not claiming that Epicurus lifted the thought from there.

though the concord was never perfect, most kept the compact with a kind of purity of heart that as yet had nothing to do with fear of the consequences of breaking it.[315] In this mostly peaceful village-like setting language developed as people tried to communicate within a stable family and with constant neighbours. Among those who achieved prominence of mind and influence in this setting, making social changes and technological innovations, there were some who were prominent enough for Lucretius to call them kings. Such men transformed villages into cities, built fortified places, allotted land and livestock according to the standards of physical and mental excellence.

With increased prosperity came the use of gold as a medium of exchange: money had been invented.[316] This was a significant step in the human invention of society, for with the invention of money it became possible to have a lot more than you can use, and turn that into a source of influence and power. Wealth now replaced excellence of body and mind as the primary cause of pre-eminence in society. It was possible to be ambitious with this new standard in a way it had not been with the old, and ambition for wealth and power changed society into a struggle for prominence which bred its own downfall by engendering envy and resentment to the point where society collapsed in feuding and civil war. "So things came to the uttermost dregs of confusion, when each man for himself sought dominion and exaltation."[317]

This state of affairs was eventually found intolerable by most and, "tired of

---

[315]bona magnaque pars servabat foedera caste, Lucr. 5.1025.

[316]Lucr. 5.1113.

[317]Lucr. 5.1141-2.

living in violence,"[318] mankind was ready for the next innovation in the structure of society. The old contract had been broken by all. Things had changed so that it could never be revived, for it was not meant to contain ambition for private gain. So a new contract was invented: the rule of law.[319] Now the concept of justice was articulated, defined, codified in law and distinguished from friendship as primarily a mere contractual matter.

It is to the concept of justice developed in the transformation of society into an organization under positive law that the Epicurean discussion of justice applies. Its purpose is to give a philosophical analysis of the concept and to show that even as a contractual concept it has not entirely been reduced to a means of not being harmed, that is, that in the formula 'neither harm nor be harmed', the first part is not only a means to the second but also has intrinsic merit. This set up a tension in the Epicurean discussion of justice which many commentators have noticed and been disturbed by.

## Justice

In K.D. 33 Epicurus writes that "Justice was never anything in itself but a kind of contract, regularly arising at some place or other in people's dealings with one another, about not harming or being harmed." This doctrine asserts that justice was not found but invented, that it did not exist prior to being invented but that it first comes to be as a kind of contract anywhere and anytime people find some way of living together without harming each other or being harmed. The

---

[318]Lucr. 5.1145, 1149.

[319]Lucr. 5.1143 ff.

indefinite reference to a kind of contract allows for the inclusion both of the first rudimentary forms described by Lucretius, as well as of the later more definite forms established under law which people agree to in order to put an end to mutual violence. In this legal contract justice and injustice are interpreted as obedience and disobedience of the law. The legalistic interpretation of justice makes no appeal to an intrinsic rightness of justice or intrinsic wrongness of injustice, but understands the concept in purely contractual terms. In those terms the reason an individual may have for avoiding injustice is not that it is wrong in some non-legal sense, but that injustice is punished. This is what Epicurus expresses in the next doctrine, K.D. 34: "Injustice is an evil not in itself but in the fear that arises from the suspicion that one will not escape the notice of those who have the authority to punish such things." Injustice is here understood as evil because it has painful consequences, the pain either of punishment or the fear of punishment. The fear of punishment is very real because any group that agrees to set up laws under which to live must provide not only for punishment if the law is broken, but also for ways of discovering when and by whom the law has been broken, so that the parties to the contract cannot publicly support the contract and secretly break it for private gain. This consequence of institutionalizing the legalistic interpretation of justice is expressed in the next doctrine, K.D. 35: "No one who secretly infringes any of the terms of a mutual contract made with a view to not harming and not being harmed can be confident that he will escape detection even if he does so countless times. For right up to his death it is unclear whether he will actually escape."[320]

Justice cannot be fully reduced to the legalistic conception of it, because even

---

[320]cf. Lucr. 5.1151-60.

though justice is nothing in itself and apart from a contract which is an artifact, it is not an arbitrary artifact. Just as any artifact can be made well or badly, so can this one; people who make contracts to establish justice can do so well or badly. And just as not any artifact will in fact succeed in doing what it was designed to do, so not any contract will succeed in establishing justice. A particular contract may in retrospect be seen not to do what it had been designed to do, or no longer to do what once it had done owing, perhaps, to a change in circumstances, and so on. In short, it is possible to have unjust laws.

Epicurus does not subscribe to the notion of natural law, but neither does he subscribe to the view that law is entirely a matter of convention. Rather, he combined the two in a concept of law as a convention with natural roots. These natural roots, of course, are not the nature of justice somehow discoverable in the natural or supernatural world, but rather the intentions of the parties to the contract, intentions rooted in the affective nature of the contracting individuals in terms of which the function the new artifact was designed to have is understood. K.D. 31 is about these natural roots: "Nature's justice is a guarantee of utility with a view to not harming one another and not being harmed."[321] What is meant here by nature's justice is what the participants in the production of positive law naturally want from the contract of mutual submission to law. It functions as their intention in the design of the contract to achieve "utility of social relationships" (cf. K.D. 37) and, so, furnishes the sign or guarantee that utility has been achieved by a law. In this way nature's justice functions as a criterion of the justice of positive law because it is an expression of the ultimate ethical criteria of pleasure

---

[321]On the translation of 'sumbolon' ('guarantee') see Long and Sedley, The Hellenistic Philosophers, Cambridge University Press 1987, Vol. II, p. 129 n.l.; and Reimar Müller, Die Epikureische Gesellschaftstheorie, Berlin 1972, p. 92 n. 206a.

188

and pain.

The natural ethical criteria of pleasure and pain are the same for all human beings because they exist by nature rather than convention. And because their expression in what Epicurus calls nature's justice is equally a matter of nature rather than convention, justice is the same for all. But justice is only the same for all in a general way, much as nutrition is the same for all because of shared biological characteristics which give all human beings the same basic needs. And much as the cuisine may vary greatly among different societies depending on a variety of circumstances, so legal systems may vary. Different cuisines may supply nutritional requirements, and different legal systems may provide justice. Some foods which are a traditional part of the diet of a region may at some time be discovered to be rather harmful. You may, if you have to suffer through a time of institutional food at a hospital or corporate cafeteria, find that you have to eat toast made from white bread soaked in butter spread with very sweet jam, or a fruit cup with pesticide residue, or beef from doped cattle and so on. The analogue between nutrition and justice must, of course, not be pushed too far, since there are many important differences. But the similarities can be helpful in understanding what Epicurus had in mind when he wrote K.D. 36:

> Taken generally, justice is the same for all, since it is something useful in people's social relationships. But in the light of what is peculiar to a region and to the whole range of determinants, the same thing does not turn out to be just for all.

One way in which the second part of this doctrine can be read is that laws differ from region to region much as what is good to eat differs from region to region. Justice taken generally, that is, the basic requirement of neither harming nor being harmed, is the same for all, but the laws and customs by which different societies try to institutionalize justice vary from society to society, so that institutional justice is not the same for all but shows some cultural relativity. From this, of course, it does not follow that justice is a social convention and nothing more, any more than it follows that diet is a social convention and nothing more. Both have natural roots in an analogous way.

The notion of justice is plainly being used in two senses in K.D. 36, first in a general sense or in the sense in which it was called nature's justice in K.D. 31, and second in the sense of legal justice. This distinction is made clear in the next doctrine, K.D. 37.

> What is legally deemed to be just has its existence in the domain of justice whenever it is attested to be useful in the requirements of social relationships, whether or not it turns out to be the same for all. But if someone makes a law and it does not happen to accord with the utility of social relationships, it no longer has the nature of justice. And even if what is useful in the sphere of justice changes but fits the preconception for some time, it was no less just throughout that time for those who do not confuse themselves with empty utterances but simply look at the facts.

Epicurus distinguishes nature's justice from legal justice. The former is the content of the preconception, the prolēpsis of justice, and it is the mark or guarantee of social utility. The latter is the body of positive law which institutionalizes what is just and unjust in a society. The ideal is for legal justice to articulate and institutionalize nature's justice and to the extent that it succeeds it "has its existence in the domain of justice", that is, to that extent the laws are just. But to the extent that laws fail to articulate and institutionalize nature's justice they fail to be just. A particular law or set of laws may have been badly made from the beginning and thus never have been just except in the legal sense alone. Or they may have been just at the beginning but certain changes have since then come about in the social situation which prevent their functioning as they were designed to function, which robbed them of their usefulness or, worse, have made them positively harmful. Think here of laws like an early nineteenth century law permitting people to drive cattle down Yonge Street in Toronto, or an early twentieth century law limiting the speed to 30 mph on major roads, or the constitutional right to bear arms south of the border and so on. This is not difficult to understand once Epicurus' distinction is allowed. K.D. 38 speaks precisely to this point.

> If objective circumstances have not changed and things believed to be just have been shown in actual practice not to be in accord with our preconception [of justice], then those things were not just. And if objective circumstances do change and the same things which had been just turn out to be no longer useful, then those things were just as long as they were useful for the mutual associations of fellow citizens; but later, when they were not useful, they were no longer just.

Both nature's justice and legal justice are a kind of contract in the sense that each is underwritten by an agreement between people, but they are different kinds of contracts. We have seen a description of each kind in Lucretius' account of the genesis of civil society. Justice, either natural or legal, can therefore obtain only between parties capable of making an agreement about not harming or being harmed. It cannot obtain between two inanimate objects on both counts, for they can neither agree nor be harmed. It cannot obtain between lower animals which, even though they can be harmed, cannot agree. It cannot obtain between a human being and an inanimate object such as a car for, even if the human being can both agree and be harmed, the car can do neither, though it can be damaged. A difficulty arises when we have two parties, both of which can be harmed, but only one of which can agree, such as a human being and an animal. Epicurus insists that the relationship between a human being and an animal is as little a matter of justice as the relationship between human beings without an agreement. In K.D. 32 he writes that

> Nothing is just or unjust in relation to those creatures which are unable to make contracts about not harming one another and not being harmed; so too with all peoples which are unable or unwilling to make contracts about not harming and not being harmed.

A tension develops here in the contractual analysis of justice, for we perceive some things to be wrong which are not covered by the analysis of justice as a contract, and so did Epicurus. The absence of a contract does not condone any treatment whatever either of animals or foreign nationals. We may, whether in Epicurus' time or today, condemn the use to which animals are put in experimentation by the cosmetics industry, and we may condemn the treatment of prisoners of war by countries which haven't signed something like the Geneva convention, and our condemnation has nothing to do with the violation of any agreement. One has a choice at this point between limiting the notion of justice to a contract and giving an account of some things as wrong on grounds other than injustice, or of extending the concept of justice beyond the contract. Our inclination today would be not to extend the concept, I think, but to find that some things are morally right or wrong without being just or unjust, for we perceive justice as only a species of the morally right.

But Epicurus extends the concept, for he understands justice also to be a psychic state. Justice understood as a psychic state is, however, not unrelated to justice understood as a contract. As a psychic state justice is basically a disposition not to harm, as distinct from positive benevolence or the disposition to benefit, which is already a matter of friendship rather than justice.

It will be recalled that in Lucretius' account of the genesis of civil society neighbours came together "eager not to harm one another and not to be harmed."[322] This must not be understood merely as an eagerness not to be harmed, which could easily be understood as the natural disposition to avoid pain,

---

[322]Lucr. 5.1020.

but also as an eagerness not to harm. The agreement not to harm must not be understood as merely a concession that each is willing to make in order to get what he really wants, not to be harmed. That would be reading something into the text which isn't there. One could as easily say that each party is eager not to be harmed so that he is relieved of the need to do harm in return. That would be just as lopsided a reading. According to Lucretius the founders of civil society were eager for both. That they were willing to extend the agreement not to harm even on its own without making a similar agreement by the other party a condition of such an offer is shown by their willingness to agree not to harm someone from whom they had nothing to fear because they were too weak to do them any harm.[323] The unreciprocated agreement not to harm, however, is also a part of justice (aequum), at least during the time of the first contract. Later, when positive law was invented as a second contract primarily as a defense against being harmed, it is unclear whether an eagerness not to harm is part of the contract. Lucretius simply tells us that people were worn out and nauseated by their violent way of life and, therefore, agreed to submit to laws and constraining rights.[324] This exhaustion and nausea with violence might well have included an aversion to being violent as well as to suffering violence. In fact, the text positively suggests it by twice telling us that people had had it with living violently rather than making the point that people felt that they had been hurt enough. The old readiness not to harm others is never lost entirely, from which it does not follow, of course, that some people at least, then as well as now, would not be prepared to harm others.

---

[323]Lucr. 5.1023 for children and women,

[324]Lucr. 5.1145-50.

The readiness not to harm others is not entirely altruistic in the sense of doing something desirable for another to which I am quite indifferent. Nothing ever is, according to Epicurus. Later we shall see, for example, that it is a pleasure to love another person for that other person's sake. The opposition between egoism and altruism is an invention of a later fancy. They are not concepts with which Epicurus works, indeed I think that, had they been proposed to him, he would have rejected them as ill conceived. The readiness not to harm others is not purely altruistic because acting justly, quite apart from being treated justly, is a means to katastematic pleasure. In K.D. 17 Epicurus writes that "The just [life] is most free from disturbance, but the unjust life is full of the greatest disturbance." Justice brings tranquility (ataraxia) and injustice disturbs this tranquility for two reasons. First, in a society with laws their breach brings punishment and, second, the link between justice and tranquility is a function of the very nature of a healthy psyche, both human and divine.

We have already seen that a society which agrees to live under a body of positive laws must provide for the detection and punishment of law breakers. K.D. 34 and 35 have pointed out how the unjust life of a law breaker cannot be a tranquil one but is lived in constant fear of detection by the authorities whose job is to punish violations of the law, and Lucretius (5.1151-60) gives a vivid account of the troubled life of law breakers who, even if they can hide their crimes from gods and men may yet reveal them "speaking in dreams or raving in delirium." S.V. 7 points out that even if it is possible for a criminal actually to escape detection, which though difficult is possible, it is impossible to escape the fear of detection. The tranquil confidence of the just person is not possible for the unjust, even if they are never caught.

194

But having nothing to fear from others is not the only source of tranquility for the healthy soul. The very act of harming another is a source of disturbance, quite apart from subsequent punishment or the fear of it. No one intentionally harms another except from motives such as "enmity, resentment and disparagement, which the wise man masters by reason";[325] or for private gain which the wise man does not need because he has developed a simple life of self-sufficiency; or simply to see another suffer, but the wise man finds no pleasure in the suffering of another except so far as it serves to increase the others' wisdom.[326] Any possible motive for harming another is itself a disturbance in the soul and a sign of weakness, and a soul which is itself untroubled will make no trouble for another. This is not only true of human beings but, because it is a function of the nature of any healthy soul, Epicurus confidently attributes it to the gods as well.[327] The person who experiences the untroubled tranquility of katastematic pleasure will therefore not be unjust since justice is a necessary condition for tranquility.[328] This is not sufficient to make justice an intrinsic good but it remains instrumental. The Epicurean is just for the sake of his tranquility. But justice is not merely incidental, but necessary and, therefore, "inseparable from pleasure."[329]

We can now consider a puzzle which has been transmitted by Plutarch in his Reply to Colotes (1127e). He is at this point discussing with great indignation what he perceives to be Metrodorus' disrespect for the revered lawgivers of

---

[325]D.L. 10.117.

[326]D.L. 10.121b.

[327]K.D. 1.

[328]K.D. 5; Ep. Men. 132.

[329]D.L. 10.138.

Sparta and Athens, Lycurgus and Solon, and goes on to say that the Epicurean quarrel is not only with lawgivers but with the laws themselves, which one may learn from Epicurus himself, "for in the Puzzles Epicurus asks himself whether the wise man will do some things which the laws forbid, if he knows that he will escape detection. And he answers: 'the plain statement [of the answer] is not easy',[330] i.e., I will do it but do not wish to admit it." Plutarch's interpretation of what Epicurus meant need not be accepted[331] for he is not so much giving a responsible account as venting his indignation.

It is a pity that we no longer have any of Epicurus' discussion of the problem. Nevertheless, it seems clear that the problem is not whether the wise man would ever be unjust but whether he would ever disobey a law, which is a different problem. It is also clear that the problem is not whether he would break any law whatever, whether he would do anything and everything forbidden by law if he were certain not to be discovered, but some things only are at issue, though it is not clear what these things are. And it is further clear that there was no simple answer Epicurus cared to give because, presumably, the problem was not a simple one.

We would do well to keep the issue of unjust acts distinct from the issue of

---

[330]There is a textual difficulty (recently reviewed by Anna Angeli in Cronache Ercolanesi 11 (1981) pp. 84-6) in the quotation from Epicurus. The difficulty is whether to retain the manuscript epikatēgorema (as do Einarson and de Lacy in the LCL edition, for example) or to accept Stephanus' emendation esti katēgorema (as do Usener, and Bailey, for example). There seem to be no compelling reasons for either reading, but this is not crucial for us since either reading would indicate that Epicurus was unwilling to give an unqualified answer. The translation given here is that of Inwood and Gerson.

[331]Though it has been accepted. J.M. Rist, for example, writes: "If an Epicurean could be certain of avoiding detection, he would act illegally" (Epicurus, p. 116). Rist gives no reason for this astonishing claim other than a reference to Plutarch. We have already argued that Rist quite misunderstands Epicurean pleasure and, thus, the springs of action recognized by Epicurus.

illegal acts since they are different and the present problem is specifically about disobeying laws. Nevertheless, a look at the possibility of a wise man's injustice can be helpful. If we can show that a wise man will not be unjust and that to break a just law is to be unjust, then we will also have shown that a wise man will not break just laws. A wise man would then not do "some things which the laws forbid" if the laws in question were just, though he might still break unjust laws. A wise man will not be unjust because it would mean harming someone, and doing harm disturbs his tranquility, which is worth more than anything he could gain by injustice. This much we have already seen. It is allowed even by Bailey who finds Epicurus' attitude to the law "cynical" but concedes that it "must not be understood to mean that fear is the only motive for just action in Epicurus' eyes."[332] But P.A. Vander Waerdt, who argues that "the Epicurean wise man will not commit injustice, secretly or openly, because it is in his self-interest to be just,"[333] nevertheless thinks that he "might commit injustice for the sake of a friend in need."[334] The need, I suppose, would have to be very great, so great perhaps that, were it not the friend's need but the wise man's own need, he would also commit the injustice. The need in question might be for an object necessary for life itself. Indeed, there is no reason to think that Epicurus would not condone a starving Epicurean's petty theft to feed himself, for example.[335] But once one

---

[332]Epicurus: the Extant Remains, Oxford 1926, p. 370.

[333]"The Justice of the Epicurean Wise Man," Classical Quarterly, 37 no. 2 (1987), p. 402.

[334]P.A. Vander Waerdt, op. cit., p. 416.

[335]The theft would be a petty injustice in that it did the deprived person a small harm. Vander Waerdt argues that this kind of injustice was widely condoned in ancient times. He writes: "In fact, all of the leading classical natural right theorists would agree ... If Epicurus is unwilling to rule out entirely the possibility that the wise man might be forced to violate a law were it to thwart some natural desire necessary for life itself, his view has its counterpart in the natural right reading that no principle of justice is beyond exception in an extreme case." (op. cit., p. 418.) He refers to Plato, Aristotle and, in a qualified way, the Stoics as evidence for this view.

condones a petty injustice, one may be confronted with a sorites argument that one must condone any injustice whatever, and Epicurus may have realized that discussing the issue of where to draw the line is "not easy," especially with people like Plutarch.

It may also be that breaking a just law is not always unjust. For example, I consider the legal status of traffic lights to be just. Yet this morning, when walking to the university in the early morning with no traffic on the streets as yet, I crossed two intersections against a red light without, I believe, being unjust to anyone. No one was harmed by my act, and I had excellent reason to think that no one would be. Similar cases are not difficult to think up, and it is possible that Epicurus also had something like this in mind when he found the issue "not easy."

There are difficulties, then, in asserting without qualification that an Epicurean will always obey just laws. But neither can one claim without a further discussion that an Epicurean will always break an unjust law if he is certain not to be found out, though it is certain that he would more readily break unjust laws than just ones.[336] There is good reason for thinking that in most situations the best way of getting rid of unjust laws is not by breaking them but by repealing them through some legally established procedure. If anyone could break any law he considered unjust a kind of social chaos would be threatened, since the question whether a particular law is just is often a difficult one and many people are poor judges of whether or not laws are just, and if one valued the law at all (as it is clear the

---

[336]Phillip Mitsis accepts that an Epicurean will break unjust laws if he is safe from detection and then goes on to construct a case to show that he might break an unjust law even if he is sure of being found out, if the punishment for breaking it is less than the pain of obeying it. (Epicurus' Ethical Theory, Cornell University Press 1988, p. 90 n. 75).

Epicureans did[337]) one has good reason for obeying even some unjust laws for a period of time. This issue is very complex and there is no reason to suppose that Epicurus was ignorant of this complexity, which may have been partly responsible for the guarded response and Plutarch's perplexity.

We can safely accept, then, that an accomplished Epicurean would not be unjust except perhaps in extremis, and that he would always obey the law unless he had excellent reason not to, and that this follows quite readily from his philosophical principles. But there is a touch of millennialism in at least the later Epicureans. The institution of positive law was after all an emergency measure adopted by society against the power struggle made possible by the invention of money, as Lucretius tells us. It is therefore an emergency measure against what an Epicurean would consider a symptom of mental illness which they thought Epicurean philosophy could cure. In a society of healthy souls, sometime in the future, there would be no further need of laws. In that happy state, Diogenes of Oenoanda assures us, "truly the life of the gods will pass to men. For everything will be full of justice and mutual friendship, and there will be no need of city-walls or laws ..."[338] In fact, this millennial vision may already have been entertained as early as Hermarchus,[339] which would make it much less of a late fancy than it appears to be.

---

[337]After the collapse of social harmony with the invention of money described by Lucretius, and before the advent of a sane Epicurean society of which we shall speak presently, laws are valuable as the main source of peace and justice. Plutarch quotes Colotes that "those who drew up laws and customs and established monarchical and other forms of government brought life into a state of much security and tranquility and banished turmoil; and if anyone should remove these things, we would live a life of beasts, and one man on meeting another will all but devour him." (Col. 1124d). It is worth reading Plutarch a little beyond this quotation to get the measure of the man.

[338]Long and Sedley, The Hellenistic Philosophers, 22 S.

[339]cf. Long and Sedley, op. cit., 22 M(4).

# Friendship

The Epicurean story of society is not only the story of justice but of friendship as well. The story begins with a compact in which justice and friendship are not yet clearly distinguished,[340] and ends in a millennial vision of perfect justice and friendship without the need of laws to enforce justice. In between these two stages is the rule of law in which justice comes to be defined and distinguished from friendship. The society born of a benevolent eagerness not to harm or be harmed becomes positively violent and has need of justice as a defense against being harmed. Justice becomes institutionalized in an explicit contract not to harm which is the positive law of society, though it is never entirely reduced to a legal contract, but lives on, in at least some people, as the virtuous readiness not to harm for its own sake. Beyond this readiness not to harm, friendship develops as a readiness to benefit. Both justice and friendship are a kind of contract from the beginning, however, and always will be, in at least the sense that this readiness must be returned. Unless the offer of peace and friendship is returned it will not last. Friendship, however, never becomes institutionalized as an explicit agreement, as does justice; and friendship is reserved for a relative few, while justice is extended to all fellow citizens whether you know and like them or not.

Both justice and friendship are desirable for the sake of the other's agreement to extend justice and friendship in return. To be safe from a neighbour's attack, and

---

[340]That this is not just an invention of Lucretius is confirmed by Epicurus in S.V. 61: "The sight of one's neighbours is most beautiful if the first meeting brings concord or [at least] produces a serious commitment to this." This is the translation of Inwood and Gerson. For a different interpretation and discussion of the text see Bailey, Epicurus, Oxford, 1926 p. 385.

to have a friend ready to help if ever you need help, are desirable goods. But the desirability of neither justice nor friendship is restricted to its being the source of goods conferred by the other. We have already seen how being just benefits the just person, quite apart from the threat of punishment for injustice and quite apart from the reciprocal justice of the other. Justice is also a virtue, a psychic state which is necessary for the Epicurean's katastematic pleasure. As a virtue, as well as a contract, justice remains a means to pleasure without actually becoming an object of pleasure. Justice is a means to pleasure in that it keeps disturbance at bay, both the disturbance of being harmed by others and the mental disturbance produced by the motivation to harm others.

We must now see how friendship is desirable not only for the sake of benefits conferred on us by friends, but for its own sake as well. Friendship, unlike justice, can be an intrinsic good because it can be an object of pleasure. We must see now how friendship, which begins as a kind of bargain, can nevertheless escape the simple categories of egoism and altruism because, while genuine friendship is the love of another for that other's sake alone, it is also a genuine pleasure to be a friend. Friendship is altruistic, if you like, because it loves the other for the other's sake; and it is egoistic, if you like, because the lover is not indifferent to loving, and if ever the lover becomes indifferent to this love, the love would die.

The main problem in understanding the Epicurean theory of friendship is to understand how it can be based on need, on utility, how it can have the character of a kind of small bargain for mutual support which it never loses; and how it can nevertheless be the genuine article, the love of another for the other's sake; and that all of this is intelligible in terms of pleasure.

This is not a new problem, of course. Cicero's main objection to the Epicurean account of friendship was that in all their talk of the consequences of having a friend, of profit and utility, he missed any mention of genuine affection which would make friendship desirable for its own sake and not for the sake of the benefits one could expect from a friend.[341] He does not deny that Epicurus says some laudable things about friendship, but insists that Epicurus had no right to say them on the basis of his philosophical principles, since they are inconsistent with a philosophy which sees the good in pleasure.[342] This charge had already been made before Cicero, and the source[343] from which Cicero drew his report of Epicurean friendship seems in fact to be a reply to just such a charge. Cicero thinks that the charge to which his source is responding is that if pleasure is the chief good then there can be no friendship.[344] But, judging by the response, the charge was a little more complex than that and might be articulated as follows: if we take our own pleasure to be the highest good and do everything for the sake of our own individual pleasure, then none of us can be a true friend, because friendship requires that we treat the friend as an end in himself and not just as a means to our own pleasure. The response of Cicero's source to this charge is essentially that friendship cannot be separated from pleasure, and that this does not prevent genuine friendship because the individual is not concerned only with

---

[341]De fin. 2.83.

[342]Cicero thought that Epicurus could say things inconsistent with his principles because he, Epicurus, was not very bright (De fin. 2.80). We must not forget, however, that Cicero fails to understand Epicurean pleasure, as we have shown, and is himself a man who believes that the test for truth in moral theories is that they provide the stuff for fine speeches, as do Peripatetic and Stoic theories (De fin. 2.76-7). And, as we shall see, he also bungles his discussion of Epicurean friendship in ways that give us reason not only to doubt his scholarly sincerity but his cerebral wattage as well.

[343]For a brief discussion of the sources of the De finibus see the Loeb Classical Library edition p. xiii.

[344]De fin. 1.65.

his own pleasure but with his friend's pleasure as well, that is, the presumption of what we today would call egoistic hedonism is mistaken.[345]

Cicero writes that his source deals with the issue of friendship in three ways.[346] The first way begins by recording a controversy in the Epicurean school. Both parties to the controversy apparently agree that to have friendship requires that each person not make his own pleasure the only goal of his acts, but that he must also seek to bring about his friend's pleasure. The controversy, however, is about the relative importance of the friend's pleasure. One party to the controversy thinks "that our friends' pleasures are not in themselves as worthy of pursuit as are our own," and the other party thinks that putting our friends' pleasure into second place like that "undermines the stability of a friendship." Notice that both parties to this controversy could quite consistently agree that if every human being only sought his own pleasure as the goal of all his acts then there could be no friendship, and both parties deny that Epicureans only seek their own pleasure. To that extent even reporting the controversy is a reply to the charge, namely that the charge rests on a misunderstanding. The controversy is not about whether to include a friend's pleasure in my telos, but what priority it is to have there.

At this point Cicero apparently becomes confused. He says that someone, presumably the first party to the controversy, defends their position easily, and then he goes on to give an argument. He seems to think that it is the argument

---

[345]Phillip Mitsis writes: "any recommendation of unselfish friendship sharply conflicts with Epicurus' much repeated claim that only one's own pleasure is the telos of action and desirable for itself." (Epicurus' Ethical Theory, Cornell University Press 1988, p. 101; this chapter is a reprint of "Epicurus on Friendship and Altruism," Oxford Studies in Ancient Philosophy, Vol. 5, 1987). The words 'only one's own' are Mitsis' invention.

[346]De fin. 1.65-70. The following discussion draws on this section. It will be appropriate to remember that we are dealing here with replies to a specific charge rather than with an independent exposition of Epicurean doctrine.

given by the first party in defense of their position. But it cannot be. What follows is either a separate position, in which case we don't have three replies to the objection, as Cicero thinks, but four. Or it is the argument of the second party to the controversy, as it easily could be, but then Cicero really does seem to be rather confused at this point. We shall here treat it as the argument of the second party so as to preserve the count of three replies, which is generally accepted.

The argument is essentially that life with friends is more pleasurable than solitary life, that friendship produces pleasure as much for our friends as for ourselves, that we enjoy friends both present and absent, but that in order to maintain friendship we must cherish our friends as much as ourselves. Epicureans will therefore rejoice at their friends' joy as much as at their own, and grieve as much at their friends distress as at their own. For all these reasons the wise man will have the same feelings for his friends as for himself and will pursue their pleasure as sincerely as his own. In any case, making pleasure the highest good does not prevent friendship as construed by these Epicureans.

The second response to the charge is portrayed by Cicero as given by some Epicureans who, though quite intelligent, have been intimidated by the criticism, presumably because they see that it is not entirely without foundation. What they see is that friendship is not a simple relation between people, but one that develops from a rudimentary beginning and grows, when it does, into a mature friendship. The problem, as they see it, is that the rudimentary beginning of friendship really is a self-seeking little bargain in which each is as yet only concerned about the benefits to be had from friends. This presents a problem because the charge could be read as claiming that this rudimentary character is all that Epicurean friendships ever have and that the development of genuine friendships from such a beginning is unintelligible on Epicurean principles. They see their task, therefore, as giving an account of the genesis of the kind of friendship described in the first reply. One could read this, therefore, as a supplement to the first reply rather than a fully separate reply. Friendship, it is admitted, begins in the quest of each individual for his own pleasure, but then develops into love of the friend for the friend's sake such that, even if there is no benefit to be gained from the friendship or, at least, quite apart from any consideration of such benefit, the friend is still loved for his own sake. And the mechanism of this development is said to be constant association. We do, as a matter of fact, come to love places and buildings and cities and animals and games etc. once they have become familiar and are part of our feeling at home and at ease among them. In a similar way, say these Epicureans, we come to love our friends.

The explanation of the flowering of genuine friendship from rude beginnings by constant association and familiarity is probably the invention of some later Epicureans and not to be ascribed to Epicurus himself, as Cicero notes,[347] but the general developmental thesis, which claims that the mature and genuine form of friendship develops from humble benefit-seeking beginnings, was most probably already held by Epicurus himself.[348] The contribution of the explanatory mechanism of association is in any event a very feeble one. I may come to love familiar places and things, but it is unclear how I came to love them not for the pleasure they give me but for their own sakes quite apart from any benefit or utility in having them in my environment. The general point of this reply to the

---

[347]De fin. 2.82.

[348]See, for example, D.L. 10.120b.

original charge, however, is that the critic would be right if Epicurean friendships remained nothing but benefit-seeking associations, but they do not. The difficulty here is giving a plausible explanation of how and why they develop into mature friendships.

The third reply proposes a different explanatory mechanism through which to understand the development into mature friendships: a contract. Presumably what happens according to this explanation is that some people, "wise men," realize both that friendship is desirable and that, unless they love the friend for his own sake and not only for the sake of the benefits he can bring, friendship won't last. Wise men who understand this therefore make "a kind of contract" to love each other for each other's sake, and that seems to be enough actually to produce this love and the genuine friendship of which it is the condition.

This third reply may have been an attempt to find an explanation in the Epicurean literature rather than to devise a new one, for one may think one hears an echo here of K.D. 33 on justice or perhaps the source from which Lucretius wrote of the original contract in which justice and friendship were as yet not properly distinct. But the proposal of a sort of contract as the mechanism does little more than add a word to what had already been proposed in the second part of the first reply. Like the proposal of constant familiarity as the mechanism by which genuine friendship grows, the proposal of a contract is quite feeble. It may explain how a wise man, faithful to the terms of an advantageous contract, acts as agreed, but it does not explain how the genuine love of another for another's sake comes about from self-seeking beginnings. It may explain the appearance of friendship, as if between actors on a stage, but not genuine affection, as Cicero also notes.[349]

We have been given this discussion through the eyes of Cicero, who was careless even in reporting it, as the confusion over the first reply shows, but who also is hampered in understanding Epicurean friendship because he has quite failed to understand Epicurean pleasure, in particular, katastematic pleasure. He wants to limit all pleasure to kinetic pleasure,[350] which may account for the slip in his discussion of the second reply. The second reply tried to explain how it was possible to love another for the other's sake quite apart from any consideration of benefits to be got from the other, but Cicero discusses it as an attempt to explain such love quite apart from any prospect of pleasure.[351] This is a serious slip, but Cicero would probably have considered it a trivial slip of his pen, for he was quite innocent of any idea of pleasure other than the pleasure to be got from such benefits and the like. But if, as we shall argue, one cannot understand Epicurean friendship without understanding katastematic pleasure, then we would do well not to rely too much on what Cicero has to say on the topic and try, rather, to get an understanding from more orthodox Epicurean material.

Epicurus supplies the key to understanding his theory of friendship in S.V. 23:

---

[349]De fin. 2.78.

[350]De fin. 2.77.

[351]De fin. 2.82. John Rist pounces on him for this and "convicts Cicero of misreading Epicurean theory." ("Epicurus on Friendship," Classical Philology, 75, 1980, p. 123.)

"All friendship is intrinsically desirable, but it originates from benefiting."[352]
Even though friendship originates as an arrangement for bringing about benefits
and thus is something instrumentally valuable, that is, a means to pleasure, it
eventually becomes intrinsically valuable, that is, itself a pleasure. Diogenes
Laertius[353] describes these two aspects of friendship with an agricultural
metaphor. According to him our needs provide the original motivation to befriend
someone. This act is analogous to sowing the earth in that it is done for the sake
of the harvest it will bear. The need which motivates our befriending someone is
the need for the benefits which having a friend can bring. These benefits, of
course, can be understood as benefits only in terms of pleasure. It is, therefore, for
the sake of pleasure that we first befriend someone.

A friend can be both a source and an object of pleasure. He is a source of
pleasure so far as he provides objects of pleasure or helps to make such objects
more pleasant. A pleasant dinner, for example, is more pleasant in the company of

---

[352]There is a textual problem here about whether to accept the manuscript reading of <u>arete</u>, or
whether to accept Usener's emendation to <u>hairete</u>. For a discussion of this problem and references
to further discussion see Long and Sedley, <u>The Hellenistic Philosophers</u>, Cambridge University
Press 1987, Vol. 2, p. 132. See also Phillip Mitsis, <u>Epicurus' Ethical Theory</u>, Cornell University
Press 1988, pp. 10-1 n.6; and Inwood and Gerson, <u>Hellenistic Philosophy</u>, Hackett Publishing Co.
1988, p. 30 n. 25. On the manuscript reading we would have to try to understand friendship as an
intrinsic virtue. The difficulty with this is that the value of virtue in Epicureanism is not intrinsic
but instrumental. Virtue is a means to pleasure, that is all. This reading would make friendship a
virtue, which is odd, and the only virtue whose value is not instrumental by being a means to
pleasure, but intrinsic and thus itself a pleasure. The emended reading gives friendship out to be
intrinsically valuable without calling it a virtue. But since in Epicureanism the only intrinsically
valuable thing is pleasure, the emended reading also gives us to understand that friendship is itself
a pleasure. We accept the emendation here as being the less complicated way to the point of S.V.
23 that friendship is intrinsically valuable, though it begins by being instrumentally valuable.

[353]10.120b.

friends,[354] and friends can also make conversation more pleasant[355] than conversation with strangers. A friend can also be an object of pleasure. The mere sight of a friend can be a pleasant thing and Rist may well be right that "Epicurus would certainly include the provision of heterosexual favours, and sometimes of homosexual favours, among the pleasures that friendship can provide."[356] There is no doubt that Epicurus thought life in the company of friends to be preferable to life among strangers or to the solitary life, and that this was quite compatible with the value he placed on self-sufficiency.

But the pleasures of life in a community of friends are incidental to the original motivation for befriending someone, a pleasant bonus and decoration, so to speak. The original motivation seems rather to be the assurance of help in case of need. Even if someone is a pleasant conversationalist and dinner guest or even sexual partner, he is no friend if you can't depend on him in time of need. This readiness to help must not be understood in a small way for "he is no friend who is continually asking for help."[357] A friend's readiness to help in times of need can be abused by constant petty requests. And yet if this readiness is withdrawn, as though friendship had nothing to do with help in time of need, friendship is destroyed as surely as by the abuse of this readiness.[358] The ideal friendship is one in which friends are constantly ready to help, but this readiness is reserved for

---

[354]Epicurus "says you should be more concerned about inspecting with whom you eat and drink, than with what you eat and drink. For eating without a friend is the life of a lion and a wolf." Seneca, Letters 19.10 (Us. 542).

[355]D.L. 10.22.

[356]J.M. Rist, Epicurus, Cambridge University Press, 1972, p. 127.

[357]S.V. 39.

[358]Ibid.

209

times of emergency and real need and is therefore rarely, if ever, made use of. The real value of friendship, so far as it is a kind of contract for mutual benefit, lies not so much in the actual help received, which is in any event a rare occurrence if it happens at all, but in the confidence that help is available if needed, which is not at all rare and occasional, but a constant and uninterrupted benefit of friendship.[359]

The benefits of friendship do include kinetic pleasures such as dinner and conversation, but the Epicurean stress is not on these. Rather it is on the constant pleasure of confidence and the expectation of help. The memory of a pleasant event is a kinetic pleasure, as is the expectation of a pleasant event to come such as dinner, a concert, a game of tennis. These pleasures have definite objects and come and go, and thus are kinetic. Thus, if, for example, I have a bottle of rare wine which I intend to drink on some unspecified future occasion, then the knowledge that I have this wine for some fitting future occasion is a pleasant thought, an anticipation of future kinetic pleasure which is itself a kinetic pleasure. It is continuous while it lasts, but its continuity has a definite termination in a pleasant event with a definite object, the drinking of the wine. In that respect it is like the anticipation of a dinner that will be ready "soon", a kinetically pleasant anticipation. The pleasures of friendship no doubt include such pleasant anticipations. But the confidence that help will be provided, if ever it is needed, has the continuousness of katastematic pleasure as well as its lack of a proper object, for the expectation is not of a definite act or object, but rather of whatever it takes to help in whatever emergency should arise. It has the character of the removal of evil which shows us the nature of the good and provides gēthos,

---

[359]S.V. 34.

the highest form of katastematic pleasure.[360] The constant anticipation of katastematic pleasure, so far as it is pleasant, is itself a katastematic pleasure since it is constant and has no object, or only a quasi-object. Even in its rudimentary nature as a kind of bargain for mutual aid, therefore, the value of friendship is understood in terms of pleasure and prized by Epicureans more for its katastematic pleasure than its kinetic.

This, though a necessary feature of friendship, is still rudimentary and not yet the distinctive character of a mature friendship. It will be recalled that the distinctive feature of katastematic pleasure is that it is a constant joy taken in the quasi-object of the self, in one's existence as such. Friendship, however, provides not only kinetic but also katastematic pleasure from its inception. The friend can be not only a source of pleasure, but also an object of pleasure. That he can be an object of kinetic pleasure we have already seen and is easily understood. But he can also be the quasi-object of katastematic pleasure.

A friend is not only valued for the help he can provide in times of need or for the good times that can be had in his company, but in a mature friendship "The mere existence of a friend should bring pleasure ... the mere existence of friends is one of the attractive things in life."[361] This is finally what makes friendship intrinsically valuable beyond any kinetic pleasure that may be got from it, it is the genuine affection for another apart from any consideration of utility, the love of another experienced as the katastematic pleasure taken in the existence of a particular other individual. Just as in our awareness of ourselves we become

---

[360]Plutarch, non posse 1091a; we have already discussed this in chs. 4 and 6.

[361]J.M. Rist, "Epicurus on Friendship," Classical Philology 75 (1980), pp. 124-5; cf. S.V. 61.

aware of our own uniqueness, our peculiar character as individuals which we value as the core of our self-hood, so in genuine friendship we become aware of and value the peculiar character of the friend, and take pleasure in his existence as we do in our own.[362] And it is because we love the friend for his sake in this way, that we can be as concerned with his good as we are with our own for its own sake above and quite apart from any bargain of utility.

Because friendship multiplies katastematic pleasure as it were, it is esteemed by Epicureans as the greatest good which wisdom can provide,[363] an immortal good,[364] incorruptible in its constancy and shared with the very gods.[365] It is because in mature friendship we are as concerned with a friend's good and ill as with our own, that a wise man is as pained by a friend's pain as by his own[366] and will on occasion be prepared to die for a friend.[367] Remarks such as these have the strong flavour of ancient controversy about stock situations. To get some idea of the kind of occasion on which an Epicurean might be ready to die for a friend we need only look, for example, to Cicero.[368] The ancient world had its heroes of friendship and, I suppose, philosophers were now and then confronted with them as challenges to their philosophy. One such hero was Damon, a Pythagorean

---

[362]S.V. 15; for a discussion of the textual difficulties see Bailey, Epicurus; The Extant Remains, Oxford 1926, p. 377. With John Rist, we follow Bailey's text.

[363]K.D. 27.

[364]S.V. 78.

[365]Philodemus, de dis 3, frag. 84, col 1, 1-9. Hermann Diels, Philodemos über die Götter (Abhandlungen der Königlich Preußischen Akademie der Wissenschaften 1916, no. 6), writes "man darf ergänzen: 'wenn das Schönste fehlt, die Freundschaft'." (p. 6).

[366]S.V. 56.

[367]D.L. 10.121b.

[368]De fin. 2.79, 5.63.

philosopher who had been condemned to death by Dionysus, the tyrant of Syracuse in Sicily. Damon had some personal affairs to settle before his death, so he asked Dionysus whether he might go and settle them and leave his friend Phintias, also a Pythagorean, as surety against his return. Should he fail to return, Dionysus was to execute Phintias in his place. Dionysus agreed, not because he really believed that Damon would return, but because he thought there was sport in testing their friendship. When Damon returned in the nick of time Dionysus was so overcome that he pardoned Damon and asked to become the third member in so close a bond of friendship. The ancient world was quite taken by this story, [369] and one imagines Epicurus being asked whether this would have been possible had Damon and Phintias been Epicurean philosophers true to their principles. Epicurus's answer is yes.[370] The same could be said of another story to which Cicero refers, the story of Pylades and Orestes from the play Dulorestes by Pancuvius. The two friends had been taken captive by Thoas, King of the Tauri, who wanted to kill Orestes, whereupon both claimed to be Orestes. Most philosophers, with the possible exception of Cyrenaics, would want to allow for the possibility of such friendship in their philosophies. But most scenarios would run in terms of duty and virtue and nobility and glory and so forth, while Epicurus' could be a simple 'because I love him as myself.'

Note, however, that an Epicurean might be prepared to die for a friend, and not for just anybody. The Epicureans readiness to die for a friend is not purely

[369]In Chapter 33 of his Life of Pythagoras Iamblichus quotes the story from Aristoxenus' A Pythagorean Life; Porphyry, in para. 60 and 61 of his Life of Pythagoras, also tells the story. For an example of modern admiration, see Schiller's poem "Die Bürgschaft".

[370]It should be clear from the above that I cannot agree with Mitsis' speculation about why an Epicurean might die for a friend. (Epicurus' Ethical Theory, Cornell University Press 1988, pp. 99-100.)

altruistic because love is not purely altruistic. If I were told that some random stranger would die unless I donated my kidney, and I agreed, that might be a purely altruistic act if I had no other motives, but it would not be friendship. And if I befriend someone for his bank account, prepared to drop him if ever I cease to see the benefits of this money, then I am trading friendly relations for a payoff.[371] This might be construed as egoistic friendship, but in fact it is no friendship at all, only the pretense of friendship.

Friendship is both for the other's sake and for my sake,[372] love is both fully altruistic and fully egoistic, if we insist on using those terms, but it would be better to drop them and understand that love is neither.

---

[371]S.V. 39.

[372]Lactantius wrote that "Epicurus said that we do not love another except for our own sake" (Institutiones Divinae 3.17.42). No doubt he did say so somewhere, but he surely did not say that we love others, when we do, for our own sake alone in a purely egoistic way, and it is ill considered to read him so, as does, for example, Phillip Mitsis (Epicurus' Ethical Theory, Cornell University Press 1988, p. 98 n. 1.)

# Chapter Eight

# The Good Life

In the Introduction we said that by Hellenistic times the main philosophical question was no longer 'what is there?' but 'how shall I live?' We are now in a position to consider Epicurus' answer to this question.

The first thing that strikes one is that there is no complete Epicurean recipe for living. Not every problem encountered in life has a general solution, not every vital question has a philosophical answer, because circumstances differ and because none of us is simply a human being, a more or less successful approximation of a Platonic form, but each of us is a unique individual.[373] Both of these considerations importantly shape the meaning of the question 'how shall I live?' each time it is or could be asked. The Platonic cast of mind, which might ask 'how shall a human being live?', and for which the many particular individuals who ask 'how shall I live?' are only asking more or less confused versions of the one question, has become obsolete. The real question now is in every case 'how shall I, this unique individual in these particular circumstances, live?', and the general question 'how shall a human being live?' is the abstraction, dealing with the partial common content of the many real questions and for that reason always incomplete.

The general and, therefore, abstract and incomplete question is a matter of philosophy. The particular and, therefore, in each case the real question is a

---

[373]S.V. 15.

matter of practical wisdom, of prudence. Prudential deliberations will always take general considerations into account but take precedence in the end, when what is wanted is an answer which may be beyond the reach of philosophy. That is why Epicurus judged prudence to be more precious than philosophy.[374] This must, however, not be understood as a disparagement of philosophy. The general element in individual deliberation, which is the province of philosophy, is most important. But it is not exclusively the province of philosophy: both semi-articulate folk wisdom and religion have long had great influence here and still do. When Epicurus praises philosophy and the philosophical life he does not do so because he thinks that philosophy can answer every question and solve every problem, but because he thinks that philosophy can give an understanding of the nature of reality and generate ethical principles better than either folk wisdom or religion, and in particular, that his philosophy can do so better than other philosophies. But because philosophy only gives a general understanding and general principles of action, there always are issues in the lives of particular individuals beyond the reach of philosophy. That is why in Epicureanism we find principled philosophical doctrine side by side with what looks like mere advice and even shoulder-shrugging.

In the present chapter we must give an account of what an Epicurean life looks like, an account of the Epicurean idea of the good life. There is a common element that runs through all Epicurean lives simply in virtue of their being human lives. This common element is independent of individuating considerations such as political and economic situation, gender, state of health,

---

[374]Ep. Men. 132; a look at the lives of many accomplished philosophers today may make one sympathetic to this judgement.

character and so forth. The common element is the proper subject of philosophy which, so far as it deals with this common element, pretends to timeless wisdom. But the common element is an abstraction which never exists by itself but always as embedded in the life of a particular individual for whom philosophy is wisdom. Philosophy itself will, therefore, have an ahistorical perennial core from which it radiates out into a more or less variable, time and circumstance bound periphery. The core of the Epicurean idea of the good life, the core which it has merely in virtue of the humanity of the individual whose life it is, is the idea of pleasure. The next ring, which may still be considered part of the core because necessarily connected with pleasure rather than by accidental circumstance, is the idea of virtue. Pleasure and virtue (some virtues, though not all) constitute the matrix of the Epicurean idea of the good life. Next comes a layer which is already affected by circumstances of social setting and individual character. It is already more a matter of life-style than a matter of insight into the nature of the good in every human life and, therefore, more a matter of advice than philosophical doctrine. Here, with varying degrees of importance, belong the lesser virtues such as frugality and reclusiveness and cheerfulness, and matters of life-style such as marriage and involvement in public affairs. Let us first consider the principled philosophical core.

## The Pleasant Life

The good life is in the first place a life dedicated to pleasure, to katastematic pleasure rather than the kinetic pleasure of the fun seeker and bon vivant. Qua pleasure, kinetic pleasure is of the same nature as katastematic pleasure: a felt pre-deliberate natural approval, and as such it is the good, and takes precedence over all deliberate and conventional aims which must themselves be justified in terms of pleasure. But kinetic pleasure differs importantly from katastematic in that it is a non-sustainable intermittent approval of some object or event which may be more or less difficult to acquire. Katastematic pleasure, on the other hand, is the felt natural approval of an object which never has to be acquired, the constant object which is the condition for the possibility of there being any objects at all, and with the loss of which everything is lost. And the felt natural approval of this quasi-object, the individual self, is in its nature continuous, though it may be interrupted by katastematic pain (by boredom, despair, psychic turmoil, duress and so forth) which is an existential illness to be cured by philosophy[375] rather than something in the nature of being human.

Kinetic pleasure, because it involves the acquisition of an object of pleasure, is bound up with the possibility of pain in a way katastematic pleasure can never be. The enjoyment of kinetic pleasure may have painful consequences, for example, not only in the direct way in which too much food and drink may cause hangovers, indigestion or obesity and physical enfeeblement, but also indirectly through the claim of others on the object of pleasure. This claim may be institutionalized in law,[376] for example, in which case the kinetic pleasure will involve illegal activity with the attendant problem of punishment or its threat. Or the pursuit of kinetic pleasure may involve trouble because of the way society is organized, as seems to have been the case with the pursuit of a rich and varied sex

---

[375]Lucr. 3.1072. When Epicurus considers the fear of death not as the fear of a painful afterlife of divine punishment but as the fear of the utter absence of any future existence, he sees that this fear is without a proper object, i.e. that it is the katastematic pain of despair. The philosophical understanding that we have neither full control nor knowledge of the future can help to keep this despair at bay. Ep. Men. 127.

[376]Epicurus advises against sexual intercourse forbidden by law (D.L. 10.118), presumably adultery or incest and the like. But the same advice would, of course, apply to any pleasure involving illegal activity, if only because of the trouble involved in law breaking (e.g. K.D. 34, 35).

life. Epicurus points out that the price of such pursuit is too high because it will surely bring trouble of some kind, since it may involve breaking laws or customs, or cause grief to your neighbour if you choose to carry on your pursuit in his household, or cause health problems if you're not too particular about where and with whom you play, or deplete your bank account if you are particular.[377] Much the same could be said of any passion you insist on indulging, of course, and a person who is sentenced to a life of hard labour for the crime of an opulent life style, whether he enjoys it or not, was as sad a sight in Epicurus' day as now. One problem with opulence, of course, is its relativity. My opulence usually seems to be opulence only to someone worse off than I, whereas the opulence I crave is always slightly out of reach. In general, most kinetic pleasures will require a little more again and again in order to have the same effect.

The Epicurean reservations about the pursuit of kinetic pleasure generated by considerations of this kind may make Epicurus seem like a "a hedonist malgré lui" if we associate the notion of pleasure with kinetic pleasure in a way not characteristic of Epicurus.[378] These considerations are important, but there is another consideration more important yet. If the Epicurean reservation about the pursuit of kinetic pleasure were justified only by circumstances of law or custom or finances or the imprudence of overindulging and so forth, then Epicureans would in the end be nothing more than untalented Cyrenaics who might profit from lessons by a superbly accomplished fun seeker such as Aristippus the elder.

---

[377]S.V. 51.

[378]cf. Malte Hossenfelder, "Epicurus — hedonist malgré lui", in M. Schofield and G. Striker ed., The Norms of Nature, Cambridge University Press 1986. The judgement that Epicurus was "originally concerned not with pleasure but with inner peace" (p. 250) indicates an inadequate appreciation of the Epicurean notion of pleasure. It is important for an understanding of Epicurean ethics to see that it is not a grudging concession to hedonism.

But Epicurus sees a problem in the very nature of kinetic pleasure, not, to be sure, in its nature as pleasure, but in its kinetic nature. The most important problem with kinetic pleasure is that it can interfere with katastematic pleasure.

Kinetic pleasure, especially a regular and trouble-free round of kinetic pleasure, will distract and divert one from katastematic pleasure, and absorb one in its objects. The absorption in the objects of kinetic pleasure brings with it a distraction and diversion from oneself, one becomes eccentric, it is as though one's centre and selfhood had become dislocated into the trappings of a dissolute life. Kinetic pleasure can distract one not only from katastematic pleasure, but also from katastematic pain. When it does so distract one and begins to function as a cover for and diversion from katastematic pain, it tends to perform this function inadequately, and indeed to produce the very thing it is trying to cover up. The person becomes increasingly easily bored, requires greater excitement, more novelty, and may suffer from bouts of boredom, despair and a sense of general futility. The ancient world was as aware of this problem as the modern, especially among people who were not kept distracted by hardship and work, but had nothing better than kinetic pleasure to divert them.[379] For Epicurus, therefore, the good life, though dedicated to pleasure, cannot be a life dedicated to kinetic pleasure, for such a life is self-defeating.[380] To keep the pleasant life from becoming self-defeating is the important function of virtue in Epicurean philosophy.

---

[379]It is no accident that Lucretius illustrates boredom with a wealthy person (3.1053-75).

[380]Hegesias, the Cyrenaic philosopher who advocated suicide, recognized only kinetic pleasure and, so, probably failed to recognize the soul's disturbance as a pain of a different order from the disappointments of fortune. (D.L. 2.94).

# Virtue

The value of virtue, in Epicureanism, is instrumental, and only instrumental. "The virtues too are chosen because of pleasure, and not for their own sakes, just as medicine is chosen because of health."[381] Even moral beauty (to kalon), which was widely considered to be intrinsically valuable, had merely the instrumental value of any other virtue. Athenaeus reports Epicurus as saying that "beauty and virtue (to kalon kai tas aretas)" and the like are to be honoured if they give pleasure; but if they do not give pleasure, we must bid them farewell; and a little further on he gets more emphatic yet: "I spit on the beautiful and those who pointlessly respect it when it produces no pleasure."[382] Moral beauty holds a high place in the Epicurean hierarchy of virtues. In fact, as we shall see in a moment, it is one of the set of three virtues which Epicurus considers necessary for the pleasant life. Nevertheless it has no intrinsic value but is merely a means for producing pleasure. This may be difficult to accept if one insists on interpreting Epicurus in a small way. As long as one thinks that the Epicurean designation of virtue as a means to pleasure amounts to the view that a virtue is a sort of knack for getting kinetic pleasures, one will continue to misunderstand Epicurus. It is worth pointing out somewhere (and why not here?) that Epicurus was not a muddled Cyrenaic with a taste for Ionian physics.

Pride of place in the hierarchy of virtues is given to practical wisdom, to prudence (phronēsis). It holds a special place not only because it is the most important virtue, the greatest instrumental good, but also because it is the source

---

[381]D.L. 10.138; a possible exception is friendship. If we accept the manuscript reading of S.V. 23, we must accept that friendship was considered to be a virtue and that it had intrinsic value.

[382]Athenaeus, 12.546f = (Us. 70); Athenaeus, 12.547a = (Us. 512).

222

and principle of all the other virtues.[383] A virtue, for Epicurus, is a quality of character produced and justified by practical wisdom, consistent with and productive of the pleasant life. Prudence is the chief virtue because it purges the character of vices or bad habits,[384] those productive of pain and misery, and because it forms the character with virtues or good habits, those productive of pleasure and happiness. A virtue, then, is really a specialized form of practical wisdom.

Prudence, along with two specialized virtues, moral beauty and justice, are said by Epicurus to be necessary for the pleasant life.[385] What pleasure might prudence, moral beauty and justice be productive of? We have already seen in our previous chapter that justice is not a means to kinetic pleasure but to ataraxia, that is, to katastematic pleasure. Justice helps to produce the inner peace of ataraxia by removing the disturbing motives and emotions which trouble the souls of those who harm others, and by providing security from other parties to the contract which is the basis of justice, as well as from those whose job it is to apprehend and punish law breakers. The virtue of justice is a means to katastematic pleasure.

[383]Ep. Men. 132.

[384]S.V. 46.

[385]Ep. Men. 132; K.D. 5; both of these texts contain an apparent omission. These omissions were filled in by Stephanus (Ep. Men. 132) and Gassendi (K.D. 5) in the same way so as to make these virtues not only necessary but also sufficient for the pleasant life. It is hard to explain these two omissions. Bailey thinks that they are due to homoeoteleuton, but while that might be an acceptable explanation in the case of one text, it is improbable in the case of two widely separated texts. Also there is some difficulty in the idea that these three virtues are sufficient for the pleasant life without some qualification to indicate that what is meant is that they are ethically sufficient or that they are all the virtues you need, which might in any case be acceptable since prudence is the source of all other virtues such that to have prudence is to have all the others as well. But it cannot be meant that the possession of these three virtues is sufficient for the pleasant life without qualification, since presumably one could have these three virtues and still fear death, for example, or be troubled by any number of religious superstitions, which could be enough to sour anyone's life. Because of the textual and doctrinal difficulty of the claim to sufficiency, we shall here make nothing of it.

To kalon, literally 'the beautiful', "has far more than an aesthetic sense, being more or less the equivalent of our term 'goodness'."[386] This moral beauty and integrity produces an honest and upright life, one without skeletons in closets; it produces a nobility of character which inspires trust and confidence in others and a general smoothness of life and sentiment in oneself. This too has nothing to do with the production of kinetic pleasure. Moral beauty too is a virtue which is a means to katastematic pleasure.

And prudence is the master virtue. It produces the other necessary virtues, moral beauty and justice; it anticipates the consequences of kinetic pleasures and pains, and regulates their choice and avoidance;[387] and it produces the many other virtues which are not necessary but more or less important to the pleasant life. Prudence is a virtue which produces other necessary virtues that are a means to katastematic pleasure; other recommended virtues that are also a means to katastematic pleasure, as we shall see; and its involvement with kinetic pleasure and pain is with their regulation rather than their production. Prudence, far from being a knack for producing kinetic pleasure, is rather the practical wisdom of its regulation, not for the sake of its efficient maximization, but in order to keep it from interfering with the continuous enjoyment of katastematic pleasure. Kinetic pleasure needs to be regulated, not eliminated, for some of it is got in the satisfaction of natural and necessary desires which cannot be eliminated without eliminating life itself, and with that katastematic pleasure would be eliminated as well. Some kinetic pleasures are necessary for the very possibility of katastematic pleasure. The wise regulation of kinetic pleasures, both to make them intrinsically

---

[386]John M. Rist, Epicurus, Cambridge University Press, 1972, p. 124.

[387]Ep. Men. 129, 132.

more enjoyable and for the sake of sustaining katastematic pleasure, is the function of prudence.

Prudence also produces the recommended virtues. As we move from the necessary to the recommended virtues we leave the domain of principled philosophical doctrine which applies to all human beings always and everywhere, and enter the situation-bound domain of philosophical advice which depends on time, place, circumstance, temperament and so forth.

The most important of the recommended virtues is self-sufficiency (autarkeia), the lived expression of the conviction that every human being, naturally and prior to conventional distortion, is a unique individual, a whole rather than a part, an end in himself. Self-sufficiency, "a great good",[388] is a fundamental attitude with which to engage in daily life, a quality of character which produces two further important recommended virtues: frugality and freedom. Of these, the more important is freedom: "The greatest fruit of self-sufficiency is freedom."[389] When Epicurus writes about freedom he is not concerned about the political right to self-determination, or the abolition of slavery, or rebellion against oppressive governments and the like. At least nothing of what remains of his writings has that kind of political flavour. He is, rather, concerned with freedom as a virtue or quality of character on the one hand, and with freedom as an ontological fact about human beings on the other.

Epicurus believed that the ontological fact of human freedom is incompatible with a determinism according to which every event is necessarily brought about

---

[388]Ep. Men. 130.

[389]S.V. 77.

by antecedent causes, a determinism which operates in principle in the same way at every level in nature. His indeterminism, his denial of necessity, is not the claim that, while many events are determined by necessity, some, such as the occasional atomic swerve, are random accidents. This kind of variation from necessity to random accident and back again would be an utterly unintelligible state of affairs. Atoms are not determined by a necessity which randomly and at any moment could fail. Rather, his indeterminism is the claim that no event, from the simplest to the most complex, happens with necessity.[390] Both the regular motion and the swerve are equally natural ways for an atom to move, and both are equally unnecessary. Epicurus considered an atom's motion to be determined by antecedent causes such as its own weight and collisions with other atoms, but not sufficiently determined or necessitated by them. This doctrine of non-necessitated causation is the doctrine of the swerve.[391] At first, at the hypothetical stage of a world of atomic dispersion and uniform motion, the effect of this absence of necessity is simply the infrequent non-uniform motion of atoms. This does not mean that an atom is fully determined except at a time of swerving out of

---

[390]There is a lacuna at Ep. Men. 133, produced by careless copying rather than a mutilated text, which scholars tend to fill in with the claim that "some things happen by necessity." But this is a guess and a claim made nowhere else; it gives us the rather awkward reading: "some things happen by necessity ... since necessity is accountable to no one"; and Epicurus is doing ethics here rather than physics, and may well have had practical compulsion rather than physical necessity in mind when he wrote whatever it was that originally filled the lacuna. For these reasons I don't think that this supplement justifies a change in my interpretation.

[391]The swerve is mentioned in none of the extant writings of Epicurus, but the denial of necessity is. There is, however, no reason to doubt the report of the swerve given by Lucretius and Cicero. Walter G. Englert (Epicurus on the Swerve and Voluntary Action, Scholars Press, Atlanta, Georgia, 1987) argues that "randomness is an important feature of the swerve" (p. 26) based for the most part on Lucretius' repeated claim that the swerve occurs at "uncertain times and places" (e.g. 2.219-20). But Lucretius' claim need not be interpreted to mean that the swerve is a random feature of an otherwise necessary atomic motion. That claim is quite compatible with our view that atomic motion, whether regular or swerving, is equally unnecessary at all times. Lucretius' statements must be interpreted in light of Epicurus' rejection not only of necessity, but also of necessity tempered with random accident, (see below).

uniformity, when it is not determined at all. It means that an atom is always insufficiently determined such that it moves regularly most of the time but not always.

There had been atomists, probably Leucippus and Democritus, who tried to give an account of atomic motion and all the events of the natural world in terms of necessity alone. And there had also been atomists, perhaps later Democriteans contemporary with Epicurus, who added an element of randomness to the theory and tried to give such an account in terms of necessity and accident. Epicurus may have thought that Democritus had already introduced the random element of accident into his physics, for in his rejection of necessity, with or without accident, he refers to "the great man" and it is hard to think whom other than Democritus he might have meant.[392] In a Herculaneum manuscript[393] of part of one of his books On Nature, Epicurus writes:

> The first men to give a satisfactory account of causes ... turned a blind eye to themselves ... in order to hold necessity and accident responsible for everything. Indeed, the actual account promoting this view came to grief when it left the great man blind to the fact that in his actions he was clashing with his doctrine.

The doctrine which attempts to explain everything in terms of causal necessity, even when supplemented with an element of random accident, is unacceptable to Epicurus because it cannot account for human agency. If a bolt of lightning blasts a tree then we can quite properly say that the lightning was responsible for the destruction of the tree; and if a human being destroys a tree, then the human being is responsible for the tree's destruction. These, however, are very different kinds

---

[392]Unless it is an ironic reference to his Democritean teacher Nausiphanes. For the place see footnote 393.

[393]Most conveniently available now in Long and Sedley, The Hellenistic Philosophers, Cambridge University Press 1987, 20C, Vol. I, pp. 102-4, Vol. II, pp. 105-7.

of responsibility, which is brought out by our holding the human being, and not the lightning, responsible for the tree's destruction, by our attributing a kind of responsibility to a person which is subject to praise and blame, while it would be inappropriate, even silly, to treat a bolt of lightning in this way. This would be true whether the event of the lightning strike were understood as necessary, as random, or as some mixture of the two; for neither necessity, nor randomness, nor their mixture produce a responsibility appropriately praised or blamed. The difficulty Epicurus sees in the doctrine of necessity is that it may be able to account for the responsibility of the bolt of lightning, because it amounts to nothing more than the claim that the bolt of lightning was the cause of the tree's destruction, but that it cannot account for the responsibility of human agency. Democritus had failed to appreciate this and so was "blind to the fact that in his actions he was clashing with his doctrine." But Epicurus was fully aware of this clash, indeed he was probably the first philosopher fully to appreciate the problem for human freedom of deterministic physics,[394] and the work done on the problem by philosophers in subsequent centuries is little more than footnotes to his discussion. There is one set of human acts with which the doctrine clashes in a special way, namely the acts of holding the doctrine and arguing for it. What is special about this clash is that it not only shows the doctrine to be inadequate, as does the clash with other acts, but that it shows that "this sort of account is self-refuting", as Epicurus argues at some length and in some detail in the

---

[394]For a persuasive argument to this effect see Pamela Huby, "The First Discovery of the Freewill Problem", Philosophy 42 (1967).

manuscript from which we have just quoted.[395]

Epicurus' non-necessitarian view of the regularity of atomic motion cannot explain human responsibility either, of course, nor was it meant to. Unlike the necessetarian doctrine it is not meant to account for every event. It is, rather, meant to allow for human agency in a natural world, a world which opposes and promotes human agency in the many ways familiar to every human agent, without producing it as it produces the events of inanimate nature. And it is also meant to allow for the development of autonomous responsible selves from a world of atoms, selves which operate according to regularities distinct from and not reducible to the regularities of inanimate nature without being immaterial substances.[396] These new psychological regularities interact with the physical regularities of non-mental atomic motions. Since atoms are not fully determined they may behave in statistically variant ways among which the influence of a free mind selects, without the regularities of physics being violated or suspended, allowing free human agency.[397]

Free agency, of course, is not arbitrary agency. The deliberation and decision

---

[395]See also S.V. 40. For a detailed discussion see D. Sedley, "Epicurus' Refutation of Determinism", ΣΥΖΗΤΗΣΙΣ; Studi sull' epicureismo greco e latino offerti a Marcello Gigante, Naples 1983, pp. 11-51; an abbreviated version of this argument is given in Long and Sedley, The Hellenistic Philosophers, Cambridge University Press 1987, Vol. I, pp. 107-112.

[396]Based on a difficult and intriguing account of the development of human psychological autonomy in the Herculaneum manuscript we have quoted, Long and Sedley argue very plausibly that Epicurus thought of minds as sets of properties of atomic complexes not reducible to atomic motions, nor mere epiphenomena of such motions, but non-physical properties which bring entirely new causal laws into operation and which are best understood on the modern notion of Emergence. Long and Sedley, The Hellenistic Philosophers, Cambridge University Press 1987, Vol. I, p. 110.

[397]For an argument that Epicurus is committed to downward causation of this kind, see D. Sedley, "Epicurean Anti-Reductionism" in Jonathan Barnes and Mario Mignucci ed., Matter and Metaphysics, Bibliopolis 1988, esp. pp. 318 ff.

which produces acts are determined without necessity by the various considerations relevant to the deliberation as well as by our character. The character is not an invariant given from the start but produced from "seeds" by its own activity[398] and not by alien regularities such as the laws of biology or physics, and it is always subject to change. The human character is self-made from pre-disposing "seeds", always subject to change, such that at every moment we are responsible for our own characters and the acts to which it disposes us. This responsibility, which is subject to praise and blame and distinct from the kind of responsibility attributed to the causes of natural events, is a property human agents have in virtue of the ontological property of freedom, and it is crucial to the notion of freedom as a virtue or quality of character, of freedom so far as it is a "fruit of self-sufficiency."

To be free, to have freedom as a quality of character, is to accept responsibility for your acts and your life. It is making no excuses and not living with necessity.[399] It is a mentality quite distinct from the Stoic acceptance of necessity, which accepts going with the flow as the highest wisdom, but rather a stance of being the author of your own life in a contingent world.[400] It is living without compulsion and the constant need to do this and that, which is why so far as it is, as a virtue, a means to pleasure, it is a means to aponia. The virtue of freedom too is not a means to kinetic pleasure but to katastematic pleasure. And because freedom is the virtue of living without compulsion and the urgency to do and

[398]See Long and Sedley, op. cit., 20C (1), p. 102.

[399]S.V. 9.

[400]Ep. Men. 134; Porphyry to Marcella 30.

achieve, freedom requires frugality.[401]

Epicurus frequently points out[402] that wealth in the ordinary sense of prosperity, of lots of money and property and a luxurious life, is not the great good most people take it to be, but rather is a trap to be avoided by those who seek the good life with philosophical insight. There is, he thinks, another conception of wealth[403] which by the standard of the ordinary conception is poverty, but by the natural standard of the philosopher is plenty and natural wealth rather than the deprivation and hardship of real poverty. To understand the difference and put it into practice we need the virtue of frugality.

Epicurus must have known people who wore themselves out in the single minded pursuit of wealth, for he thought that work of this kind was fit only for sub-human animals and that human beings, even if they are made wealthy, are also made miserable by such servitude to money.[404] Wealth, in the experience of Epicurus, simply did not tend to make people happy,[405] because its possession is quite compatible with the katastematic pain of a disturbed soul and a life devoid of any kinetic joy worth having. Even the greatest wealth, Epicurus writes in S.V. 81, does not calm the disturbed soul or produced any joy worth considering (<u>axiologan charan</u>). The good life is not a consumer good with a price tag.

---

[401]S.V. 67.

[402]S.V. 53; S.V. 81; Gnomolog. Paris. 1168 f 115 etc. = Us. 488, Bailey fr. 76; Porphyry to Marcella 29 = Us. 207, Bailey fr. 48, Inwood and Gerson A45, and Us. 480, Bailey fr. 73, Inwood and Gerson A115; Plutarch, <u>De aud. poet.</u> 37a = Us. 548, Bailey fr. 85, Inwood and Gerson A124.

[403]K.D. 15; S.V. 25; S.V. 68; Stobaeus Anthology 3.17.23 = Us. 135, Bailey fr 28, Inwood and Gerson A36; Porphyry to Marcella 27 = Us. 202, Bailey fr. 45, Inwood and Gerson A93.

[404]Porphyry to Marcella 29 = Us. 480, Bailey fr. 73, Inwood and Gerson A115.

[405]Plutarch, <u>De aud. poet.</u> 37a.

Epicurus' rejection of wealth did not take the form of advocating poverty as it did with the Cynics. It is possible that Epicurus had witnessed the debilitating effects of real poverty, or even experienced them himself in his youth on Samos. When he does say positive things about poverty he does not have in mind the hardship of backbreaking work with not enough to eat, but rather a simple and frugal life which seems like poverty only to the rich and ambitious. Rather than advocate poverty he speaks about a different kind of wealth, a condition which by natural standards and philosophical reflection can be called wealth, though to conventional perception it appears rather as poverty. The distinction between wealth in the conventional sense and wealth in the philosophical sense is clearly drawn in K.D. 15. Wealth in the conventional sense is based on groundless opinions, mere conventional values, and has no limit either in itself or in the work that may be demanded in its pursuit. Wealth in the philosophical sense, on the other hand, has its basis in nature, in the natural needs of the human being for whose sake wealth exists, and it is limited and usually easy to acquire. What to convention appears as poverty will be seen by philosophical reflection, using the standard of the natural goal of human beings, to be instead wealth. And conventional wealth, if limits are not set for it, is seen to be poverty because it requires the same endless toil to which real poverty condemns people.[406]

To be wealthy, by the natural standard of philosophy, is to have all you need, to have enough. Self-sufficiency in respect of the means for satisfying one's needs is the virtue of frugality, and frugality is being satisfied with having all you need and understanding that it is enough. It is important to have this virtue because if having only enough seems too little to you and you are dissatisfied with it, then

---

[406]S.V. 25.

you will always be dissatisfied, for "nothing is enough to someone for whom enough is [too] little"[407] and "nothing satisfies the person who is not satisfied with little."[408] There is nothing wrong in itself with occasionally having more than you need, with for example satisfying your hunger with luxurious food rather than plain fare; but there is something wrong with missing fancy food when you can't have it, or with having it so regularly that it seems ordinary and plain fare becomes unacceptable. The Epicurean ideal is to be perfectly content with plain nutritious food, never to miss luxurious food, but to be able to enjoy it as a rare treat and enjoy it more than the person who has it regularly. This ideal of self-sufficient frugality is described in the Letter to Menoeceus.[409]

Epicureans are not frugal for the sake of the pleasure of eating barley cakes and water so much as for the sake of the contentment of finding it enough, of keeping the disruption of wanting and having to work for more and ever more out of life. The frugal person is not discontent with having little, does not envy[410] people who have more, has no need for things for which he must work in competitive struggle with others,[411] but can pay more attention to life than to supporting life, as can the gods. Self-sufficiency and freedom and frugality, as virtues, are all a means to katastematic pleasure rather than kinetic.

It is a matter of prudent judgment, and may vary with circumstances, just what

---

[407]S.V. 68.

[408]Aelian Miscellaneous Histories 4.13 = Us. 473, Bailey fr. 69, Inwood and Gerson A111.

[409]130-32; cf. [Epicurus] said that he was ready to rival Zeus for happiness, as long as he had a barley cake and some water. (Aelian Miscellaneous Histories 4.13 = Us. 602, Inwood and Gerson A125).

[410]S.V. 53.

[411]K.D. 21.

is enough. The point of frugality is not to try to survive on as little as possible. Frugality too has a limit and a right proportion, and it is as bad to go wrong on the side of too little as on the side of too much.[412] A certain generosity, the ability to give rather than to receive,[413] is among the graces of life according to Epicurus, and he disapproved of stinginess.[414] The Epicureans were not a mendicant philosophical order.[415] They did work for a living if they had to, and the accomplished Epicurean philosopher would do so by giving philosophical instruction.[416] The poverty of Epicureans is a frugal life style based on understanding what is enough and not wanting any more.

## General Advice

There is a style to an Epicurean life which cannot be derived from philosophical principles with any logical rigour, but is at best recommended by them, subject to other considerations such as individual temperament and circumstances. One expression for this general style is the phrase lathe biōsas, which we owe to Plutarch[417] who was indignant enough about it to devote a special essay to it. This phrase is usually translated "live hidden" or "live unknown", but its sense is less one of hiding in obscurity than of keeping a low profile. There are good prudential reasons for withdrawing into the privacy of a quiet life since fame is

---

[412]S.V. 63. The text of the first few words is a matter of disagreement (see Bailey p. 386 and Long and Sedley Vol. 2, p. 120) but there is agreement on the point of the aphorism.

[413]S.V. 44.

[414]S.V. 43.

[415]D.L. 10.119.

[416]D.L. 10.121.

[417]De lat. viv. (ei katos eiretai to lathe biōsas) 1128 ff; Us. 551, Bailey fr. 86.

234

not intrinsically desirable and brings with it the vulnerability of conspicuousness which no Epicurean would recommend. It is in the name of security that Epicureans recommend private life over public, and in the name of freedom they warn against the merry-go-round of affairs and politics.[418] An Epicurean will not try to become a good public speaker and make moving speeches on public occasions,[419] nor will he try to become a crowd pleasing philosophical orator,[420] though he is not in principle against public lectures and will give one if asked.[421] Nor is an Epicurean in principle against taking part in public life. He will do his part in the administration of justice. He will take an active part in the judicial system when called to jury duty,[422] for example, or serve a monarch[423] if circumstances demand it. But in general, and where possible, he will cultivate the private sphere over the public and prefer the country to the town[424], and gardens to market places.

All of this is a matter of prudence, with a great deal of leeway to accommodate circumstances and individual temperament and preference. Epicureanism is a philosophical core with a certain style, not a uniform.

•

---

[418]K.D. 7, K.D. 14, S.V. 58, D.L. 10.119.

[419]D.L. 10.118, 10.120a; how could Cicero be expected to forgive this distain for oratory?

[420]D.L. 10.121b; this could be a reference to Theophrastus who drew about two thousand auditors to his lectures (D.L. 5.37).

[421]D.L. 10.121b.

[422]D.L. 10.120a.

[423]D.L. 10.121b.

[424]D.L. 10.120a.

235

Epicurus gives similar advice with regard to sex.[425] That the target is extra-marital sex is made pretty clear by S.V. 51, and the kind of person to whom the advice is given seems to be the young Epicurean novice, who feels not only the call to philosophy but also "the movement of his flesh." The advice, briefly, is: "act upon your inclination in any way you like." as long as you don't invite trouble by doing so. The possible troubles indicated by Epicurus,[426] which a young man intent on erotic diversion may find it difficult to avoid altogether, do not, however, apply to the conjugal couch. But whether or not an Epicurean should marry is another problematical question. The manuscript reading at D.L. 10.119 clearly states that the accomplished Epicurean will marry and have children, but this reading has been questioned and emended.[427] C.W. Chilton, in the article just cited, argues in favour of emending the manuscript reading to the opposite of what it says, that is, to the denial that the wise man will marry, on the grounds that marriage is inconsistent with Epicurus' view on happiness and sex, and also that later writers like Epictetus, Seneca, and Clement of Alexandria make Epicurus an opponent of marriage and the family. It is quite unclear, however, that marriage and children will in every case compromise the Epicurean's ataraxia and autarkeia, as Chilton thinks, and that the hostages to fortune mentioned in S.V. 47 can reasonably be thought to refer to one's children. And it really is a misunderstanding of S.V. 51 to call it "a bitter attack upon sex." The later writers mentioned by Chilton give opinions without evidence and may well be accounted

[425]D.L. 10.118; S.V. 51; Us. 62, Bailey fr. 8.

[426]Or Metrodorus, cf. A. Vogliano, "Frammento di un nuovo, gnomologium epicureum'", Studi Italiani di Filologia Classica 13 (1936) pp. 268-81.

[427]For a discussion of the textual question see C.W. Chilton, "Did Epicurus approve of Marriage? A Study of Diogenes Laertius X, 119", Phronesis, 5 (1960), pp. 71-74.

for by Epicurus having got the reputation for being against marriage and children because he refused to give them unqualified approval. That the question is problematical is indicated by Diogenes Laertius' report that Epicurus discussed the matter in his Puzzles, a book devoted to problematical issues. The reasons given by Chilton are simply not persuasive and his suggestion to reject the manuscript reading has rightly not been accepted by recent translators like Long and Sedley and Inwood and Gerson. The recommendation given in the manuscript is qualified in any case: "he will marry [only] when it is indicated by the circumstances of his life at a given time."[428] The issue of marriage is not decided by philosophical principles, but is a matter for prudence and circumstances. Metrodous married (we think) and had children (we know[429]), but Epicurus abstained.

Economic circumstances varied as widely in Epicurus' day as they do now. Some were wealthy enough not to have to work for a living. Such people might still have had problems,[430] but work was not one of them. Ordinary people, however, must work to earn a living, and this too is a topic for advice in Epicurean philosophy.

Epicurus' own work was philosophy which, initially, is an occupation of instrumental value,[431] but with progress and understanding comes to have

---

[428]D.L. 10.119. The indication at 10.118 that the wise man will not fall in love is puzzling in conjunction with the recommendation of marriage. But this report is probably not about loveless marriage but about the disinclination of the wise man to have amorous affairs before and during marriage.

[429]Us. 117, Bailey fr. 36; D.L. 10.21; 10.23.

[430]Lucr. 2.34-6; Porphyry to Marcella 29 = Us. 207, Bailey fr. 48.

[431]K.D. 11.

intrinsic value as well.[432] In that respect work, at least philosophical work, shows the same progression as friendship. It begins for the sake of utility, but can come to be valued for its own sake. This, for an Epicurean, must be the proper relation to work. It must be done freely, without compulsion and stress, because it must be compatible with <u>aponia</u>. It cannot, therefore, be the obedient test of endurance exemplified by the life of Hercules, nor can it be the occupation worthy of a beast of which Porphyry writes to his wife,[433] nor the life-long labour of procuring the means to life, forgetful of life itself, and unmindful of oneself to the point of not living in the awareness of one's own mortality noted by the melancholy Metrodorus.[434] Rather, work should be like the philosophy in which Epicurus found his peace,[435] or the philosophical verse-making which Lucretius found such "delightful toil."[436] It should be possible to combine the intrinsic value of work with its instrumental value of earning a living. At least, there is no indication that when an Epicurean has to earn a living by giving philosophical instruction[437] that philosophy will for that reason cease to be enjoyable. And also there is no reason to suppose that what is true of philosophy and poetry might not also be true of many other kinds of work, and that when work becomes a routine

---

[432]S.V. 27. This aphorism contrasts philosophy with other pursuits, the contrast being that in philosophy the very activity is enjoyable while other pursuits are difficult and not rewarding until the end. This should be understood rather as a piece of propaganda for philosophy than a reasoned assessment of the nature of every other occupation as irredeemably instrumental for surely that is not true. We shall mention Lucretius' verse-making as an exception in a moment, and there surely are many other exceptions as well, depending on circumstances, temperament, and other such considerations.

[433]Porphyry to Marcella 28 = Us. 28.

[434]S.V. 30; S.V. 10.

[435]Ep. Hdt. 37.

[436]Lucr. 2.730, 3.419.

[437]D.L. 10.121b.

of chores rather than fulfilling activity, one might not nevertheless do it cheerfully[438] and compatibly with katastematic pleasure. Being able to sustain katastematic pleasure through grey times, even times of great misfortune, was something an Epicurean learned to do. The general advice with regard to work, then, is to make it enjoyable, to make it supply the necessary means to life, and to do it cheerfully. But an Epicurean would certainly avoid the compulsive approach of competitive ambition, in philosophy or anything else.[439]

## The Good Life

Human life, in each case, is lived by a particular human being. It is the human individual who is the subject of pain and misery or pleasure and happiness, and it is the individual who pursues and enjoys, when he does, the good life. Epicureans understand themselves as individuals and aim at being fully individual, at being self-complete, a whole rather than a part, an end rather than a means; and the good life for such an individual is above all to be alive with the pleasure of being, rather than the pleasures of having and consuming. This must not be construed in any narrowly selfish or exclusively egoistic way, but as being fully compatible with, indeed augmented by, the capacity to see others as such individuals as well and to value them for themselves in bonds of friendship.

The cultivation of the pleasure of being, of katastematic pleasure, requires in the first place the removal of mental disturbance and physical toil and compulsion. Mental disturbance, tarachē, can of course have many causes, but

---

[438]S.V. 41.

[439]S.V. 45; K.D. 21; Lucr. 2.10-13.

Epicurus treats the fear of gods, of death, and of other human beings as the most prominent and, therefore, as important targets for philosophy. Philosophy provides an understanding of the indifference of the gods and of the causes of certain natural phenomena such as thunderstorms, earthquakes and the like which may be thought to be divine manifestations, and of nature as a process devoid of divine intention. In consequence of this understanding fear and disturbance in face of the gods and nature is lost. Philosophy, both theoretical and therapeutic, also provides an understanding and appropriate attitude to human mortality, enabling the accomplished Epicurean to live in face of his own death without terror on the one hand, or the dispersion of his individuality in work and business, forgetful of his mortality,[440] on the other. Security from other human beings, and with it the removal of another major source of fear and disturbance, is achieved for the most part by the institution of laws in the community and the virtue of justice in the individual. The virtue of justice prevents an Epicurean from harming another human being, whether stranger or friend, for the sake of his own tranquility, because to harm someone involves disturbing motives and feelings. This refusal to harm another is quite distinct from considerations of legality, since an accomplished Epicurean needs the law not to prevent his doing harm but to prevent harm being done to him.[441] Because the disturbance accompanies the act of harming whether or not there is a contract of justice, an Epicurean would not harm another human being from another society not bound by the law of his own community, nor would he harm an animal incapable of making a contract.

Because killing an animal, even for food, is a violent act not in keeping with

---

[440]S.V. 30.

[441]Stobaeus 4.1.143 = Us. 530, Inwood and Gerson A121.

tranquility of soul, Epicureans were vegetarians.[442] They had other reasons for vegetarianism as well, such as our being quite capable of living well without eating animals and meat being an impediment to health rather than good for you. But the moral reason was that eating animals "involves a violent gratification" rather than the kind of reason a Pythagorean might have had, based on a belief in reincarnation, which Epicureans rejected.[443]

Within a secure human community friendship becomes possible as the very crown of human relations, much valued and earnestly cultivated by Epicureans. Friendship adds the further security that not only will a friend not harm you, but he will help you if ever you need help.

The removal of physical hardship and compulsion required the cultivation of the virtues of freedom and frugality. If you understand that you don't need luxury and superabundance to be wealthy, but that real wealth is to have all you need, to have enough, and that this is normally easy to come by,[444] then you have a chance to introduce into your life the kind of stressless leisure, the divine idleness of the self-complete person which Epicureans prized highly and called aponia.

To cultivate the pleasure of being, the combination of ataraxia and aponia, required in the second place the control of the pleasures of having and consuming, that is, the control of kinetic pleasures; and this required above all the right understanding of desires and their prudent management. This management involves in the first place asking of every desire what the consequences of

---

[442]Porphyry, de abst. 1.51.6 = Us. 464, Long and Sedley 21 J (1).

[443]Lucr. 3.670-740.

[444]Stobaeus 3.17.22 = Us. 469.

satisfying and not satisfying it are,[445] since those consequences may be pleasurable or painful and that is relevant to deciding whether or not to satisfy the desire. This inquiry into desires and the consequences of satisfying or not satisfying them is greatly facilitated by a theoretical understanding of the classification of desires because there is a set of desires which are necessary and we must arrange our lives so as to guarantee their satisfaction. Among the unnecessary desires some are natural, such as the desire for sex or perhaps even the desire for immortality; and some are only conventional, such as the desire for reputation. Such desires an Epicurean will have to learn to manage in a variety of ways depending on circumstances and always with an eye to the maintenance of katastematic pleasure. With the desire for sex, for example, it is mostly a matter of avoiding painful consequences which, outside of marriage or perhaps the happy arrangement of a group of friends, will be nearly impossible;[446] and with the desire for immortality it is a matter of getting rid of the desire;[447] and with the desire for reputation it is mostly a matter of avoiding a bad reputation.[448]

Necessary desires are all natural and they come in a variety of kinds as well. In the Letter to Menoeceus Epicurus divides necessary desires into those necessary for happiness (eudaimonian), those necessary for the untroubledness (aochlēsian) of the body, and those necessary for life itself. The last of these is fairly straightforward, referring surely to our need for food and air and shelter. The others are less easy to understand, and Epicurus does not elaborate anywhere else,

---

[445]S.V. 71.

[446]S.V. 51.

[447]See Chapter 3.

[448]D.L. 10.120a.

but plausible examples come to mind without difficulty. Epicurus is pretty clear about our need for philosophy and that a consequence of philosophy is happiness.[449] The desire for philosophy, when we are lucky enough to have it, would therefore be a plausible example of a desire necessary for happiness. Seneca[450] reports Epicurus as holding that the need for a friend is compatible with self-sufficiency, Cicero reports that "we rejoice at our friends' joys just as much as at our own, and grieve just as much for their anguish. That is why a wise man will have the same feeling for his friend as for himself and will undertake the same labours for the sake of a friend's pleasure as he would undertake for his own."[451] Some of this is echoed in S.V. 56 and S.V. 66. The desire for a friend and for the friend's pleasure is, therefore, another plausible example of a desire necessary for happiness. And plausible examples of desires necessary for the untroubledness of the body might by the desire for security against attack, the desire for law and order in the community, and the desire for the appropriate leisure to devote oneself to life rather than endure the hardship of acquiring the means to life.

The third and final thing required for the cultivation of the pleasure of being, besides the removal of mental and physical trouble and the control of kinetic pleasure, is the prudent management of life in the circumstances in which you find yourself. This prudent management involves keeping things simple, cultivating enlightened leisure, keeping a low profile, not rushing into marriage,

---

[449]e.g. Ep. Men. 122, S.V. 74.

[450]Seneca, Letters on Ethics 9.1 = Us. 174, Inwood and Gerson A39. Even if only for the reasons given at 9.8 = Us. 175, Inwood and Gerson A40. But there surely is more to it than that.

[451]N.D. 1.67-8.

staying away from politics, curbing the desire for prominence and the ambition to have more than you really need.

An Epicurean good life is a life of pleasure taken in mere existence for its own sake, a pleasure which is the very opposite of boredom and despair, the very opposite of a fearful, troubled life of toil and duress. It is a simple life lived by a self-complete individual in friendship with other such individuals. And it is a mortal life lived in the face of death, which removes it from the everyday temptation to pettiness and greed. It is life lived in a kind of garden oasis in a world which is a brute fact, a spiritual desert without a trace of divine intent.

# Chapter Nine

# Conclusion

In the foregoing chapters we have attempted to give a reasoned account of Epicurean ethics based on the best evidence still available to us. As indicated in the Introduction, however, our purpose is not only to ascertain the facts about and secure an interpretation of an ancient philosopher. Our intention all along had been to ask whether Epicureanism could still present a genuine philosophical possibility today, or whether we have outgrown Epicurus in all significant respects, and whether we must therefore treat him as a more or less interesting museum piece. Many, probably most, ancient philosophies are such museum pieces. There is still much that a philosopher can find interesting, insightful, even instructive in such cases, but it never adds up to the whole world view and self-understanding to which such a philosophy pretended. Take Stoicism, for example. There is much that is still interesting and insightful in Stoicism, and we can still study Stoicism with profit and pleasure, but I do not believe that we could today be Stoics. The thesis of divine providence is fundamental to Stoic ethics and its removal would undo it entirely. But we can no longer live as though in a divinely providential universe if once we have resolved to live by philosophy, because our scientific conscience would make of any such attempt a mere game, and to live as a Stoic would today amount to little more than a piece of theatre for a philosopher.

There is no clash between Epicurean physics and our scientific conscience. Epicurus is the most thoroughly modern philosopher among the ancient Greeks, the difference is one of detail and sophistication, not principle. Our scientific conception of the natural world is precisely the spiritual desert of Epicurus, and his question whether and how a human being could live in such a desert without what to philosophy seem illusions, is the most modern of all questions (even if not the most fashionable now). The question which animated Epicurus' philosophy is also ours, the root question: how can I live and be mortal in a world which is as our best science makes it out to be, and what, if anything, is most fundamentally good in such a world?

The Epicurean answer, that the very pinnacle of human possibilities is a brief life of pleasure, seems initially as deeply disappointing today as it did twenty-three centuries ago. We're disappointed with life's brevity because, like the ancient Greeks, we have a wish for immortality, and the intervening centuries have seen the flight of all other religions in the western world before the Christian promise of eternal life. The idea of immortality is as familiar to us as to Epicurus' contemporaries, the hope of it as ardent and widespread, and the disappointment at the prospect of its loss as keen. And the intervening centuries have been no less dominated by the spirit of seriousness, of duty and service and self-sacrifice to someone or something, even if only the common good, to make the idea of pleasure's being the highest good counter-intuitive and disappointing.

An important consideration to bear in mind if we're going to criticize Epicureanism with respect to its present possibility is that it has a philosophical core and a periphery which is variable in response to circumstances. The crucial question must be whether the core, the mortal life of katastematic pleasure, can stand up to criticism; but it is peripheral matters which one might assume would be most affected by moving from Epicurus' Greece to the industrialized world of the closing years of the second millennium. The questions which most readily come to mind in an attempt to relocate Epicureanism into today's world are in any case peripheral ones. Could, for example, a competitive capitalist economy survive a wholesale adoption of Epicurean frugality, lack of ambition, and non-competitiveness? Could a democratic political system remain viable with Epicurean non-political attitudes and unconcern about public affairs, or would it not soon turn into a power monopoly of the recalcitrant few? And would not an Epicurean country with its probable lack of interest in military matters soon fall prey to more aggressive neighbors?

An Epicurean might, of course, feel uncomfortable with such questions because they are formulated in a way so alien to Epicureanism. An Epicurean might point out that the question is in each case a question asked by an individual human being and that the appropriate question is: Is Epicureanism a viable possibility for me? The peripheral questions we have just mentioned might then be captured by asking: If I live as an Epicurean, will I undermine our economic and political system? The answer to that question is obviously no. Perhaps that is too easy. We might want to insist: what if all, or a great many of us, were to live as Epicureans? Well, if enough were to do so to have an impact on the country's economic productivity, then there would also be enough not to care about this productivity as much as people used to. And dictators and power elites usually take over countries at times of high and widespread political involvement rather than during the sort of low level politics one might expect in an Epicurean community; and self-defense is a matter for prudent deliberation as much for Epicureans as for anyone else. Such issues are in any event very hypothetical, and practical solutions would depend on prudent consideration of circumstances as they arose.

Even on this hypothetical level, however, something could be said in favour of a country of Epicureans. There is something very attractive about a society in which people live in peace and friendship, content to have enough, a society in which the government could think of abolishing jobs rather than creating them, because so much of the old productivity is seen to have been an appalling waste of human energy. Don't we human beings have better things to do than to live as consumers of goods we spend our lives producing?

But these are millennial considerations fine for an idle moment, not the real business of philosophers. At least, philosophers have always been a lot less effective at the reorganization of society than is sometimes supposed. Besides, can one really suppose that a society of Epicureans, were it to become a reality, would reflect Epicurean principles any more than Christian societies have reflected Christian principles? It was, after all, societies of Christians which produced competitive economics, consumerism as a way of life, world wars, nuclear weapons, and so on. What reason is there to think that a society of people claiming to shape their lives on philosophical principles would reflect those principles any more than a society claiming religious principles? Epicurus had a mild distain for "the many" and perhaps he was right. The many may be no more capable of living by philosophy than by religion.

Philosophy, certainly philosophy as it was conceived by the philosophers of the Hellenistic period in general and Epicurus in particular, that is, philosophy conceived as the pursuit of wisdom to live by, is in each case a solitary affair based on general timeless principles. This is the home ground of Epicureanism where we must meet it critically. We shall first look at the philosophical core and then go on to peripheral matters of interest.

## The Core

Reservations about hedonism, in Epicurus' time as much as today, tend to be reservations about the life devoted to kinetic pleasure, and these reservations are based on two grounds: first, the pursuit of kinetic pleasure is not worth it, and second, this pursuit distracts from what is really important. It should be clear by now that Epicurus, even though he was a hedonist, shared those reservations, and shared them precisely for the usual reasons.

The pursuit of kinetic pleasure is the pursuit of the objects of kinetic pleasure, and this pursuit is full of trouble for a variety of reasons. The first is that the objects of kinetic pleasure have to be acquired, they cost money and money is labour, either your own or another's. A life of labour, however, is not worthy of a human being in Epicurus' estimation, nor in the estimation of other hedonists, the Cyrenaics, for example. To engage the labour of others in your pursuit of the objects of kinetic pleasure tends to producing a division in society of a class of workers and a class of enjoyers, which is a state of affairs no Epicurean could condone. Further, a truly successful life of kinetic hedonism is very difficult to achieve because it generates new difficulties in mental and physical dissipation, requires more and more to have the same effect and makes one increasingly sensitive to the variety of pains which seem to fall into even the most protected of human lives. Hegesias,[452] for example, thought that the truly successful life of kinetic hedonism was so difficult to achieve as to be an ideal ever out of reach

---

[452]D.L. 2.93-6.

rather than a practical possibility and he thought the whole struggle not be be worth the effort. But even where such a life is successful by the standards of kinetic hedonism, it undermines the human spirit in subtle ways which shows from time to time in eruptions of boredom, a general sense of futility or even full-blown existential despair. Epicurus understood this, and realized that the final threat of kinetic pleasure is that it distracts from what is really important.

That the pursuit of kinetic pleasure distracts from what is really important is, of course, not a new idea with Epicurus. What is new with Epicurus is that the really important thing from which the pursuit of kinetic pleasure distracts is not the heroic life of steadfast labour in the service of something other than yourself, whether the common good or the gods, but pleasure itself, katastematic pleasure. And this is the core of Epicureanism at which responsible criticism must be directed, for criticism of kinetic hedonism simply fails to touch Epicureanism properly understood.

None of the reservations about kinetic hedonism take hold when aimed at katastematic hedonism. The quasi-object of katastematic pleasure cannot be acquired, for its possession is the condition for the possibility of acquiring any object, and it cannot be reacquired once it is lost, for with its loss everything is lost. The pursuit of katastematic pleasure is not the pursuit of the object of katastematic pleasure, nor does it therefore suffer from any trouble associated with the pursuit of objects.

Katastematic pleasure, like kinetic pleasure, is in its nature a positive evaluation but, unlike kinetic pleasure, it is not an evaluation of some object or other, rather it is a self-evaluation. Katastematic pleasure is continuous pleasure taken in the continuous object by that object: it is in its nature a positive self-evaluation. In the experience of katastematic pleasure life itself, the existence of the self, is seen to be good. This evaluation is not simply a piece of information, a perceptual or cognitive item of which I am informed in the experience of katastematic pleasure. It is not simply the insight that some object matches some standard of goodness, for it is an experience which is as primordially evaluative as it is cognitive, or, to put it into more Epicurean language, it is an evaluation which is felt directly, not just known about. Pleasure, all pleasure, is self-evidently good. The pursuit of the object of pleasure may sometimes be seen to be bad in the Epicurean prudent deliberation on courses of action, which is why kinetic pleasure is always qualifiedly good, that is, a good to be chosen only if I have no reason to avoid it, which well I may. No such qualification applies to katastematic pleasure, for there is no pursuit of the object of katastematic pleasure.

There is, however, another reason why kinetic pleasure is a qualified good, a reason having to do not with the pursuit of the object of kinetic pleasure, but with the consequences of enjoying the object, of taking pleasure in the object. Obvious examples are the hangover after too much drink, the terrifying dark patch on the x-ray after too much smoking, any of the difficulties of imprudent sex or playing tennis instead of obeying a subpoena. Could katastematic pleasure have undesirable consequences?

With katastematic pleasure, because it is continuous pleasure, there isn't the post-enjoyment period there is with kinetic pleasure and, therefore, not a time after the pleasure which might be different in consequence of having enjoyed the pleasure. If there are any consequences of katastematic pleasure they would have to be contemporaneous. For example, there might be consequences of omission such that enjoying katastematic pleasure might prevent your doing something else, perhaps a moral duty which is incompatible with sustaining the unruffled tranquility of <u>ataraxia</u>. Suppose, for example, that an accomplished Epicurean has married. Might his quest for uninterrupted tranquility cause him to neglect his family, to fail as a husband and father? No doubt family life has its own ups and downs, spouses and children are not invariable sources of steady joy, and there may be times when providing for a family demands effort and hard work. Epicurus' own family had difficulty making ends meet while they were settlers on Samos. Nothing of what is left of Epicurus' writings speaks directly to this issue, but some things are left which are relevant to it. An Epicurean will undergo trouble on behalf of a friend if necessary and demonstrate loyalty and absolute reliability in relation to his friends. It is not difficult to suppose that a similar attitude to spouse and children would be normal in an Epicurean life. Epicurus had no children of his own, but he showed an interest in the welfare of the children of Metrodorus who had pre-deceased him. In his last letter to Idomeneus[453] he asks him to take good care of the children of Metrodorus after his death. Epicureanism is meant for the real world where pain and trouble cannot be entirely avoided by anyone, and the accomplished Epicurean has learned to sustain his katastematic pleasure through troubled times. There is no reason to suppose that an Epicurean, who does not take on the obligations of family life lightly, will ever neglect them because he is an Epicurean, though he may because he is human like the rest of us.

Similarly there is no reason to think that an Epicurean will neglect his work because he is an Epicurean. He may well reject certain kinds of work and show much less drive to succeed and ambition to excel because he is an Epicurean, but

---

[453]D.L. 10.22.

what work he does he will do cheerfully and well.[454]

Is it possible that an Epicurean, aglow with the pleasure of finding himself and his life good, will become rather complacent about himself and neglect self-improvement to his own detriment? It seems at least a shame, for example, if a talent is left uncultivated because its cultivation is felt to be too troublesome. Here we must be careful. Surely there is no joy in children driven to years of practicing the piano, only to give it up when finally they are old enough to assert themselves, even if initially they showed some promise. It may be impossible to tell in many cases whether we are dealing with a talent whose cultivation will bring joy and which needs encouragement, or whether we are dealing with a certain facility which produces progress but no joy. This is a matter for prudence unalloyed by false ambition, and neither Epicureanism nor any other philosophy can make the distinction easy to make. One can infer from Epicureanism that the only justification for developing an apparent talent is the pleasure it will bring and, failing that, even the greatest gift for something is not worth developing, if it is possible for there to be a talent whose exercise is not pleasant.

The issue may, however, not be just a particular talent but something wider and more general like self-improvement as a human being, one's general physical, mental, moral and spiritual cultivation. The question here, of course, is what constitutes improvement. Is it to be the currently fashionable idea of how human beings should be, an idea shaped by social or religious convention, or should it be measured by criteria arrived at in insightful deliberation on the nature and end of human life? Katastematic pleasure is finally the criterion by which self-

---

[454]S.V. 41.

improvement and human perfection is determined in Epicureanism. It would, therefore, be logically impossible for the cultivation of katastematic pleasure to interfere with self-improvement. The Epicurean road to self-perfection uses katastematic pleasure as the criterion of improvement rather than some alien ideal imposed by authority or convention. The goal of self-perfection is the state where you can maintain katastematic pleasure continuously and since katastematic pleasure has degrees of intensity, to maintain it at the level of g\=ethos or whatever is possible.

There are, however, people who would place the good and the end of their lives in something other than katastematic pleasure, not because it was imposed by any authority or convention, but because they have experienced it and now see life without it to be dust and ashes. A variety of such cases can be imagined. Think, for example, of Faust having been granted a look at Helen of Troy by Mephistopheles and judging now that "all is dross that is not Helena". This would be an example not of friendship or love in the Epicurean understanding of it, but rather of a powerful infatuation with what must be understood as an object of kinetic pleasure, the pleasure of "the sight of beautiful form".[455] Or think of a person addicted to alcohol or heroin whose life has found a focus in this object of kinetic pleasure. Seeing your good in such infatuation or addiction brings with it a dependency on fortune and the trouble of more or less elusive objects which no Epicurean could recommend because it involves a loss of self, a handing over of yourself as a hostage to fortune[456], a situation an Epicurean would think rather of curing than of supporting or recommending. There is this to be said for it,

---

[455]Athenaeus 546e = U.S. 67, Bailey, fr. 10.

[456]cf. S.V. 47.

however. The good in this situation is still pleasure, and the difficulties an Epicurean would have with it have all to do with its being kinetic rather than katastematic pleasure.

There is yet another object of pleasure, similar in some respects to the objects of infatuation and addiction. Think of Plotinus or St. John of the Cross approaching the object of his ecstasy, all aquiver with the anticipation of his vision. Could one blame a mystic for preferring his kinetic pleasure to anything Epicurus has to offer? Perhaps not. His object may require the hardship of discipline and deprivation to attain, and leave what is left of his ordinary life in shambles, but who other than the mystic himself, having experience of both ecstasy and ordinariness, is a competent judge of their respective worth? Epicureanism is not an ecstatic philosophy but rather a solution to the problem of the humanly good life in ordinary circumstances. There is, however, no reason to think that for the extraordinary Epicurean the mystic ecstasy could not be a possibility fully compatible with his Epicureanism, though not with the prosaic ordinariness in which Epicurean lives are normally conducted. Mystics, however, may not have a need for Epicurean philosophy or any other philosophy; and Epicurean philosophy, being aimed at the ordinary attainable good, may ignore the mystic as an exception out of range. It is a standard part of the account of mystics that in the ecstasy the difference between himself and the object of his vision falls away. It may be, therefore, that in the mystic ecstasy the difference between kinetic and katastematic pleasure no longer exists and that this state may for that reason be understood as easily as a limiting case of katastematic pleasure as of kinetic pleasure. But Epicurus, having had no experience of it, says nothing about it.

# The Periphery

An Epicurean thinks of himself as mortal, not just in the sense of being an animal which will one day die and be buried, but in the sense of the utter finality of the event of his death with the occurrence of which he will cease to be forever. The magnitude of the difficulty presented by the prospect of mortality so understood, can be gauged by the magnitude of the success of the Christian promise of eternal life. Philosophy, of course, does not make promises, but considers the evidence and gives arguments. Epicurus was fully aware of our natural desire for immortality, but judged that the evidence did not justify a belief in immortality, and that the person who would live by philosophy will therefore not order his life as one with a prospect of continued existence after death, but will live his life as a mortal. What if Epicurus were wrong, what difference would it make?

We indicated in our third chapter that Epicurus did not consider the prospect of our final extinction to be a certainty because the arguments, though powerful, did not establish their conclusion with certainty, if only because no future tensed proposition can be true or false, but will always only be probable. Given the evidence he had, Epicurus was quite right that a person with a well developed intellectual conscience is not available to the siren call of mere promises; but for Epicurus, the philosophical theoretician, the issue is never finally closed. Were new evidence to come to light, his philosophical conscience would as surely enjoin him to listen as it would prevent his being impressed by a mere promise. Our question now is: if sufficient evidence were to come to light to make post-mortem existence more probable than extinction,[457] if Epicurus were wrong

---

[457]In fact there is some impressive evidence of which Epicurus was unaware. See, for example, my Reincarnation, The Edwin Mellen Press, 1989.

about the theoretical conclusion of human mortality, what difference would it make to the practical conclusion of the Epicurean life?

It would make a difference if there were any evidence that in the next life we would enter the presence of gods who insist on being served and placated in the present life and will take their revenge in the next if we had failed to perform properly in this. If this were so, it might well be in our interest to make our present life one of service and placation, and cultivate the pleasant tranquility of Epicureanism only so far as such a life would allow. But there is no evidence for this at all, and Epicurus is surely right that such a role is incompatible with our best understanding of the nature of a divine being.

If I am to continue to exist after my death then, however discontinuous the next life is with the present one, it must be continuous with it in at least this respect, that the same person who lives the present life will continue into the next. If there is to be a next life then I shall take with me at least one thing: myself. The best preparation for living the next life well is most likely having learned to live this one well. A philosopher could not believe that the best preparation for the next life is a present life of service and labour, an instrumentally good life aimed at earning the reward of an intrinsically good post-mortem existence, except on evidence. But there is no evidence at all that there is a next life related to the present life in this way. Without such evidence it would be reasonable to think of a possible next life as essentially an extension of the present one, and much as the quality of my life next year is at least in part determined by how I live during the present year, one might suppose that the quality of the next life would at least in part be determined by the quality of the present one. The best preparation for a possible next life is probably a good life in the present. The conclusion, then seems to be that even if Epicurus were wrong about human mortality, it would make no significant difference to Epicurean practice in the present.

This Epicurean practice, however, is the pleasant life of an autonomous individual, and there may well be some difficulty in the very notion of such an individual. We are, in the first place, not self-complete individuals who accidentally live in the proximity of other such individuals. Epicurus, no less than the rest of us, was a child of his age and a product of his society. Much as he protested that he was self-taught, he was very much a Greek of the Hellenistic period, an heir to Greek culture and language despite his disapproval of paideia, versed in the philosophical discussion of his contemporaries and their teachers for all his claim to originality and his refusal to quote anyone else in his writings.[458]

He was not only a Greek, he was also a human being with certain necessary limitations to his self-sufficiency, if only a need for the objects of natural and necessary desires. And for all his cultivation of self-sufficiency he was not capable of the best life alone, but knew that we need others for such a life. The value of friendship was such that no solitary life could be the best, and an Epicurean's need for friends was second only to his need for food and air and the like. The Epicurean ideal of self-sufficient individuality would seem to be an illusion.

These considerations, however, are too obvious for Epicurus to have missed. To point them out in criticism of the idea of self-sufficient individuality may, therefore, be hasty and ill-considered. Epicurean autarkeia must be understood as the self-sufficiency of a human being, as a human virtue rather than a formal

---

[458]D.L.10.26.

abstraction divorced from the natural human context.

Within that context of natural human limitations we can understand the Epicurean ideal of individual autonomy as the conscious project of living as an end and never only as the means to anything, of being responsible for what you do and think and are, and of not waiting for the good life as a reward or a gift, as something received from god or man or circumstances, but of pursuing it as something achievable independent of the vagaries of fortune. It is a practical ideal without the crisp outlines of a theoretical abstraction, and to fault it for that is a misunderstanding rather than a criticism. The extent to which any human being lives in solitary seclusion is in any case not so much a matter of philosophical principle as a function of temperament and preference. To find the appropriate degree of self-sufficiency is an important element of an Epicurean life, but less an exercise in philosophy than in prudence, an exercise performable as easily today as then.

Epicureanism is an attempt to understand how it is possible to be human in a universe which is a mere fact without meaning, a universe composed of atoms which move with a kind of primal regularity that is neither necessity nor randomness, atoms which form compounds that move with new regularities in the emergence of mind and freedom, and with them the human world of secondary qualities and values. Minds are conscious, that is, they are both cognitive and evaluative. They not only experience, and human beings not only move with regularity of atoms in causal contact with other atoms, but they move deliberately and it matters to them what they do. In this human world there are ends and designs and purposes, because what we have here is not only atomic events, but lives which matter to those who live them.

Epicureanism is a tale told of this world, told by a philosopher, full of understanding and tranquility, a tale told in the deliberate prose of philosophy. There are other tales, tales told in the ecstatic poetry of spirit, the imaginative gestures of art, the resigned flow of conformity.

It may be that there are people who find the Epicurean style of tranquil equanimity too prosaic, too ordinary to satisfy in face of impending death, people who have an intimation of the intensity of which human life is capable and who seek in life a springboard to ecstasy. Such people do not all resort to poppies or nightly vigils but some, such as Plotinus, may work to turn philosophy into ecstatic doctrine and live by philosophy even at times of highest transport. There are others who find that life overflows philosophy, that philosophy is therefore in need of a supplement with which to confront the enigma of being human. Thus Socrates, for example, turns to poetry during his last days in prison when not in the company of those to whom he must set a philosophical example. The Greek need for art as a supplement to philosophy is passionately argued for by Nietzsche in The Birth of Tragedy. And there are yet others who take philosophy so seriously and cultivate their intellectual consciences to the point where philosophy turns into its own skeptical demise, leaving the philosopher in a state of enlightened ignorance and the philosophical life a tranquil resignation to conformity and convention. Philosophers, like other people, are free and even the life of the intellect is never fully determined. That is why there will always be variation in weight given to evidence available to all, variation in requirements to be met before we choose to be persuaded, and so forth. Philosophers, who perhaps more than any other set of people seek agreement by persuasion, tend to disagree, not out of ignorance or perversity, but probably because more than philosophy goes into the making of philosophical conclusions. Sometimes this additional ingredient is no more than a current fashion soon to be obsolete and gone forever. But sometimes it seems rather to be a perennial human possibility, and when such is combined with philosophical thought of high quality we get a timeless philosophical possibility which, even if it falls out of fashion from time to time, keeps being rediscovered. Epicureanism is one of those.

# Abbreviations

| | |
|---|---|
| Col. = | Plutarch, Adversus Colotem |
| De abst. = | Porphyry De abstentia |
| De aud. poet. = | Plutarh, De audiendis poetis |
| De div. = | Cicero, De divinatione |
| De fin. = | Dicero, De finibus |
| De lat. viv. = | Plutarch, De latenter vivendo |
| D.L. = | Diogenes Laertius, Lives of Eminent Philosophers |
| E.N. = | Aristotle, Nicomachean Ethics |
| Ep. Hdt. = | Epicurus, Letter to Herodotus |
| Ep. Men. = | Epicurus, Letter to Menoeceus |
| Ep. Pyth. = | Epicurus, Letter to Pythocles |
| K.D. = | Epicurus, Kuriai Doxai |
| Lucr. = | Lucretius, De rerum natura |
| M = | Sextus Empiricus, Adversus Mathematicos |
| N.D. = | Cicero, De natura deorum |
| Non posse = | Plutarch, Non posse suaviter vivi secundum Epicurum |
| P.H. = | Sextus Empiricus, Outlines of Pyrrhonism |
| S.T. = | St. Thomas. Summa Theologiae |
| S.V. = | Epicurus, Sententiae Vaticanae |
| Tusc. = | Cicero, Tusculanae disputationes |
| Us. = | H. Usener, Epicurea, Leipzig 1887. |

# Select Bibliography

Arrighetti, Griziano, Epicuro Opere, 2nd edition, Turin, 1973.

Cyril Bailey, The Greek Atomists and Epicurus, New York: Russell and
Russell, 1964, (first published in 1928).

Cyril Bailey, Epicurus; The Extant Remains, Text and Commentary,
Oxford: The Clarendon Press, 1926, Hyperion Press
Reprint, 1979.

J. Bollock, ed., Etudes sur l'epicurisme antique, Lille 1976.

Emile Bréhier, The Hellenistic and Roman Age, trans. Wade Baskin,
The University of Chicago Press, 1965.

Jacques Brunschwig, "The Cradle Argument in Epicureanism and Stoicism", in
Malcolm Schofield and Gisela Striker, ed., The
Norms of Nature: Studies in Hellenistic Ethics,
Cambridge University Press, 1986.

Myles Burnyeat, ed., The Skeptical Tradition, University of California
Press, 1983.

Eugene Carver, "Aristotle on Virtue and Pleasure", in David J. Depew,
The Greeks and the Good Life, California State
University, Fullterton, 1980.

C.N. Chilton, "Did Epicurus Approve of Marriage? A Study of Diogenes
Laertius X, 119", Phronesis 5 (1960) 71-74.

F.M. Cornford, From Religion to Philosophy, New York: Harper
and Row, 1957 (first published in 1912).

J.L. Cowan, Pleasure and Pain: A Study in Philosophical Psychology,
MacMillan, New York: St. Martin's Press, 1968.

Giorgio de Santillana, The Origins of Scientific Thought: From
Anaximander to Proclus, 600 B.C. to 300 A.D., The University of
Chicago Press, 1961.

David J. Depew, ed., The Greeks and the Good Life, California State
University, Fullerton, 1980.

Norman Wentworth DeWitt, Epicurus and His Philosophy, University of
Minnesota Press, 1954.

E.J. Dijksterhuis, The Mechanization of the World Picture, Oxford:
The Clarendon Press, 1961.

W.J. Earle, "Epicurus: 'Live Hidden!' ", Philosophy, Vol. 63, No. 243,
January 1988, 93-104.

Rem B. Edwards, Pleasure and Pains: A Theory of Qualitative Hedonism,
Cornell University Press, 1979.

W.J. Englert, Epicurus on the Swerve and Voluntary Action, Atlanta:
Scholars Press, 1987.

Don Fowler, "Sceptics and Epicureans", Oxford Studies in Ancient
Philosophy, Vol. 2, 1984, pp. 237-167. A discussion of M.
Gigante, Scetticismo e Epicureismo, Elenchos, VI, Bibliopolis
Naples, 1981.

David Furley, "Nothing to Us?", in Malcolm Schofield and Gisela Striker, ed.,
The Norms of Nature: Studies in Hellenistic Ethics,
Cambridge University Press, 1986.

David Furley, Two Studies in the Greek Atomists, Princeton, N.J., 1967.

K. Gaiser, "Plato's Enigmatic Lecture 'On The Good' ", Phronesis 25
(1980), 5-37.

David K. Glidden, "Epicurus and the Pleasure Principle", in David J. DePew,
The Greeks and the Good Life, California State
University, 1980.

J.C.B. Gosling and C.C.W. Taylor, The Greeks on Pleasure, Oxford: The
Clarendon Press, 1982.

Leo Groarke, Greek Scepticism, McGill-Queen's University Press, 1990.

R.M. Hare, "Pain and Evil", Proceedings of the Aristotelian Society,
supp. vol. XXXVIII (1964) 91-106.

Richard J. Hall, "Are Pains Necessarily Unpleasant?", Philosophy and
Phenomenological Research, Volume XLIX, No. 4,
June 1989, 643-659.

R.D. Hicks. Stoic and Epicurean, New York: Russell and Russell, 1962.

A.V. Holden and W. Winlow, The Neurobiology of Pain,
     Manchester University Press, 1984.

Malte Hossenfelder, "Epicurus - hedonist malgré lui", in
     Malcolm Schofield and Gisela Striker, ed.,
     The Norms of Nature: Studies in Hellenistic Ethics,
     Cambridge University Press, 1980.

P.M. Huby, "The first discovery of the freewill problem", Philosophy 42
     (1967), 353 - 62

P.M. Huby, "Epicurus' Attitude to Democritus", Phronesis 23
     (1978), 80-86.

J.F.M. Hunter, "Pleasure", Dialogue, Vol. XXVI, No. 3, 1987, 491-500.

Brad Inwood and L.P. Gerson, Hellenistic Philosophy, Indianapolis
     and Cambridge: Hackett Publishing Company, 1988.

A.A. Long, Hellenistic Philosophy: Stoics, Epicureans, Sceptics,
     University of California Press, 1974, Second
     Edition 1986.

A.A. Long and D.N. Sedley, The Hellenistic Philosophers, 2 Vols.,
     Cambridge University Press, 1987.

A.A. Long, "Pleasure and Social Utility--The Virtues of Being Epicurean", in
     H. Flashar and O. Gignon, ed., Aspects de la philosophie
     hellenistique, Foundation Hardt, Geneva 1986, pp. 283-324.

Ronald Melzack and Patrick D. Wall, The Challenge of Pain,
     New York: Basic Books, 1983.

Philip Merlan, Studies in Epicurus and Aristotle, Wiesbaden:
     Otto Harrassowitz, 1960. (This is No. 22 of
     Klassisch - Philologische Studien, edited by
     Hans Herter and Wolfgang Schmid).

Johannes Mewaldt, "Die geistige Einheit Epikurs", Königsberger
     Gelehrte Gesellschaft, Geistige Klasse, Vol. 4, no. 1, 1927/8.

Philip Mitsis, Epicurus' Ethical Theory: The Pleasures of Invulnerability,
     Cornell University Press, 1988.

Reimar Müller, Die Epikureische Gesellschaftslehre, Berlin, 1972.

Wilhelm Nestle, Vom Mythos zum Logos, 2nd edition, Stuttgard:
        Alfred Kröner Verlag, 1942.

Martha C. Nussbaum, "Therapeutic Arguments: Epicurus and Aristotle" in
        Malcolm Schofield and Gisela Striker, ed., The Norms
        of Nature: Studies in Hellenistic Ethics, Cambridge
        University Press, 1986.

Martha C. Nussbaum, "Mortal Immortals: Lucretius on Death and the Voice of
        Nature", Philospophy and Phenomenological Research,
        Vol. L., No. 2, December 1989, 303-351.

Edward R. Pearl, "Is Pain a Specific Sensation?", Journal of Psychiatric
        Research 8 (1971), 273-287.

George Pitcher, "The Awefulness of Pain", The Journal of Philosophy, 67.
        No. 4 (1970), 481-492.

Giovanni Reale, A History of Ancient Philosophy, Vol. 3, The Systems
        of the Hellenistic Age, trans. John R. Catan,
        State University of New York Press, Albany, 1985.

John M. Rist, Epicurus: An Introduction, Cambridge University Press, 1972

John M. Rist, "Pleasure: 360-300 B.C.", Phoenix, 28 (1974), 167-179

John M. Rist, "Epicurus on Friendship", Classical Philology 75 (1980)
        121-129.

Stanley Rosen, The Ancients and the Moderns: Rethinking Modernity,
        New Haven and London: Yale University Press, 1989.

S.E. Rosenbaum, "How To Be Dead And Not Care: Defense of Epicurus",
        American Philosophical Quarterly, Vol. 23, No. 2,
        April 1986.

S.E. Rosenbaum, "The Symmetry Argument: Lucretius Against the Fear of
        Death", Philosophy and Phenomenological Research,
        Vol. L, No. 2, December 1989, 353-373.

Malcolm Schofield, Myles Burnyeat and Jonathan Barnes, eds., Doubt and
        Dogmatism: Studies in Hellenistic Epistemology,
        Oxford: The Clarendon Press, 1980.

Malcolm Schofield and Gisela Striker, The Norms of Nature: Studies in
    Hellenistic Ethics, Cambridge University Press, 1987.

David Sedley, "Epicurus' Refutation of Determinism", in
    ΣΥΖΗΤΗΣΙΣ; Studi sull' epicureismo greco e latino offerti
    a Marcello Gigante, Naples 1983, pp. 11-51.

David Sedley, "Epicurean Anti-Reductionism", in Jonathan Barnes and Mario
    Mignucci ed., Matter and Metaphysics, Bibliopolis 1988,
    pp. 295-327.

Stephen Smith, "The Concept of the Good Life", in David J. Depew,
    The Greeks and the Good Life, California State University,
    Fullerton, 1980.

Suzanne Stern-Gillet, "Epicurus and Friendship", Dialogue XXVIII (1989),
    275-288.

Gisela Striker, "Commentary on Mitsis", in Proceedings of the Boston Area
    Colloquium in Ancient Philosophy, Vol. 4, 1988, 323-328.

C.C.W. Taylor, 'All Perceptions are True', in Malcolm Schofield, Myles
    Burnyeat, Jonathan Barnes, eds., Doubt and Dogmatism, Oxford:
    Clarendon Press, 1980.

P.A. Vander Waerdt, "The Justice of the Epicurean Wise Man",
    Classical Quarterly 37 (1987), 402-422.

Patrick D. Wall and Ronald Melzack, Textbook on Pain,
    Edinburgh: Churchill Livingstone, 1984.

# Index of Passages

Note on translation: Wherever possible published translations have been used in quotation.

# General Index

| | |
|---|---|
| Anaxagoras | 160 n 263 |
| Angeli, Anna | 195 n 330 |
| aponia | 134, 144-145, 147, 152, 160 n 263, 167-171, 176, 229, 237, 240 |
| Aristippus | 76-77, 168, 219 |
| Aristotle | 1, 58, 69-70, 79-80, 82-83, 85-87, 91, 121, 128, 156-157, 159-160, 169, 172, 183, 196 |
| Aristoxenus | 79, 212 n 369 |
| Armstrong, Louis | 92 |
| ataraxia | 134, 144-145, 147, 152, 166-171, 176, 193, 222, 235, 240, 252 |
| atoms | 2, 3, 22, 44-45, 55, 100, 108, 225-226, 228, 259 |
| autarkeia | 163, 173, 224, 235, 258 |
| Bailey, Cyril | 5 n 5, 33 n 46, 135 n 233, 199 n 340, 210 n 362, 222 n 385, 230 n 402-404, 232 n 408, 233 n 412 & 416, 235 n 425, 236 n 429 & 429, 254 n 455 |
| Bollack, Jean | 9 n 9, 60 n 101, 147 n 247 |
| boredom | 100, 164-166, 170-171, 175, 218, 220, 243, 250 |
| Brunschwig, Jacques | 82 n 150 |
| Burnyeat, M.F. | 9 n 10, 20 n 18, 23 n 27, 28 n 39 |
| Chilton, C.W. | 235 n 427 |
| Cicero | 10, 15, 43-45, 48, 51, 68, 79, 92, 97, 110-112, 123-129, 134-143, 146-149, 168-169, 172-173, 200-206, 211-212, 225, 234, 242 |

## STUDIES IN THE HISTORY OF PHILOSOPHY